International
Codes
and
Multinational
Business

Recent Titles from QUORUM BOOKS

International
Codes
and
Multinational
Business

Setting Guidelines for International Business Operations

John M. Kline

Q

Quorum Books
Westport, Connecticut · London, England

Library of Congress Cataloging in Publication Data

Kline, John, M.
  International codes and multinational business.

  Bibliography: p.
  Includes index.
  1. Foreign trade regulation.   2. International
business enterprises—Law and legislation.   1. Title.
K3943.K58   1985   341.7′54   84-18061
ISBN 0-89930-085-5 (lib. bdg.)

Library of Congress Catalog Card Number: 84-18061
ISBN: 0-89930-085-5

First published in 1985 by Quorum Books

Greenwood Press
A division of Congressional Information Service, Inc.
88 Post Road West, Westport, Connecticut 06881

Printed in the United States of America

10 9 8 7 6 5 4 3 2 1

Contents

Acknowledgments

This book has benefitted from the comments and cooperation of many people, too numerous to acknowledge individually, but whose willing contribution of time and experience is greatly appreciated. Many corporations have shared their materials with the author and granted permission to reprint excerpts from them. Early survey work on corporate codes was undertaken as part of a project at the Landegger Program in International Business Diplomacy on ''International Business, Ethics and U.S. Foreign Policy,'' supported by a grant from the Exxon Education Foundation. The views expressed herein are, of course, the sole responsibility of the author.

Selected Abbreviations

BIAC	Business and Industry Advisory Committee
CIME	Committee on International Investment and Multinational Enterprises
CoE	Council of Europe
EC or EEC	European (Economic) Community
ECOSOC	Economic and Social Council
FCPA	Foreign Corrupt Practices Act
GATT	General Agreement on Tariffs and Trade
IBI	Intergovernmental Bureau for Informatics
ICC	International Chamber of Commerce
ICFTU	International Confederation of Free Trade Unions
ILO	International Labor Organization
IMF	International Monetary Fund
ITO	International Trade Organization
MNC	Multinational Corporation
NIEO	New International Economic Order
OAS	Organization of American States
OECD	Organization for Economic Cooperation and Development
RBP	Restrictive Business Practice
SEC	Securities and Exchange Commission
TBDF	Transborder Data Flows
TNC	Transnational Corporation
TNE	Transnational Enterprise
TUAC	Trade Union Advisory Committee
UN	United Nations
UNCTAD	United Nations Conference on Trade and Development
UNEP	United Nations Environment Program
WHO	World Health Organization

1

Introduction

Over the span of three decades multinational corporations (MNCs) revolution-ized international business patterns and generated a global debate over their proper political control. In a world of national governments and international business, a certain level of conflict over operating methods and results is inevitable. Nevertheless, global interdependence places a premium on harmonious conflict resolution and national governments have struggled to find new mechanisms for managing troublesome MNC issues.

In the mid–1970s, international codes of conduct emerged as uniquely useful new instruments of international relations. Codes emanated from various inter-governmental organizations such as the Organization for Economic Cooperation and Development (OECD), International Labor Organization (ILO), and United Nations Conference on Trade and Development (UNCTAD). In a correspond-ing move, many MNCs, especially those based in the United States, formulated private codes of conduct. Initially dismissed by many observers as toothless rhetoric or public relations gimmicks, these codes promise to be a central facet of the continuing debate over MNCs for the remainder of the century. In this book the development, implementation, interrelationship, and impact of inter-national codes of conduct are explored at both the intergovernmental and pri-vate firm levels.

PROBLEMS AND OPPORTUNITIES IN INTERNATIONAL CODES

Intergovernmental codes will continue to be negotiated in the 1980s because they are useful to governments. By shifting much of the burden for resolving transnational conflicts in values and expectations from governments to MNCs, these codes bridge international differences while still preserving the sovereign rights of national governments to intervene on a case-by-case basis.

Intergovernmental codes developed because of the rapid expansion of multinational business over the past two decades. National governments evolved broader concern for, as well as more direct access to, tangible segments of a corporate entity that was subject to regulation in many different countries. Problems arose in both the "home" country of the parent company and in the nation serving as a "host" to the MNC's subsidiaries or affiliates abroad.

Home governments felt they were losing substantial control over the corporations because regulation either stopped at the border or involved claims of extraterritorial jurisdiction that often overlapped and conflicted with other nations' regulatory authority. Home governments could also be drawn into diplomatic conflicts in support of corporate actions abroad at times and in places beyond the government's direct control.

On the other hand, host governments felt too far removed from the real MNC decision-makers located at the home headquarters facility. This distance, in both geographic and legal terms, left the host country susceptible to outside manipulation, whether by the MNC itself or, through it, by the home government.

Proliferating Intergovernmental Codes

An obvious solution to these difficulties would be to have corporate regulation follow MNC activities to the international level. In a world of sovereign nation-states, however, such an international option is far from easy when there exist such wide divergences in national political systems, economic priorities, and socio-cultural characteristics. Any international law system that could control MNCs would also constrain national sovereignty at the same time.

Most governments, particularly those with the most effective power over MNCs, have been unwilling to limit their sovereignty in the investment area through extensive international law regimes. It appeared that diplomatic conflicts would therefore continue to expand as spreading MNC operations generated more cross-national problems. Unexpectedly, however, governments discovered the use of voluntary intergovernmental codes of conduct that can help guide MNC actions without the national sovereignty compromises inherent in any mandatory international regulation.

Intergovernmental codes have come to mean many things to many people. For the United States and other governments primarily supportive of MNC operations, the codes constitute an important reaffirmation of the potential global benefits derived from MNC activity, as well as a framework within which governmental obligations to MNCs can be addressed and public confidence in international business enhanced. For many European nations, codes recognize problem areas between MNC operations and national needs, focusing especially on the MNC's social and economic obligations. Developing countries perceive code developments as a way to state past grievances and current concerns over

MNC power, seek a redress in their international bargaining position, and secure the assistance of home country governments in obtaining and enforcing agreements with MNCs that are more advantageous to developmental priorities.

These differing orientations to intergovernmental codes reflect the different self-interest objectives of national governments in structuring the role of MNCs in the international economic system. Disagreements pertain partly to business operating modes and methods, and partly to the division of the resulting economic benefits. Lacking the basis for an early harmonization of these differences in agreed international law, governments are opting for code documents that clothe differences in generalities, and then call upon MNCs to behave in a manner that will satisfy the legitimate interests of all parties.

Business Reaction and Response

Even today many members of the international business community are confused about the adoption of intergovernmental codes and their implications for the future. Corporations tend to view these documents from a legal perspective as possible forerunners to international law regulating MNC operations. While in some instances relevant international law may eventually develop, in most areas the requisite harmonization of national policies and procedures concerning business operations is still a long way off. Therefore, MNCs will be dealing for the foreseeable future with a growing set of general voluntary standards recommended to them by governments as the type of behavior expected from a "good corporate citizen."

The most positive and effective business response to intergovernmental codes will come about if MNCs learn to view such codes more from a public affairs than a legal perspective. Too often anti-MNC attitudes are fostered or exacerbated by the cloud of mystery that seems to envelop international business dealings. This perception is heightened when corporations react to public concern over their operations by preparing defensive positions based on limiting their legal liability. Thus far business input to intergovernmental code discussions has been dominated by a drive to ensure that the codes are not mandatory and to keep code provisions ambiguous enough that they do not set a damaging precedent if the documents eventually do lead to mandatory controls.

Business concern with the legal implications of intergovernmental agreements is understandable, especially when coupled with the announced desires of many MNC-critic groups to turn the codes into mandatory instruments. Yet a legal concern is a necessary, although not sufficient, business response to codes of conduct. Indeed, a legal orientation can be distorting if it prepares the corporation primarily for defensive action geared to formal court-of-law proceedings rather than for the type of public affairs communication needed in the unstructured public forums where most code debates will take place.

International enterprises must prepare themselves to explain more fully and concretely the policy bases for their actions. While such a task is often viewed as a bothersome and frustrating distraction from the business of business, an effective response to this demand is rapidly becoming part of an evolving international social contract for MNCs. Enterprises must develop or revise internal policies and positions to reflect more accurately the international character of the firm, and to be more responsive to public concerns about the globe-spanning nature of daily MNC operations.

Individual Corporate Codes of Conduct

Individual corporate codes of conduct can serve as the galvanizing device for internal policy reviews and as an initial vehicle for corporate communication to the general public. It is important to realize that for most corporations the development of a meaningful international self-identity has lagged woefully behind both the adoption of MNC business structures and the spread of political concerns about them. The dichotomy between a corporation's international business commitment and its self-concept as primarily a national institution is reflected in internal policy statements and, somewhat ironically, in most individual company codes of conduct.

A review of numerous corporate codes issued by leading MNCs reveals a surprisingly parochial self-identity, with few firms reflecting an international policy commitment that matches their business stake in the global marketplace. Most corporate codes, at least those of U.S.-based MNCs, are primarily a response to the U.S. Foreign Corrupt Practices Act (FCPA). Following the public controversy over questionable business payments abroad and the U.S. Securities and Exchange Commission's (SEC) voluntary disclosure program many MNCs adopted written policies and procedures to control such practices. Often these new FCPA-related statements were combined with existing corporate policies on antitrust and conflict of interest standards, framed with a few other good citizenship topics, and issued as a corporate code of conduct. Thus, despite the international origins of the controversy that stimulated most corporate code formulation, few existing company codes deal extensively with international policy questions.

A good test of the adequacy of corporate policy for meeting international challenges to MNCs would be to read company statements from the perspective of an interested foreign observer. How well does a corporate code address the enterprise's international operations—enough for an MNC which may derive 30 to 60 percent of its profits from international business activity? Are the policies that set forth the corporation's procedures defined with international characteristics in mind or have most corporate policies been inherited from past management and adjusted, if at all, simply to meet U.S.-dictated international business changes such as the FCPA? Until a corporation's internal policies and self-identity better match the importance of its international business operations the firm will be unlikely to understand adequately, much less effectively respond to, the challenges posed by international codes of conduct.

As intergovernmental codes continue to proliferate, experience with their initial implementation is proving them to be more than ineffectual rhetoric. Multinational enterprises are being called upon to account for their actions under these officially endorsed standards by government officials, labor leaders, and other public and private representatives in both industrialized nations and in developing countries. Corporations will be forced to respond to these calls.

Current debates on MNCs do not seem as volatile as during the 1970s, but this lowered level should not be mistaken for a permanent resolution of problems. Recessionary times and capital shortages can dampen the rhetoric from some sectors, but basic international differences remain and new issues are emerging, such as how MNCs respond to proliferating trade performance requirements. Corporations should use the present relative lull to reexamine international investment issues and position themselves to operate clearly within acceptable standards. It is especially important for MNCs to get away from past preconceptions about intergovernmental codes that led firms to worry more about their legal implications than about pursuing an active public affairs response to these expressed international concerns.

The opportunity now exists for an MNC to develop and communicate a clear corporate identity that sets forth the relevant policies upon which its international business is conducted. Voluntary corporate codes can bridge the differences between national political systems and international business requirements, but only if MNCs use the inherent flexibility of self-regulation to meet societal concerns about cross-national business operations. International codes of conduct should be viewed and responded to as societal guidance mechanisms, not as government regulation of international business dealings.

ORGANIZATION OF THE BOOK

This book is organized into two major sections that are followed by a concluding argument. Chapters 2 through 5 focus primarily on the emergence of a new form of intergovernmental accord that sets voluntary standards of conduct for MNCs. Chapters 6 and 7 examine the development of codes in the private business sector, looking particularly at the formation and function of individual corporate codes. The relationship between these two areas is then elaborated in Chapter 8, which argues for a corporate identity code of conduct as the best response to a proliferation of intergovernmental codes, as well as a desirable objective in and of itself.

Chapter 2 provides the necessary historical setting for the emergence of intergovernmental codes. In the post–World War II years the victorious nations structured an international economic system based on solid agreements covering trade and monetary affairs, but a similar accord on investment matters encountered insurmountable obstacles. The spread of MNCs in the postwar economy led to special problems and created intergovernmental friction in different parts of the world, particularly in the absence of an internationally accepted framework for foreign investment. In the 1970s events in the United States, Europe, and the developing countries caused shifts in attitudes and interests that catalyzed a further search for common answers at the international level.

The renewed struggle for intergovernmental accords in the investment field is the subject of Chapter 3. National, bilateral, and regional actions are explored, as is the effort to formulate international investment law. This search resulted in the discovery of a new diplomatic instrument that could permit intergovernmental agreement on non-binding codes that were directed primarily at MNCs.

Chapter 4 offers a brief description of the major intergovernmental efforts relating to this new code form. Most important actions are centered in the OECD and various bodies within the United Nations (UN) or groups affiliated with its system. Chapter 5 analyzes the significance of these codes as they are perceived and used as law or levers to influence corporate operations. Greater potential is found for using such codes as political levers on corporate conduct, but this finding is counterbalanced in some respects by a discussion of how codes might be better used as guidance.

The notion of codes as guidance rather than regulation underlies the discussion in Chapters 6 and 7 about the use of codes of conduct within the business community. Chapter 6 explores a few instances of collective business codes, but finds limitations to the use of such documents. Individual MNC codes are then examined, using aggregate survey data from about 120 corporations to compare code objectives, content and implementation. An argument is made for wider adoption of a particular type of approach, characterized as a corporate identity code.

In Chapter 7 a closer look at individual MNC codes reveals interesting and informative examples of how some corporations construct policies and programs to guide their international operations and meet global social responsibilities. Drawing upon this illustrative material, the chapter discusses the purpose, form, application, and implementation of individual codes of conduct. This examination places particular emphasis on the special challenges that confront international companies in devising and applying such a code.

Finally, the concluding chapter seeks to draw together the preceding material with an integrated analysis of codes of conduct, both intergovernmental and corporate, that clarifies the vital relationship between the two. International political forces that are driving the proliferation of intergovernmental codes will force corporations to take a more forthright and self-adaptive approach through individual MNC codes if the harsher aspects of codes as law or political levers are to be avoided.

Looked at from a more positive standpoint, MNC codes of conduct can help guide corporations to more sensitive and responsible participation in their host societies throughout the world. A clearer international self-identity and the willingness to search out new ways of guiding operational conduct will help MNCs to meet this challenge in the coming years.

2

The Evolution of International Codes of Conduct

International codes often seem to have appeared suddenly on the global agenda, and there are many people who believe, or at least wish, that these codes will disappear just as suddenly. In fact, the codes did not spring into existence full grown without proper parenting. Most code issues developed from fundamental concerns about the way multinational corporations (MNCs) operate in a world system based upon nation-state sovereignty, where neither the MNC form of business organization nor the nation-state system seem likely to disappear in the near future.

The apparent suddenness of the current code debate stems not from its component MNC issues, but rather from the discovery and rapid use by governments of a voluntary international code instrument, directed primarily at business entities, that can help respond to MNC problems without impinging on national sovereignty. For reasons to be examined in later chapters governments are unlikely to forego use of such code devices in the future.

THE RELEVANCE OF HISTORICAL ROOTS

The multinational corporation rapidly captured global imagination. Debates over MNC power and effectiveness have become a staple agenda item at intergovernmental discussions throughout the world and have permeated the literature on international relations. Unfortunately, this pervasive impact generates a casual familiarity with the subject that obscures the relatively recent origins of public debate over MNCs.

A proper time perspective on MNC growth is essential to understand the link between concerns about multinational business operations and the current challenge posed for MNCs by international codes of conduct. Both the development of modern MNCs and discussions about international economic codes date from the immediate post–World War II era. The two developments proceeded along roughly parallel tracks until the early 1970s, when several key world events caused their clear intersection. Out of this MNC–economic code merger came a concern with international business codes of conduct, a new voluntary instrument of international relations directed principally at non-governmental international actors.

Most of the issues in current code discussions result from the world community's failure to reach traditional international agreements that would establish binding rules governing foreign investment transactions. Blocked by a deadlock over foreign investor protection rights, the search for international investment rules did not keep pace with the rapid spread of MNC operations. Growing concerns were voiced about MNCs in the developing countries, in Europe, and finally in the United States.

Although perspectives and priorities among countries often differ, some common threads exist in their growing criticism of MNCs that trace the evolutionary path of the contemporary debate over MNCs and international codes of conduct. An appreciation for the historical stages in this evolutionary process is important in order to understand that current concern with international codes is not a temporary aberration that will soon disappear. International codes of conduct have been seized upon by political authorities as a mechanism that can be used to address concerns about international business dealings in areas where binding international rules would require too great a compromise of national sovereignty.

INITIAL ROADBLOCKS TO INTERNATIONAL INVESTMENT LAW

Visions of a new world order were kindled in the dying days of both world wars, but resurgent nation-state sovereignty soon blocked the types of binding commitments required to structure such a reordered international system. International commercial accords ranked particularly high among the issues under negotiation after World War II, when economic problems of the interwar years were identified as a major cause of the second conflagration. Institutional agreements were reached covering many trade problems as well as methods of financial cooperation, but the central economic charter for a new global order was rejected and virtually every investment-related issue was left unresolved. The world community was unable to reach an international law solution in the investment field primarily because such proposed accords posed too great a threat to nation-state sovereignty over resident foreign enterprises.

While the immediate origin of the international-code movement traces most directly from the post–World War II years, some authors point to earlier developments as useful precursors for what was to follow. For example, Don Wallace, in his book *International Regulation of Multinational Corporations* (1976), refers to proposals placed before the League of Nations in the late 1920s that dealt with protection of foreign investment and model bilateral tax treaties.[1] Another analysis points out that broader economic cooperation objectives were referenced in the Atlantic Charter and the Lend-Lease Agreement in the early 1940s just prior to America's formal entry into the hostilities. Subsequently, the draft Charter of the United Nations expanded upon these principles in a specific chapter, "International Economic and Social Cooperation."[2]

Certainly the early discussions helped set the stage for the major effort at structuring an international legal basis for economic relationships, represented by the proposed International Trade Organization (ITO). A draft charter for the ITO was drawn up and signed in 1948 at Havana. Aimed principally at removing trade barriers, the Charter also contained provisions that addressed the protection of foreign investment. Particularly important to the treaty's eventual rejection was its failure to find an acceptable compromise on expropriation issues. Many nations, especially in Latin America, insisted that foreign investors should be guaranteed no more than the rights available to local investors, and that any disputes should properly be resolved under the host nation's legal system. This principle is often referred to as the Calvo doctrine after the Argentine jurist who promoted it in the early 1900s.

The International Chamber of Commerce (ICC) opposed many portions of the ITO Charter, preferring instead its own draft, "International Code of Fair Treatment for Foreign Investments," first approved at an ICC meeting in 1949. This document proposed restrictions on nation-state sovereignty in foreign investment cases that went far beyond what governments would realistically accept, but the code's adoption indicates business problems with the ITO's investment provisions and serves as a useful backdrop to ICC discussions on later international business codes. Strong business opposition to the ITO helped assure that the U.S. Senate would not approve the treaty's commitments and, without U.S. participation, the other nations soon lost interest as well.[3]

The ITO's failure was partially rectified in the trade area by the evolution of the General Agreement on Tariffs and Trade (GATT). This organization joined the International Monetary Fund (IMF) and the International Bank for Reconstruction and Development (IBRD or World Bank) as the primary international management instruments for the postwar world economy. This institutional coverage left a "gap" in the international system, however, regarding rules to cover the rapidly expanding area of foreign investment.

The central investment issue for many years remained the dispute over investor protection in cases of expropriation. Numerous proposals were offered in the late 1950s by various European groups, but without any apparent success in resolving the major differences. As a result the search for binding international legal commitments devolved from the multilateral level to scattered bilateral treaties and investment insurance agreements that provided useful but limited coverage.

In the 1960s the Organization of Economic Cooperation and Development (OECD) adopted a "Code of Liberalization of Capital Movements" and a "Code of Liberalization of Current Invisible Operations'' to establish nondiscriminatory national treatment for foreign investors. In practice, however, even the industrialized nations to whom the codes applied often undertook actions which derogated from these standards. Taxation practices and antitrust policies also sometimes appeared as topics in international discussions related to foreign investment, but these two issues usually generated less emotion and retained a lower profile than the key expropriation dispute.

In summary, the relevant early debate over international legal standards for commercial activities yielded some new postwar agreements and institutions regarding trade and finance. A roadblock was encountered, however, when the search for international legal coverage of foreign investment fell victim to the dispute over limiting nation-state sovereignty in favor of foreign investor protection. While this expropriation/compensation debate remained the dominant factor in the investment field, discussions on taxation and antitrust issues signalled a progressively wider scope for investment-related concerns. The continued spread of multinational corporations, combined with growing public controversy over certain aspects of MNC operations, ensured that many more items would soon be interjected into negotiations over international investment codes.

THE GROWTH OF MNCs

Researchers generally take the origin of the multinational form of business organization back to the British Empire and firms such as the East India Company. For the United States, multinational corporations date from the 1850s, with about two dozen large U.S. companies possessing significant operating interests abroad by 1900.[4] The relevant starting point for contemporary MNC discussion, however, is more properly the beginning of the post–World War II era. After virtual stagnation during the interwar years, international trade expansion nearly doubled the rate of general production increases while foreign investment accounted for an increasing share of total business investment. In the center of this dynamic international growth picture was the multinational corporation.

Many factors combined to stimulate general economic expansion and lay the basis for MNC growth through foreign direct investment. The United States emerged from the war's devastation as the world's dominant economic actor. Whether for altruistic motives, a keen sense of its national interest, or a combination of both, the United States substantially aided postwar reconstruction and supported a basically open international economic system that favored a relatively free flow of goods and resources between nations.

The formation of the European Economic Community (EEC or EC) also stimulated greater use of multinational business organizations that could better exploit potential opportunities in this expanded, integrated market. Many U.S. firms found the common external trade barrier of the Common Market a significant disadvantage to export operations, so production processes were established within the EC's tariff walls. Other countries tried to emulate Europe's successful economic expansion, seeking to attract foreign firms initially for import substitution and later for export promotion objectives.

Equally instrumental to the growth of MNCs was a technological revolution in areas such as communication, transportation, and business management strategies. Information regarding the peculiarities and potential of overseas markets became more readily accessible to companies, both through data-based analysis with the assistance of computers and through personal evaluation facilitated by jet transportation. Improvements in communication technologies speeded necessary contacts between a company's organizational units, even at great distances and across national boundaries.

More centralized coordination was possible over materials purchasing, production schedules, component transportation and assembly, financial management, and other aspects of an integrated business operation. Better local sales and servicing techniques further aided the potential for expanding a beachhead gained through exports into a local production base. The multinational business form became a favored vehicle for combining these various production and management elements into an integrated package that, with the backing of sizable corporate resources, could translate into better competitive efficiencies in an expanding global marketplace.

During the early growth period, U.S. corporations dominated the spreading ranks of global MNCs. The country's economic health, relative capital surplus, and official government encouragement of corporate participation in European economic recovery, all underlay the outflow of U.S. foreign direct investment into overseas subsidiaries and affiliates. The definition of many early MNC issues was strongly influenced by this distinctive national identity characteristic. The MNC became a symbol of U.S. economic power.

More recently, the number and size of non-U.S. MNCs have increased markedly, with the U.S. share of total overseas investment falling below one-half in the mid–1970s and world market share figures showing an even more significant erosion of U.S. dominance in certain industrial sectors.[5] Nevertheless, the United States is still home to the largest and most influential group of MNCs, a fact which stamps current international code debates with an imprint nearly as large as the one which helped shape the character of earlier MNC controversies.

NATIONAL VIEWS ON MULTINATIONAL BUSINESS

The controversies which accompanied the first burst of postwar MNC growth reflected the economic and political realities prevailing at that time in the international system. Official U.S. government objectives were basically aligned with MNC interests and there was little domestic debate over the country's international economic policy. Developing countries sporadically levied exploitation charges against MNCs and reacted to political sovereignty issues, but these nations for the most part were preoccupied with broader concerns and seemingly lacked any effective leverage in the international economic system anyway. European nations, on the other hand, developed an expansive policy challenge to U.S. MNCs which defined many key issues concerning multinational business operations and in turn provided the basis for programs to support their own MNC champions.

United States Complacence

In the United States, a vigorous and expanding economy provided little cause for domestic concern about MNC activity abroad. Indeed, a free investment flow standard seemed only a natural companion to the free trade policy that formed the most fundamental premise of U.S. international economic policy. Corporate activity in Europe was encouraged to the extent that it could aid reconstruction goals, while occasional squabbles elsewhere over the protection of U.S. investment interests were accepted as the price to be paid for maintaining the traditional property rights of U.S. citizens. Not until the mid–1960s did the prevailing consensus on international economic policy in the United States begin to break down over charges that MNC operations abroad were having detrimental effects on certain domestic industrial sectors.

Developing Country Concern

The attitude of the developing countries toward MNCs usually exhibited a mixture of rather abstract policy concerns, specific historical experience, and a generally weak position to effect any real change. Comparisons showed that individual MNC sales figures dwarfed the GNP of many developing nations, causing reactions ranging from general uneasiness to paranoia when these governments contemplated how to deal with the implied power of such corporate goliaths. A number of countries held ideological beliefs antithetical to private foreign capitalism. Some new leaders feared they might be replacing one form of overt colonialism with another perhaps more subtle or insidious economic variation. Many newly independent countries, however, were too preoccupied with the immediate tasks of internal nation-building and basic economic survival to focus clearly on general concerns about the role of large foreign enterprises in their domestic economy.

Experience with particular historical problems did condition the response of some developing countries to MNC issues. Foreign investment interests in these nations traditionally centered on natural resource projects that tended to be large-scale, high-profile, and politically sensitive undertakings. When problems occurred in such ventures, the controversy could rapidly escalate into a national crisis. Home country governments often became involved in support of their MNCs, adding to the view that developing country interests were forcibly sacrificed to foreign exploitation. These difficulties with natural resource foreign investments played an important role in shaping many developing countries' attitudes toward all MNCs, as well as toward specific policy issues in later debates over international investment controls.

Despite both generalized and specific historical concerns over MNC exploitation, developing countries seemed to lack the ability to effect much positive change. Individually each country would strike the best deal possible with an MNC to gain domestic economic benefits while minimizing potential costs. Over time, this route has proved increasingly effective as developing country officials employed more sophisticated negotiating and regulatory devices to extract larger concessions from MNC guests. On the international level, however, little action was taken to attempt to correct the seeming imbalance that existed between developing countries and global MNCs backed by their home government sponsors.

The major exception to this early inactivity of developing countries at the international level was their role in the failure of the ITO and other proposed instruments for setting international investment protection rules. Investor protection proposals were presented as a way to create a climate of greater security and certainty that would stimulate a larger flow of beneficial foreign investment to developing country economies. The developing countries, however, saw these proposals as a threat to their sovereignty that would allow MNCs to circumvent national law and institutional processes in a dispute with the host government by appealing to international standards and organizations weighted in favor of investor nation interests.

The refusal of developing countries to compromise on an international rule to cover this area, combined with MNC opposition to any international investment standard without strong investor protection guarantees, blocked the adoption of international investment law initiatives. General fears of MNC power and particular natural resource sector experiences readily combined to focus many developing countries on a specific issue of national political sovereignty. By refusing to cede authority to international investor protection schemes, the developing countries sought to prevent a further erosion of their relative bargaining position with MNCs.

The European Response

Europe evolved the most clearly focused policy response to postwar MNC expansion when most countries moved to restrain the rapidly growing influence of the U.S. MNCs in the recovering continental economies. While one should not generalize too broadly about a ''European'' policy during this period, most nations took actions to check U.S. MNC expansion while stimulating their own competitive counterweight through larger national companies. European concerns over U.S. MNCs soon became associated with MNCs in general, helping to give more legitimate expression to the isolated experiences of developing countries and the abstract criticism of outside commentators. Somewhat ironi-

cally, the political decision to encourage the expansion of larger national companies eventually produced more, albeit European, MNCs, which led to later
concerns about the ability to control even one's "own" MNCs.

As Europe's postwar economic recovery quickened, concerns about the growing
presence and strength of U.S. MNCs rose proportionately. *The American Challenge* (1968), the popular book by Jean-Jacques Servan-Schreiber, both stimulated and symbolized the emerging perception in the late 1960s that U.S. MNCs
threatened Europe, and indeed the world, with perpetual American domination.
This view was not based upon economic cost-benefit calculations regarding the
role of U.S. MNCs in Europe. Instead, political control factors tended to dominate the real policy concerns of continental governments, raising issues that
echoed some developing countries' misgivings about MNCs.

Analysts have identified three major components in European concerns.[6] First,
American investments tended to concentrate in what could be considered the
"commanding heights" of the national economies; that is, in the key industrial
sectors essential to a country's economic health and vitality. The generally large
size of U.S. MNC investments, as well as their strategic economic significance,
led to fears of American industrial dominance of European markets.

Second, U.S. MNCs controlled most leading edge technologies, causing "brain
drain" problems as expertise and resources were attracted away from European
enterprises. American control over innovative processes and applications could
make Europe technologically dependent upon U.S. MNCs for future economic
growth. This fear was dynamically related to the first concern over industrial
dominance, since access to new technologies would reinforce control over basic
industrial sectors, which would in turn support the search for new technological
breakthroughs. This pattern seemed to generate the potential for perpetual U.S.
dominance of Europe's business sector.

Finally, U.S. MNCs seemed to threaten government officials' control over
national economic planning. These firms could draw on resources from their
global organization in a way that might enable them to circumvent financial or
other control instruments used by national authorities to guide the country's
economy. The importance of U.S. MNCs also introduced more uncertainty into
a nation's business-government relationships, since American firms did not have
experience with the more informal mode of administrative guidance traditional
in most European economies.

Although economic in nature, these three components really constituted a political challenge to European nations. Assured control over such economic factors was considered essential to domestic political stability and to a nation's
socio-cultural integrity. European government authorities felt threatened in a
manner similar to what developing country leaders might feel when several large
foreign MNCs dominate the landscape in a considerably smaller national economy.

The generalized response to these fears was an effort by European governments to check the growth of U.S. MNCs and to stimulate the creation of stronger

"national champion" firms to act as competitive counterweights to American corporations.[7] National variations existed in this "European" response, with France usually taking the lead in both restricting American firms and promoting its own enterprises, while West Germany often followed a less interventionist course. Nevertheless, most governments utilized instruments such as industrial rationalization or merger policies, financial incentives, procurement preferences, and other techniques to help foster the larger size and market share power thought necessary to compete with U.S. MNCs. Some efforts were aimed at creating pan-European champions to gain further economies of scale and represent common EC interests versus U.S. competition, but most of these efforts floundered under the weight of continuing nationalistic jealousies or poor economic coordination. (The European Airbus venture is a later, somewhat more successful example of this broader objective.)

The logical evolution of Europe's "national champion" efforts was the expansion of those firms into multinational business operations. Some countries already had sizable direct investments abroad and a few European corporations were among the earliest multinational enterprises. Now, however, European MNCs increased in number and scope, often with official government sponsorship or encouragement. The firms themselves were being driven by the competitive requirements of matching advantages gained by other firms through integrated factor utilization and market penetration on a global scale.[8]

As European MNCs expanded in the global marketplace, the firms' interests began to diverge from the national objectives originally conceptualized by government planners. Rather than being subject to clear national benefit calculations, the European enterprises became like the U.S. MNCs they were designed to offset, following the dictates of global market competition more than strictly home country economic objectives. After tracing the operational production and sourcing decisions of these corporations, one analysis concludes,

In short, to maintain their positions in foreign markets and to stay competitive in their home markets, European champions are driven to emulate American multinationals, whether or not that behavior meshes with the desires of home-country officials.[9]

The early European response to the U.S. MNC challenge thus expressed several political fears of foreign MNC dominance, but without finding a clear solution for the perceived problems. In fact, the resultant spread of more European MNCs in the world economy may ironically have increased overall concern with MNCs in general. These developments also laid the basis for more specific and defined challenges to MNC operations, particularly as labor and other interest groups began to question the global decision-making methods seemingly used by all MNCs, irrespective of their national affiliation. These types of questions mark the evolution of current challenges to MNCs in the developed countries, as reflected in the various code of conduct exercises.

THE CATALYST FOR RECENT CODE DEVELOPMENTS

While postwar MNC growth generated increasing concern over their global expansion, the current configuration of MNC issues relating to international codes of conduct did not emerge until the early 1970s. The catalyst for recent code developments is multidimensional, involving a combination of specific events and broader shifts in perception among public and private sector actors. Vocal criticism of MNCs in both developed and developing nations formed pressures that led to a renewed interest in the search for international approaches to controlling multinational business activity.

The discovery of oil resource power and the galvanizing effect of International Telephone and Telegraph (ITT) actions in Chile led developing countries to a more aggressive posture in various international forums. At the same time, many segments of organized labor in the industrialized nations moved to oppose MNC expansion, while other individuals and institutions, drawn specifically from the religious and academic communities, began to question MNC performance in relation to diverse social needs throughout the world. These three elements—developing country alignments, organized labor, and social activist groups worldwide—constituted the main critics of MNC expansion; they were also the main promoters and prospective users of international codes of conduct.

Developing Country Action

Developing countries have provided the primary stimulus to the international code movement. During the 1970s these nations expanded efforts in constituent organs of the United Nations aimed at constraining MNC activities and reordering the global economic system to favor developmental interests. Several documents emerged from these forums that helped shape both the general goals and the tactical strategy of developing countries in relation to international codes of conduct.

ITT and the UN Debate

A single event can be readily identified as the primary proximate catalyst to developing countries' actions in the United Nations. As recognized by Raymond Waldmann in his book *Regulating International Business Through Codes of Conduct* (1980):

Although pressures against multinational corporations had been building through the 1960s, generalized theoretical objections such as these may never have triggered concerted international action toward a code of conduct were it not for one political act—the stirring and articulate protest by the Chilean representative to the United Nations against interference by ITT in his country's internal political affairs.[10]

Interference in a nation's political sovereignty was a standard item in most listings of developing, or even some developed, countries' concerns regarding MNC power at that time. While it is difficult to justify such fears with much solid evidence, corporate control over large economic resources and several historical incidents of American "gunboat diplomacy" seemed to link MNC interests closely with the potential for foreign intervention in domestic political affairs. The ITT incident was unsurpassed, however, in its public documentation and debate.

The eventual overthrow of the Allende government in Chile added further poignancy to this example. Even as an isolated incident, the event touched the very core of national government interests and thereby made the range of other charges regarding MNC activity all the more believable. This event spurred developing countries into action on the international level, galvanizing their general concerns about MNC exploitation into a focused drive for international controls.

Beyond generating universal condemnation by both developing and developed nations, the ITT incident led to the appointment by the UN Secretary-General of a Group of Eminent Persons to study the role of multinational corporations in world development. In a sense this group was the symbolic embodiment of international community action, since its membership of public officials and private individuals was drawn from countries representing a full spectrum of global interests and concerns with MNCs. The study's central focus was an investigation of what impact MNCs have on the development process, especially in developing countries. A somewhat broader task was to consider the implications of MNCs for international relations, relaying any conclusions to governments for use in national foreign policy decisions. Finally, the Group was to formulate recommendations for appropriate international action.

The work of the Group of Eminent Persons gave organized expression to diverse concerns about MNC operations, while also helping to legitimize subsequent actions by international institutions to address these issues. Many problem areas were identified in a report, *Multinational Corporations in World Development* (1973)[11] prepared by the UN Secretariat to assist in the Group of Eminent Persons' study. While noting that UN actions had been "prompted by incidents involving certain multinational corporations," the report discussed a wide range of issues that could be grouped into the following four categories:

1. *MNC costs and benefits for the host country.* Foreign private investment is recognized as an important asset for developing economies, bringing a potential for needed capital inputs, technology transfer, managerial skills, employment creation, and market expansion. On the other hand, MNC structures could displace alternative business options and lead to monopolistic inefficiencies. The crucial issue is the compatibility of MNC operations with host country development plans which vary widely in quality and precision.

2. *Divergence between MNC and nation-state objectives.* The focus here is on two elements, decision-making authority and a division of benefits, that create tensions between MNCs and nation-states when private profit-making motives conflict with governmental social welfare concerns. Decision-making becomes a critical MNC issue
when local affiliate actions detrimental to host state interests are seen to be directed
by headquarters management located in a foreign country. Social and cultural differences in such cases can exacerbate communication difficulties between government
authorities and MNC executives. Questions concerning an appropriate division of
benefits can create tensions among all parties on issues such as corporate revenue
disbursement (taxation claims, repatriation versus reinvestment, transfer pricing decisions) or job-related production moves (input sourcing, export promotion, use of
investment incentives).

3. *Jurisdictional conflicts between governments.* While related to some decision-making
and benefit division issues, this concern also addresses the extension of one nation's
policies and interests into another nation through the vehicle of the MNC. The global
proliferation of MNCs increased the incidence of such problems. There is even some
suspicion that MNCs seek to exploit differences, playing off one nation against another. However, when questions clearly become conflicts of jurisdiction between different political sovereigns, MNCs will most likely become sandwiched between
competing national authorities in no-win propositions, as in cases of U.S. strategic
export controls involving overseas U.S. subsidiaries.

4. *MNC power versus MNC accountability.* This rather broad notion responds to governmental uneasiness with the perception that MNCs can operate on the international
level between the cracks in national regulatory coverage. As opposed to situations
where overlapping national jurisdictions create international conflicts, the absence of
truly global business regulation to match the global operations of MNCs seems to
give these corporations some ability to operate as independent actors in international
relations.

These concerns coalesced around the ITT catalyst in the UN to form the basis for the Group of Eminent Persons' study. While their final report is substantively important for its content, including the comments and reservations
attached by various individual members, the exercise was even more instrumental in setting the stage for a series of UN activities that were to follow. This
Group's study focused renewed attention on the need for an international response to MNC issues. This central theme had already been identified early in
the Secretariat report: "The question at issue, therefore, is whether a set of institutions and devices can be worked out which will guide the multinational
corporations' exercise of power and introduce some form of accountability to
the international community into their activities."[12] Lacking an apparent easy
solution to the problems raised by MNC operations in a world of nation-states,
concerned governments and individuals again turned toward discussion of how
to formulate an international approach to managing such issues.

Stimulated by the Group of Eminent Persons' recommendations, the UN
Economic and Social Council created a permanent intergovernmental body, the

UN Commission on Transnational Corporations, to follow up its work. A Centre on Transnational Corporations was also created in 1975 to help staff the Commission's activities. The initial work agenda included research on the economic, political, and social effects of MNCs; establishment of a comprehensive information system on MNCs; programs of technical cooperation with governments; and the formulation of a code. (These UN code discussions are reviewed in Chapter 4).

Oil and the New International Economic Order

The ITT incident was the most specific catalyst of the UN debate, but preoccupation with that incident would present an incomplete picture of developing countries' recent involvement in international code discussions. John Robinson, in his book *Multinationals and Political Control* (1983), has suggested that Salvador Allende's eloquent speech before the UN General Assembly touched off "a political argument which appeared to be conducted in a vacuum." He believes that the vacuum was filled in late 1973 when the world oil crisis supplied an economic dimension to this issue.[13]

Developing countries had complained before about MNC abuses, even if they were perhaps less dramatic than the ITT incident. The crucial difference now was that the context for complaints changed when developing countries perceived oil resource power as an indication that they finally had some leverage to effect changes in the international economic system. This discovery served as the catalyst for further actions that set a broader framework within which international code discussions would occur and influenced the positions of many national governments toward these discussions.

The most immediate indication of this new environment came in May 1974 when the UN General Assembly passed two resolutions calling for a New International Economic Order (NIEO) that would guarantee more favorable treatment of development-oriented goals. The "Declaration" and its accompanying "Program of Action"[14] address a broad restructuring of the global system, covering monetary arrangements, technology transfer, commodities trade, and many other issues. There is also specific reference to MNCs and the role of corporate processes in a reordered international system.

Later that same year the UN General Assembly also passed the "Charter of Economic Rights and Duties of States".[15] This document sets forth a series of principles that would alter global industry and trade patterns, seeking to increase the share of wealth flowing to developing countries. A central facet of the Charter elaborates the rights of host countries to supervise and regulate the activities of MNC operations within their national jurisdiction.

These General Assembly actions did not constitute international law that is binding on nations or corporations, and indeed a number of industrialized countries, headed principally by the U.S. delegation, opposed the documents' passage. Nevertheless, these statements received the overwhelming endorsement of most national governments and constitute an organized and articulate set of principles and goals to guide common action by the developing countries in international forums.

Many of the ideas embodied in the NIEO and the Charter had been expressed at various times dating back to the mid–1950s in meetings of Non-Aligned Countries and in the United Nations Conference on Trade and Development (UNCTAD). In the early 1970s, flushed with visions of growing natural resource power and spurred by the transgressions of ITT in Chile, these various pieces came together in a forceful call for action. The theme was carried forward in specialized UN bodies such as UNCTAD and the International Labor Organization (ILO), where work focused on specialized problems in the areas of labor relations, restrictive business practices, and technology transfer. This more aggressive developing country posture on such issues also helped lead the developed countries to participate in the various international code discussions rather than risking overt confrontation over non-negotiable positions.

Developed Nation Shifts

Catalysts for the developed nations' involvement in international code discussions came from several sources. Certainly, the oil crisis lengthened the attention span of industrialized country officials, particularly in foreign resource-dependent European nations, for the developing countries' proposals on international economic issues. The massive outflow of petrodollars from ruptured industrialized economies seemingly threatened to capsize the prevailing international economic system anyway.

More direct policy impetus on code issues was provided by internal developments within the industrialized nations. In both the United States and Western Europe, organized labor undertook concerted action against MNCs, pressuring government policy in a similar direction. In addition, the ITT incident and spiraling revelations of overseas bribery by American MNCs combined to create a U.S. public outcry for greater regulation of international business. In Europe, the EC Commission moved toward imposing more community-wide regulation on corporations, particularly affecting areas important to MNC operations.

An Awakening in the United States

The postwar U.S. consensus on international economic policy was subject to increasing strains during the 1960s. Early in the 1970s a major break occurred in the free trade alliance when many segments of organized labor turned inward. The new labor position was elaborated in its flagship proposal, the Foreign Trade and Investment Act of 1972, better known as the Burke-Hartke bill after its chief congressional sponsors. Embedded within this proposed legislation were policies to restrict MNC operations, limiting corporate flexibility and penalizing foreign investment decisions.[16]

The Burke-Hartke bill clearly reflected the twin threats perceived by U.S.

organized labor as represented by the AFL-CIO. Various protectionist measures were designed to meet the challenge of increasing import penetration, particularly in basic industrial areas such as steel, textiles, footwear, and electronics. Comprehensive quotas would have maintained U.S. market share levels in nearly all product sectors facing foreign competition.

More importantly for this analysis, U.S. job losses were not attributed just to this trade threat, but also to runaway plants moved abroad by MNCs. This phenomenon purportedly transferred jobs from U.S. factories to foreign export platforms, adding to the U.S. import bill, forfeiting potential third-country sales, and shifting the technological base for future jobs away from American workers.

The heart of labor's anti-MNC package lay in a series of tax law changes that, compared to the existing system, would have penalized corporations investing abroad. The Burke-Hartke bill would have eliminated a deferral of U.S. taxes on foreign source income, replaced a foreign tax credit with a less generous deduction system, and altered other tax formulas so as to increase the cost of foreign operations. In addition, a system of direct controls was proposed whereby corporate transfers abroad of capital or technology could be prohibited if a governmental review determined that such actions would result in a loss of U.S. jobs.

This labor initiative resulted in only limited gains achieved gradually over the next decade. Many of the problems that generated the Burke-Hartke bill appear even stronger in the 1980s, however, and organized labor's attitude toward U.S. MNCs is still rooted in that earlier landmark bill. Those concerns also shaped U.S. labor's view of international code instruments as they relate to MNC issues, modified by such developments as the increased presence of foreign MNCs in the domestic U.S. economy. This latter factor is especially important to understanding U.S. labor's broadening horizons on international code issues and its growing interaction with overseas labor organizations on common MNC concerns.

The other major U.S. catalyst for creating codes of conduct was the public outcry against MNCs that resulted from the ITT incident and overseas corporate bribery scandals. The galvanizing influence of ITT's action on developing country positions has already been discussed, but its impact was equally great on popular U.S. imagery regarding MNCs. Investigated by congressional hearings and castigated by the press, ITT's deliberate political machinations weighed heavily in the American public's reaction to apparent U.S. complicity in the overthrow of a democratically elected foreign government. As with the developing countries, the ITT incident seemed to provide critics in the United States with easily understandable proof of the sinister potential of MNC power.

The fact that MNCs were now seen to engage in such overtly political acts also added credibility to broader charges of MNC abuse in economic and social areas as well. The early 1970s were replete with literature detailing MNC exploitation, particularly in newly developing countries. In the United States, this wave crested with the publication in 1974 of *Global Reach*,[17] a compendium of charges of MNC abuses, both economic and political, at home and abroad. These exposés influenced a generation of journalists, scholars, clergy, and many public officials toward a widespread belief in the basically anational and amoral or even immoral nature of profit-seeking global corporations. Added to these efforts were rapidly growing consumer and public interest movements, symbolized early by Ralph Nader's attacks against large MNCs and later by a proliferation of more issue-specific lobby organizations.

If further cement were needed to solidify a predominantly negative image of MNCs, it was quickly provided in 1975 and 1976 with spiraling revelations of secret off-the-books accounts, internationally laundered money used for illegal political payments, and bribery of foreign government officials.[18] While corporations were protesting that the isolated, atypical ITT incident had unfairly tarred the image of MNCs in general, nearly 500 of America's top corporations were being drawn into disclosures of improper payments abroad. Specific actions ranged from small gifts or extorted payments to multimillion dollar bribes involving huge contracts and investments and implicating some high foreign government officials.

The ensuing national debate intermixed ethical, political, and economic concerns. Notions of unfair competition and fears of foreign policy complications led to closer examination of the cross-cultural problems encountered by multinational business. Social activist groups increased their interest in MNC issues, sponsoring meetings, publications, shareholder resolutions, protests, and even boycotts. These activities expanded the number of actors attempting to influence policy on MNCs and laid the basis for their involvement in discussions on the formulation and implementation of code of conduct mechanisms.

The Congress meanwhile had passed a Foreign Corrupt Practices Act with unusual criminal penalties against U.S. citizens engaging in bribery of foreign officials. This Act and related U.S. initiatives seeking international controls on corporate bribery helped condition the government's response to negotiations on international codes of conduct. Additionally, corporations themselves instituted new controls in the payments area and a few engaged in broader self-examination exercises that resulted in some individual company codes of conduct.

Overall the instances of corporate misconduct seemed to provide clear justification for the generalized charges of MNC abuses that previously had been heard primarily from distant developing countries or from academic writers removed from mainstream policy influence. The MNC had exploded onto the American public consciousness in an extremely negative fashion. Imagery created by the ITT and bribery incidents helped paint MNCs as suspicious enterprises given to serious abuses if not closely watched and regulated. Most individuals lacked any real understanding of multinational business operations, so there was little basis in substantive knowledge to help offset the onslaught of broadening charges against MNCs that followed. This first impression of MNCs on the general public placed corporations in a defensive posture and helped condition the U.S. framework within which code of conduct issues would be discussed.

A Refocusing of European Concerns

The catalysts for international code discussions in Europe displayed both differences and similarities with the American experience. Missing was the general public or official government outrage over MNC abuses elsewhere. European attitudes and institutions showed little inclination toward the type of open self-flagellation that marked the American debate over corporate activity abroad. Few revelations were made of European corporate misconduct in other nations, probably not due as much to differences in MNC activity as to differences over what type of actions were felt to constitute a serious abuse of corporate power. Even cases of local involvement in questionable payments by U.S. corporations received only fleeting public attention. Instead, the major elements shaping European positions on international code issues stemmed from greater domestic labor union pressure on MNCs and a growing role for EC institutions in regulating Community-wide business activities.

The basis for union concern over MNC policies mirrored general European perceptions of American domination and foreign control problems that arose as the postwar recovery progressed. Later, the disappointment with ''national champion'' policies led to increasing clashes with European MNCs as well. Particularly troubling to unions were the similarities between U.S. and European MNCs on some direct employment decisions. Instances of plant closures or job cutbacks directed by U.S.-based parents soon had flip-side counterparts in European MNC expansion at foreign locations while local employment lagged or declined.[19] Such employment issues on closure policy and related corporate information disclosure have become one of the linchpins of European interest in international codes of conduct.

Two elements tend to amplify the importance of organized labor in shaping European attitudes toward MNC codes. First, unions in most countries are closely linked to political parties and thereby have more direct input and influence on government policies compared to the traditional American structure. A related but distinguishable second factor is that most European nations have institutionalized extensive social welfare and justice concerns throughout their political and economic systems, laying the basis for both expanded areas of government activity and broader notions of corporate responsibility on labor issues than existed in the United States.

These two elements make it certain that when a code of conduct idea is discussed within a European setting, the range of legitimate issues will be much broader and the active role of labor unions more important than would occur from a U.S. perspective. The global integration of MNCs seemingly enabled them to escape many social and political constraints that had been so arduously built into domestic societies, even calling into question the role and power of union organizations themselves. The task of constructing comparable international coordination among unions appeared slow and difficult at best. International codes were seen to offer at least a partial way to help restrain multinational management that operated beyond traditional national control mechanisms.

The second major European catalyst of code of conduct issues was the increased regulatory activity undertaken by European Community institutions. Up until about 1970 the EEC focused on developing its Common Market aspects, eliminating internal trade barriers and constructing a common external trade position. This concentration then shifted a bit as more interventionist business measures were drafted in the form of proposals, directives, and regulations. These policies reflected more concern with social and regional factors, in effect moving from a Common Market stage to that of a more integrated community. Various institutions, particularly the EEC Commission, were in the forefront of this initiative, essentially formulating a new work agenda that included giving themselves some expanded responsibilities.[20]

The initial basis for EEC activity was outlined in a report, "Multinational Undertakings and the Community," approved by the EEC Commission in 1973. This document identified numerous areas for EEC action, including protection of workers, taxation, takeovers and mergers, information disclosure, and competition policy. Economic dislocations and uncertainty in the mid–1970s delayed movement toward implementing these proposals, but the paper provided the foundation for most recent EEC measures aimed at Community-wide business regulation. While EEC measures are usually drawn so as to apply to all businesses rather than specifically to MNCs, in reality many of the most important regulatory proposals would affect primarily those firms with multinational operations.

The Commission as a body has pressed for a legally binding approach to these issues for internal regulation purposes, while most European governments favor voluntary codes of conduct on the international level. Nevertheless, EEC progress toward adopting specific statutory measures relevant to MNC operations helps define both the issues and the parameters for government positions as these topics are addressed in international code discussions. In this manner European regional activity in areas such as plant closures or telecommunications and privacy issues led to further consideration of the topics in a broader international context.

The stimulus provided to international code discussions by European Community action suggests one final related consideration that has also played a role in shaping recent code developments. Studies of organizational dynamics have shown that an activity, once begun, and particularly when it takes place within an institutionalized setting, can soon take on a life of its own. In a sense the European Commission is now pursuing the logical next step in its organizational self-definition—to create a system of business regulation that would promote the development of an integrated community economy and, incidentally, enhance the functions of EC-level institutions. Similarly, the postwar growth of other international organizations as discussion forums for global economic development issues has rapidly multiplied the number of bureaucracies and bureaucrats, both in international organizations and in national governments, that have a stake in the further development of these issues. As will become evident in the next chapter, such international discussions, once begun, are very difficult to end without some evidence of progress, usually defined in some form of a consensus document. International codes have emerged as a wonderfully flexible and inventive device of international statecraft to fulfill this institutional need.

This historical background has been presented in a very abbreviated form because an abundance of literature already exists, some of which is identified in citations, that covers the area quite thoroughly. A complete picture of international code issues would incorporate many other topics, giving greater attention to the interrelationships of trade and monetary policies to foreign investment trends, the growth of distinctive special interest pressure groups in many Western democracies, and even the position of communist countries in international code negotiations. Other subjects have been over-simplified, such as the discussion of ''European'' or ''developing country'' attitudes and positions.

A few of these deficiencies will be corrected in later chapters where additional factors are examined as they relate to particular current code issues. For the most part, however, this background chapter is designed primarily as a brief refresher course, selecting a few pertinent historical reference points to mark the emergence of international code discussions.

NOTES

1. Don Wallace, Jr., *International Regulation of Multinational Corporations* (New York: Praeger, 1976), pp. 25–26.

2. *The Search for Common Ground: A Survey of Efforts to Develop Codes of Behavior in International Investment*, a special report to the United States Committee, Pacific Basin Council (New York: The Conference Board, 1971), p. 1.

3. Ibid., pp. 2–3.

4. U.S. Commerce Department, *The Multinational Corporation: Studies on U.S. Foreign Investment*, vol. 1 (Washington, D.C.: U.S. Government Printing Office, 1972), p. 3.

5. See *Transnational Corporations in World Development: A Re-Examination*, Economic and Social Council, Commission on Transnational Corporations (New York: United Nations, 1978), Annex III, Statistical Tables; and *Recent Developments Related to Transnational Corporations and International Economic Relations*, Economic and Social Council, Commission on Transnational Corporations, United Nations, E/C.10/1982/2, July 16, 1982, pp. 8–12.

6. Jack N. Behrman, *National Interests and the Multinational Enterprise* (Englewood Cliffs, N.J.: Prentice-Hall, 1970), pp. 30–83.

7. Raymond Vernon, ed., *Big Business and the State* (Cambridge, Mass.: Harvard University Press, 1974), pp. 3–24.

8. See ibid.; and Lawrence G. Franko, *The European Multinationals* (Stamford, Conn.: Greylock Publishers, 1976), pp. 214–241.

9. C. Fred Bergsten, Thomas Horst, and Theodore H. Moran, *American Multinationals and American Interests* (Washington, D.C.: The Brookings Institution, 1978), p. 423.

10. Raymond J. Waldmann, *Regulating International Business Through Codes of Conduct* (Washington, D.C.: American Enterprise Institute, 1980), p. 69.

11. *Multinational Corporations in World Development*, Department of Economic and Social Affairs (New York: United Nations, 1973), pp. 1–3, 42–45.

12. Ibid., p. 2.

13. John Robinson, *Multinationals and Political Control* (New York: St. Martins Press, 1983), p. 116.

14. United Nations General Assembly resolutions 3201 (S-VI) and 3202 (S-VI), May 1, 1974, and 3362 (S-VII), September 16, 1975.

15. United Nations General Assembly resolution 3281 (XXIX), December 1974.

16. Kent H. Hughes, *Trade, Taxes, and Transnationals* (New York: Praeger, 1979), pp. 16–35.

17. Richard J. Barnet and Ronald E. Muller, *Global Reach* (New York: Simon and Schuster, 1974).

18. See Yerachmiel Kugel and Gladys Gruenberg, *International Payoffs* (Lexington, Mass.: Lexington Books, D.C. Heath, 1977); and Neil H. Jacoby, Peter Nehemkis, and Richard Eells, *Bribery and Extortion in World Business* (New York: Macmillan, 1977).

19. Bergsten, Horst, and Moran, pp. 408, 422–423.

20. Robinson, pp. 19–25.

3

Guidance Versus Regulation

The rapid build-up of political pressures on MNC issues in the early 1970s stimulated a new flurry of governmental activity seeking greater regulation of international business dealings. Lacking the legal framework of a postwar international investment accord, governments struggled with supplemental and alternative approaches involving national, bilateral, regional, and global regulatory formats. Over the next decade national controls expanded significantly, selected bilateral agreements were hammered out, and certain regional instruments evolved, the latter occurring particularly within the European Community (EC). Progress was slowest at the international level where proposals for global chartering of corporations and for a GATT for investment attracted no more support than had the ITO draft.

Without an international accord, the proliferation of national regulations covering global business activities threatened to increase the number and severity of conflicts between nations over differences on MNC operations. Despite public and institutional pressures to address this issue, governments were unwilling to enter into a binding international arrangement that would limit their political sovereignty and perhaps sacrifice important national interests. To break this stalemate and prevent an embarrassing breakdown in multilateral diplomacy, government negotiators turned to discussions aimed at developing a voluntary code of conduct directed principally at non-governmental international actors (the MNCs).

This voluntary code approach offered many advantages, since such a document could set general standards of corporate conduct without compromising national sovereignty on specific policy positions. The MNCs would be challenged to behave so as to meet the interests of all parties, with the companies assuming the burden of operationally smoothing over differences between government policies and interests rather than requiring the governments to harmonize such disparities themselves. Such an accord would leave the impression of intergovernmental agreement and progress, maintain maximum governmental sovereignty and flexibility of action, and leave MNCs with the primary responsibility in the public eye to behave as "good corporate citizens."

The 1976 OECD Guidlines for Multinational Enterprises was the first significant agreement to follow this new pattern. This document's adoption and continued implementation provides a landmark standard for intergovernmental codes of conduct. Other important code variations have followed, principally negotiated in organs of the United Nations, while more are likely to emerge during this current decade.

While legally binding regulation at the national and perhaps regional level will continue, many areas relevant to MNC business dealings will not be susceptible to multilateral harmonization in the foreseeable future, making such items prospective topics for voluntary intergovernmental codes. The effects of such a code proliferation, on both MNCs and governments, are only now beginning to emerge from experience with implementation activities under the first wave of voluntary codes. Even preliminary evidence suggests, however, that the growing number of multilateral guidance efforts aimed at international business dealings will require the development of new MNC strategy and resources to meet the public affairs challenge of global good citizenship.

THE STRUGGLE FOR INTERNATIONAL BUSINESS REGULATION

The growing concern over MNC conduct outlined in the previous chapter contained many different bases for evaluating MNC actions. In some cases MNC activities simply seemed to fall short of general public expectations regarding business conduct. Other instances reflected a more basic value conflict concerning the proper role of largely private international enterprises often within socialist societies. Certain governments were primarily concerned with the impact MNC activities might have on public policy outcomes. In other cases the fundamental problem related to the division of benefits from MNC operations when the company was located in different political jurisdictions, all of which desired to maximize their own returns from the business activity.

Whatever the nature of a particular conflict, the immediate deficiency always appeared to be a government's lack of control over a multinational enterprise. Given this identification of need, the path to corrective action seemed clear, and numerous efforts were begun to formulate more effective government regulations to control MNC operations.

National Regulatory Actions

Regulatory control is most easily and effectively asserted at the national level where political process channels are established and claims of sovereign juris-

diction can be exercised. In the early 1970s increased national regulation occurred primarily in host countries that were seeking better control over MNC
operations within their borders. Overt regulation by home countries over MNC
operations abroad was significant only in the case of the United States, where
traditional claims of extraterritorial jurisdiction were expanded.

Progress in the Developing Nations

The most impressive growth in national regulatory control over MNC operations has come in the developing nations. For years many of these hosts were
unequal partners in the negotiation and administration of investment agreements
that governed MNC operations in their country. These nations lacked the information, experience, and corps of trained officials to evaluate potential projects,
negotiate terms of entry or expansion, design appropriate administrative structures, and effectively enforce a business regulatory system.

Developing country charges of MNC exploitation often rested upon historical
cases where MNCs operated within an agreed legal framework that proved to
be weighted too heavily toward corporate interests. Now it has become common to speak of an "obsolescing bargain"[1] where, over time, shifts in relative
bargaining positions between the parties will place the host government in a
stronger position, increasing its willingness and power to declare the old bargain obsolete and negotiate a more favorable new arrangement. Such renegotiations are the bane of international business executives who honor contract sanctity
and Western notions of the rule of law. More and more MNCs are recognizing,
however, that periodic renegotiations will be likely whenever conditions change
sufficiently that the old agreement no longer reflects current reality.

One of the factors that has helped increase the government's leverage in developing countries is their movement up a "learning curve," where greater experience, training, and information-sharing improve the government's effectiveness in negotiating (or renegotiating) investment agreements and establishing
a regulatory system to oversee their implementation. Host country efforts to learn
the lessons of better national regulation of MNCs were traced by UN researchers in the 1970s. The initial 1973 UN report, *Multinational Corporations in
World Development*,[2] painted a picture of corporate power beyond meaningful
national control. By 1978 the updated study, *Transnational Corporations in World
Development: A Re-Examination*, identified an important major policy trend toward greater governmental regulation of MNCs.

Most host countries have attempted some form of control, structuring or regulation of
transnational corporations and have sought to improve the terms and conditions of their
dealings with them. The main objectives are to ensure that their developmental goals,
as well as national identity and purpose, are not distorted by the global strategies of
transnational corporations, and to obtain a better share of the benefits.[3]

Indeed, the new UN Centre on Transnational Corporations actively aids this
"learning curve" process by training developing country officials in the nego-

tiation and regulation of foreign business activity and by sharing information on its effectiveness.

Host countries have learned to use a variety of techniques to exert greater control over MNCs in the areas where business conduct is judged to fall below expectations. Traditional drastic expropriations are being refined to include a range of local ownership options and joint venture arrangements, often encouraged by progressive regulation of MNC activities that can restrict expansion, limit imports of vital components, or otherwise reduce profitability in ways that amount to "creeping expropriation" of corporate assets. More formal screening of MNC entry and expansion is used, often tying approval to a variable list of trade performance requirements that might set minimum export levels, import substitution, local processing, advanced training programs, or similar such conditions. Other controls pursued somewhat less aggressively and successfully by host countries seek increased local research and development efforts, technical assistance agreements, the regulation of environmental impacts, and a greater business tax revenue gain.

The U.S. Extraterritorial Reach

At the same time that the developing countries were increasing their national controls over MNCs, the U.S. government, which played the role of both host and home country for MNC operations, was extending its own regulations over foreign business activity. Concerns about foreign ownership of American resources probably peaked in the mid–1970s, as the news media fanned stories of Arab and Japanese interests buying up real estate and undervalued corporate assets. While many U.S. state governments tightened their restrictions on foreign ownership, pressures to change national policy were largely diverted until studies showed that the stories had been exaggerated and the dollar had recovered its strength on international markets. An interagency foreign investment review committee was formed to monitor particularly large or sensitive foreign investments, but the option of establishing a formal screening process for foreign purchases of U.S. assets, or otherwise restricting their permissible scope, was rejected. In the end, U.S. national policy toward foreign MNCs remained based on a non-discriminatory national treatment standard.

On the other hand, U.S. control over its MNCs abroad continued to expand, as did U.S. attempts to influence certain foreign MNC activities as well. Historically the United States has claimed and exercised greater extraterritorial control over its MNCs than any other home nation. The topical area most often associated with this extension of national control is probably antitrust regulation, where U.S. authorities have attempted to control not only the activities of American firms abroad, but also the actions of foreign MNCs where their U.S. subsidiary operations or links to American firms bring them into the competitive equation of U.S. anti-monopoly law.

A second traditional subject for extraterritorial jurisdiction is taxation policy. While home countries hold potential revenue claims against their MNCs' foreign operations, few fully exercise their options to tax foreign source income to any great extent. While many conflicts of jurisdiction are avoided by the use of credits, deferral, and bilateral tax treaties, several areas of disagreement remain. For example, an international dispute has been raging since the mid–1970s about the so-called "unitary" taxation approach used by some U.S. state governments to determine state income tax due from U.S. and foreign MNCs, according to an allocation formula usually based on sales, payroll, and assets. This concept, which treats the MNC as a unified business entity, can reach out to incorporate worldwide income in the allocation of taxes due on business attributed to in-state activity. Although the states' unitary taxation systems have been opposed by past U.S. administrations, the practice continues and generates jurisdictional protests from foreign nations about unfair double taxation of their firms.[4]

The mid–1970s also witnessed the expansion of U.S. national control over MNCs in areas including international boycotts, foreign payments and information disclosure, and export controls. Amendments to the Export Administration Act in 1977 and tax law changes the previous year set out new regulations governing what businesses may do when encountering an international boycott situation. Although the final compromise legislation tried to establish a balance between U.S. jurisdiction claims and foreign sovereignty over business conducted in their territory, the complex implementing regulations still left much room for dispute, misunderstanding, and protests against U.S. extraterritorial practices.

The 1977 Foreign Corrupt Practices Act is symbolic of one of the most extensive U.S. claims to national control over its MNCs abroad. This Act attempts to set U.S. standards for foreign business payments and prosecute the violation of those standards, whether or not the actions conflict with local law and practice. This unilateral U.S. policy is thus seen by many as an attempt to legislate U.S. morality overseas through the vehicle of its MNCs.

Along with the FCPA, efforts were increased to secure ever greater disclosure of business information, particularly through U.S. securities laws, which usually far exceed disclosure practices abroad and sometimes run directly counter to foreign information protection regulations. These U.S. efforts are seldom challenged when they impinge only on U.S.-based firms, but are often protested or rejected when foreign MNCs or their affiliates fall within the U.S. extraterritorial net.

Finally, the mid–1970s and early 1980s also saw an expansion of U.S. export control regulations, first for foreign policy reasons and later for national security purposes, that reached into U.S. foreign subsidiary operations. Assertions of U.S. control over licensed technology and the end-use of products have strained relations in the Atlantic alliance since the 1950s. If the views of the United States and its allies differed in multilateral forums regarding the necessity for trade controls over certain products, the United States could revert to its unilateral control system. This practice reached a new high in 1982, when the Reagan Administration tried to block the shipment of goods produced in several European nations for the Soviet gas pipeline—a direct application of U.S. law on foreign subsidiaries that was angrily rejected by the host nations.

As can be seen particularly in the U.S. examples, national regulation of MNCs can lead to hostility and conflict between countries. On the one hand, the extension of home country controls over its MNCs abroad are protested as unnecessary and unacceptable impositions on host country sovereignty. On the other hand, home countries fear that their firms are escaping proper national controls, or in other instances may feel that MNCs are treated unfairly by host country regulations, as with the European view of the U.S. unitary tax system or cases of expropriation in developing countries. The increasing use of trade performance requirements presents a different version of the same problem, where home governments are less upset by possible regulatory unfairness to their MNCs and more concerned with the losses such trade distortions can impose on the home country's economy.

Thus, while unilateral national regulation is the easiest step to take towards controlling MNC activity, the actual enforcement of such regulations can create international conflict. Other national governments' interests quickly become involved due to the multilocational nature of MNC operations and the potential for overlapping claims of jurisdiction over the business activity. Therefore as national regulation expands to bring MNCs under control, the potential for international conflict in such cases increases, intensifying the need to find ways to ameliorate such problems. In 1984 the OECD issued a new call for bilateral and multilateral cooperation to respond to the problem of such conflicting requirements placed by countries on MNCs.

Bilateral Agreements

Bilateral agreements are one mechanism for avoiding conflicts between countries, or at least structuring a procedure for their effective resolution. These agreements are a useful but inherently limited instrument of international diplomacy that attempt to frame the basis for relations between two countries over a defined range of subjects.

For the United States the traditional bilateral agreement in the economic area has been a treaty of Friendship, Commerce, and Navigation (FCN). As of 1984, forty-three FCNs were in force, but these treaties appear to be of declining practical value, at least in areas common to disputes over MNC activities. For example, although many FCN treaties specify non-discriminatory treatment of foreign investment, such provisions have not been vigorously enforced. The agreements were worded quite broadly and most were negotiated long before the outline of current MNC problems emerged, making the documents of little practical utility in resolving most multijurisdictional business disputes.

A somewhat more specific approach was taken by several European nations who negotiated bilateral investment agreements with many developing countries. Nearly 200 bilateral accords exist between OECD nations and various developing countries. The United States recently embarked on a drive to conclude similar agreements. By mid–1984, five Bilateral Investment Treaties (BITs) had already been signed (but not ratified) by the United States and Panama, Senegal, Egypt, Zaire, and Haiti, with about a dozen others in various stages of discussion. These accords seek to establish the general terms of entry and treatment of foreign investors in the countries involved. A standard ''model'' agreement was drafted and later revised to incorporate U.S. objectives in these negotiations, but actual agreed provisions vary somewhat according to the relative bargaining strengths of the two countries and their mutual desire to conclude such an accord.

While a global scarcity of investment capital increases the attractiveness of such an investment-encouragement device for some developing nations, many countries attractive to investors, in Latin America and other Newly Industrializing Countries (NICs), are not welcoming a BIT negotiation with the United States. Most of these nations will find the BIT's content price too high in terms of nationalization–compensation guarantees or limitations on a country's ability to regulate MNC actions on such items as trade performance requirements. Indeed, the patchwork pattern of existing bilateral agreements demonstrates the inherent limitations of this device regarding both coverage and content. Not all, or even most countries are likely to subscribe to a model bilateral accord, and when specific provisions have been agreed to in one case, deviations from such positions in other cases will engender protests of unfairness and inequality.

A quick review of some specific MNC issues demonstrates the limited role that bilateral accords play in areas beyond FCN treaties or bilateral investment agreements. For example, bilateral accords between the United States and several other nations, most notably Canada, West Germany and Australia, establish consultation procedures that seek to avoid the direct confrontations that marked past cases of extraterritorial antitrust regulation. During the corrupt payments controversy, bilateral information-sharing arrangements were negotiated with other countries, particularly Japan and the Netherlands, to facilitate those countries' investigations. Here again, the bilateral accords focused on establishing procedural cooperation guidelines rather than agreement on the substantive issues themselves precisely because there was no agreement on the underlying policy issue and its proper implementation.

One of the most direct and substantive areas for bilateral agreements are tax treaties. These instruments actually set forth the specific common policies that will allocate revenue between the two jurisdictions. While such treaties do not exist with all countries, they have been negotiated between the United States and most of its largest trading and investment partners. And while there is not yet common ground on all tax issues, as witnessed by the unitary tax dispute, this area probably represents the most successful example of substantive policy harmonization achieved through the bilateral agreements method.

Bilateral accords are thus useful devices that can range from a generalized framework for cooperation to the specific division of benefits on a particular business operation. Agreements containing any real degree of substantive precision are normally reached between those nations where there exists the least relative divergence in outlook and practice, leaving the more difficult cases for other methods of political resolution. The two-party limitations of this mechanism are expanded somewhat when an agreed bilateral accord serves as a model for the negotiation of similar bilateral agreements with other nations. But the time and effort costs of such duplicative activity, as well as recurring pressures for special provisions or exceptions in each bilateral package, soon drive government officials to seek a broader, multilateral framework for topical agreements.

Regional Agreements

Multilateral agreements can assume many different formats, depending upon the type of multinational grouping involved. Many accords are associated with some international organization, but before considering these common forms, a regional variant should first be examined. Along these lines two regional organizations bear particular relevance to the development of MNC issues in the 1970s—the Andean Common Market and the European Economic Community.

The Andean Pact

Formed under the Cartagena Accords of 1969, the Andean Common Market was an attempt by five nations (Bolivia, Chile, Colombia, Ecuador, and Peru) to stimulate their cooperative development beyond levels attained under the loosely organized Latin America Free Trade Association (LAFTA), where the influence of Argentina, Brazil, and Mexico seemed to predominate. Venezuela officially joined with these five nations in 1973 in what came to be called the Andean Pact. This organization promoted the lowering of internal tariffs and the establishment of a common external tariff, familiar steps within any common market structure. Somewhat more unusual, the Pact countries attempted to use their better organized and coordinated market to improve their bargaining power with MNCs, agreeing to common entry conditions and regulations that sought greater host country benefits, especially in local ownership and technology transfer conditions.

The main part of the Andean Pact's agreement covering foreign investment matters was their Foreign Investment Code, commonly referred to as Decision 24. The heart of the code lay in provisions requiring a fade-out of foreign ownership whereby existing MNCs would relinquish at least majority control of the enterprise over a fifteen to twenty–year period. All prospective foreign investors would be screened and permitted selective entry only under the new rules. In return for decreased ownership, firms would have the advantages of operating within the common market area and could be eligible for certain financing and import incentives. The nations in turn would agree among themselves to a rationalization of investment patterns by industrial sector. Such a sharing of production tasks would encourage specialization, reduce economic inefficiencies, further economic integration, and assure that foreign investment is channeled to areas consistent with the nations' development planning.

In addition to the entrance, ownership and industrial rationalization agreements, the Andean code also contained noteworthy provisions on regulating specific MNC conduct. For example, technology transfer contracts could not contain certain price fixing, sourcing, output, or export restrictions sometimes sought by MNCs. Regulations limited profit remittances and governed investment and royalty payments. Controls were instituted to screen MNC transactions to prevent any evasion of these rules through the abuse of transfer pricing mechanisms. More recently, new provisions established the possibility of forming preferentially treated Andean MNCs and set uniform conditions for regulating intellectual property rights within the regional area.[5]

The Andean Pact thus constitutes one of the most extensive regional agreements established in the early 1970s to regulate international investment. The accomplishment of its adoption was marred somewhat by Chile's withdrawal from the accord in 1976, dictated by the ideological changeover in that country after the overthrow of the Allende regime. The Pinochet government felt the Pact's restrictions would prevent Chile from attracting the new foreign investment actively sought by the military regime. Subsequent disputes also arose periodically over the assignment of production rights within Pact-member countries, proving particularly troublesome in transportation sector decisions. Allocations among product sectors remain a source of controversy, with the recent global recession perhaps exacerbating the difficulties.

While the Andean Pact was a successfully negotiated regional investment accord, each member state was responsible for enacting national legislation to implement Decision 24. The resulting laws and administrative frameworks were sometimes quite similar in appearance, but significant differences marked the member countries' implementation. Varied interpretations and objectives emerged as the nations sought to meet timetables established under the Pact, with the poorer countries particularly hard-pressed to remain on schedule. The Pact further lacked a strong institutional apparatus to monitor and enforce the general decisions.

In a larger sense the Pact demonstrates many of the limitations of regional agreements as instruments to meet the types of international investment problems raised by contemporary MNC practices. These limitations stem from the nature of the regional integration process, the role of national regulation within a regional organization, and the response of MNCs to a shift in international bargaining power.

The fundamental problem in regional accords is that actual economic integration usually falls far short of agreed objectives and procedures. External trade barriers controlled at the border are far easier to coordinate than investment decisions that reach far into domestic business regulation. The divergence between planned goals and functional achievements can create political friction between the countries, particularly where implementation is left to national regulation. Suspicions easily arise that the burdens of regional economic change are not being equally shared. The equity of benefit distribution may be questioned as well. Any significant shifts in political or economic ideology within member states can also cause a falling-out, particularly in the formative stages of the integration plans.

The response of MNCs to an incipient regional grouping can also affect the agreement's operational success. In the case of the Andean Pact, the agreement specifically aimed at shifting the relative bargaining power between MNCs and member nations to the advantage of the latter. From the beginning MNC spokesmen cautioned that restrictive investment regulation would discourage new capital flows to the region. At the extremes this response could be perceived either as a realistic observation about business behavior or as a private economic threat against political authorities. In any case, the inevitable result was the establishment of a troublesome ''what if'' scenario that cast doubt on the regional organization's success. These doubts exacerbated other tensions and, as in the case of Chile, helped lead to the conclusion that perhaps a nation could attract more beneficial MNC investment if it withdrew from the framework of the agreement.

The European Economic Community

On the other hand, the European Economic Community offers a somewhat contrasting case of a regional agreement. Certainly the larger developed market area involved was more attractive to foreign investors. In addition the EEC's formation was bound up with economic recovery and regional security interests, concerns that were not perceived as being aimed directly against MNC bargaining power. Perhaps most importantly, the EEC did not move immediately to regulate foreign investment on a regional basis, but focused first on trade flows and selective investment incentives until a firm base of economic integration had been achieved. A broader, integrated market was established that attracted foreign investor interest before extensive regional regulation of the investors was undertaken.

During the EEC's formative years, American firms seemed able to exploit quickly and fully the growth opportunities of a newly integrated market. Traditional nationalistic ambitions and jealousies often prevented European national firms from reaching the pan-European level of production and marketing integration achieved by competitor American MNC operations. Since EEC regulations did not specify regional investment policies, an individual nation's attempts to restrict U.S. investment could simply result in the shift of a productive facility from one country to another, as occurred with a General Motors shift from France to Belgium, with the plant's output still reaching French markets duty-free due to the unrestricted nature of internal EEC trade.[6]

While the initial EEC approach contrasted with the Andean Pact's attempt to allocate sectoral investment among member countries, the problems of MNC investment caused the EEC to take a new look at these issues in the 1970s. The foundation for this activity is found in the so-called Colonna Report issued by the EEC Commission in 1970. The document noted the general failure of European industry to move beyond national companies to regional integration and outlined certain legal and fiscal constraints on pan-European growth. Many later proposed regulations and directives from the EEC Commission aimed at the harmonization of business law stem from the concerns identified in the Colonna Report. This initiative had to proceed slowly, however, since EEC member governments remained divided over key aspects of investment policy. One analysis notes:

Although the Colonna Report provided a coherent statement of the Community's industrial ills, as well as a concise plan for alleviating the situation, the debate among member governments showed that there was little consensus on specific objectives for EC industrial policy, and thus on the implications of MNC issues.[7]

The shift of EEC regional policies from trade integration to business regulation is traced by EEC analyst John Robinson in *Multinationals and Political Control* (1983). He notes that common trade policies were in place by 1970, leading to a next-stage development of more interventionist policies that would move the region from a common market to an integrated community. The 1973 approval by the EEC Commission of a paper, "Multinational Undertakings and the Community," is cited as the end of a "gestation" period in this development, followed by a "slowdown" imposed primarily by the oil crisis. Beginning around 1977, Robinson identifies a variety of EEC initiatives to establish harmonized regulation over many sectors of transnational business activity. He concludes that for MNCs, the EEC's shift from common market to community signified a change from increasing market freedom and growth opportunities to a focus on governments imposing new responsibilities on local MNC affiliates.[8]

The EEC's recent penchant for business regulation often takes the form of proposed directives—binding policy objectives whose form and implementation are determined by national legislation. A few proposals have already been adopted by the EEC Council of Ministers and are being implemented in areas such as corporate accounting and reporting systems, mergers, and mass dismissals. Many other directives are in various stages of consideration in the EEC's elaborate rule-making structure, including items concerning worker participation in management, auditing, parent-subsidiary relationships, information disclosure and consultation with workers, product liability, unfair advertising, and environmental protection.

The EEC business directives are an extremely important development for companies operating in that region. In addition, certain directives, such as the controversial Vredeling Proposal on information disclosure and consultation with workers, carry an additional facet of extraterritorial application that can reach into corporate operations beyond the EEC's borders. A detailed analysis of these directives will not be undertaken in this book, both because so many other works already fulfill this function and, more importantly, because regional EEC regulations do not fulfill the functions of global investment law.

The growing body of EEC business law demonstrates some inherent limitations of regional investment regulations while reaffirming the absence of true international investment standards. Internal divisions over investment-related issues such as employee relations and parent-subsidiary relationships spark more dramatic discord than most regional trade issues (except perhaps agricultural policy). Although the EEC is one of the most successfully integrated regional organizations, the extensive amendments attached to most EEC Commission directives, as well as the choice of national implementing devices rather than directly applied EEC regulations, testify to the difficulty of harmonizing business policies that reach deeply into domestic economies. Even where binding rules are established within the EEC, they are inherently limited by their regional orientation. Wherever extraterritorial application may be attempted, it will encounter the same jurisdictional conflict and implementation obstacles experienced by U.S. extraterritorial legal claims.

The distinctions between regional business regulation and international business standards are drawn quite clearly, in fact, by EEC policy itself. As John Robinson points out, the EEC favors legally binding regulation of MNCs in internal matters, but supports voluntary codes of conduct over mandatory measures in external negotiations at the international level.[9] Even if the political will develops to harmonize MNC policy internally, further progress on various EEC directives will not overcome major obstacles to a true international accord on conflictual investment issues. Indeed, while internal harmonization could reduce intraregional conflicts on MNC policy, the potential extraterritorial reach implicit in some EEC policy initiatives may end up exacerbating conflicts with other areas of the world.

International Investment Law Proposals

The struggle to devise investment law directly at the international level has stimulated discussion and debate, if not much real progress, ever since the failure of the ITO and other related proposals. Suggestions have ranged from global chartering of MNCs under an elaborate international regulatory body to an agreement by which nations would essentially decline any jurisdictional claims over MNC activities beyond their borders. An organizational middle ground was offered in a "GATT for Investment" proposal, while a somewhat different approach urged negotiators toward broader, non-binding international agreements that might eventually evolve into international law standards.

Global chartering of MNCs under a new international regulatory authority presents the most direct and comprehensive proposed solution to the absence of international investment controls. The concept is usually associated with George

Ball, who perceives global chartering as a positive step that would free MNCs from inadequate national regulations that unnecessarily constrained their activity. From a somewhat different perspective, other commentators view global chartering as a way to constrain MNCs that now operate too freely under inadequate national regulations. In either case, the suggestion has proven unrealistic since no international organization is going to be granted the budget, staff, or broad regulatory authority over MNCs needed to enforce chartering requirements when there is no underlying agreement between sovereign nations on the substantive content for enforceable regulations. In many ways the global chartering proposal goes even beyond the extensive demands for relinquishing national sovereignty that killed the early ITO charter.[10]

A conceptually opposite proposal, attributed to Raymond Vernon, suggests that local national law should become the sole governing authority in all situations. In a type of no-international-law formulation, somewhat akin to the Calvo doctrine in Latin America, home countries would renounce legal claims over MNC activity outside their own borders, leaving the resolution of any problems to the processes of the host country's laws.[11] This national law approach to international agreement sometimes develops in particular case scenarios, but this outcome is determined more by the political bargaining leverage of the contesting sovereign nations in each particular case than by any prior binding commitment. In a world where political sovereigns are unwilling to cede their authority to the vagaries of an international regulatory body, it is equally unlikely that most nations possessing much effective power over MNCs will agree in advance to forego the use of that power, especially in cases involving the more numerous, less powerful sovereign states that would generally favor a national law solution.

The proposal for a "GATT for Investment" is generally associated with Charles Kindleberger, largely because of an article he co-authored with Paul Goldberg in 1970. Their suggestion involved the establishment of an international group of experts who could formulate a limited set of principles for regulating MNCs. The agreed principles would then be backed by a limited international agency capable of impartial investigation of and recommendations on issues brought to the international body by companies or countries. The proposal did not suggest binding enforcement authority regarding decisions, but rather relied on voluntary acceptance generated over time. The initial proposal seemed to focus primarily on dealing with issues involving home versus host country conflicts of jurisdiction, although a later article by Kindleberger explicitly included MNC evasion of any national government controls, as well as cases where the international community might disagree with MNC activity even if the company is backed by both home and host nations.[12]

This proposal has maintained a consistent attraction for many people over the past decade. Conceptually the idea offers a neat symmetrical answer to the organizational void on investment issues created when establishment of GATT covered most trade-based issues left orphaned by the ITO's failure. The unde-

fined content of the proposed investment principles as well as the use of a recommendatory body makes the idea less threatening in its initial stage. In a sense
the ambiguous nature of the concept as it has evolved provides a broad banner
that many claimants can seek to stretch across their own proposed variations.
In the end, however, even this proposal for an international agency to admin-
ister an agreement on MNCs through recommendatory decisions was deemed
too ambitious by most commentators. The "GATT for Investment" proposal
has not provided the spark necessary to initiate actual steps toward its own substantive negotiation.[13]

The initial UN report on MNCs considered many of these alternative international proposals and concluded that global chartering or even a GATT for
Investment was unattainable, at least for the near term. A more limited step,
proposed for its educational value, was the preparation of a general code of
conduct for MNCs. Even without a strong international enforcement agency,
the report suggested that the code could be improved over time into a set of
guidelines by which MNC actions could be evaluated.[14]

The UN report thus recognized the serious limitations imposed on possible
international law proposals by current world political realities, particularly the
assertion of nation-state sovereignty. International regulations to control MNCs
are too often perceived simply as an extension of supplemental political power
over unrestrained private actors. This perception ignores the reality that any agreed
application of international law will supersede and replace either actual or potential national political control over these actors. An international law agreement by its very nature limits and constrains national sovereignty at the same
time that it may constrain private MNC actors. Thus an international law solution is not cost-free to national political sovereigns; and on investment issues
that reach deeply into domestic economic regulation and citizen well-being, the
perceived cost of losing potential control over internal policy choices is usually
judged to be too great by most nations.

The basic problem facing proponents of binding international investment
agreements is the simple but basic fact that major differences in aims and interests exist in today's (and likely tomorrow's) world of sovereign nation-states.
Substantively, divergent interests and objectives block the formulation of a
common basis for harmonized international controls over MNC operations.
Furthermore, linked to these substantive differences and giving them concrete
effect upon national interests, are the procedural constraints inherent in binding
international regulation. International controls may constrain MNC activities,
but such binding accords inherently constrain national political authorities as
well, simultaneously restricting their freedom of action vis-à-vis MNCs in areas
covered by the agreement. Thus even states concerned about a loss of sovereignty to MNCs may not see international controls as a necessarily desirable
option. As Cynthia Wallace put it in *Legal Control of the Multinational Enterprise* (1983):

A certain loss of sovereignty is necessarily involved in the application of any binding agreement enforced by an international or even by a regional body. Those states must realize that international regulations can be as much of a compromise of sovereignty— or more so—as the commercial activities of foreign multinationals, which at least are subject to national regulation.[15]

Thus the struggle toward international investment law offers a limited and sometimes contradictory approach to handling problems arising from the spread of MNC business activity. Burgeoning national regulation, particularly if extended through extraterritorial enforcement, is multiplying conflict situations where multilocational corporate operations become caught between competing political jurisdictions. Efforts to use bilateral or even regional agreements to ameliorate struggles between nations over MNC control or benefit distribution claims offer inherently limited solutions that can, in themselves, exacerbate tensions with governments excluded from and perhaps discriminated against because of such accords.

At the international even more than the regional level, investment law is lacking, with little prospect for much improvement in the near term. Don Wallace found that no international law exists for MNCs in the most crucial business areas, making the MNC ''in the truest sense . . . a legal nonentity.'' He further concludes that the conditions permitting establishment of an effective international regulatory organization are not likely to develop in the foreseeable future. Most other commentators would join Wallace in this prognosis.[16]

The dilemma facing global policy-makers is clear. Spreading MNC operations raise a growing number of political control and economic benefit distribution issues that cannot be adequately addressed by national laws in isolation. Yet binding international law solutions necessarily involve a sacrifice of national sovereignty to international authority, where divergences between national systems in aims and interests prevent the substantive agreement essential for a harmonization of policies. National political sovereignty is simply more bound up with international investment issues than with traditional trade relationships. In short, an international solution is needed to resolve spreading national conflicts over multilocational MNC operations, but legally binding agreements cannot be achieved without a politically unacceptable infringement on sovereignty over internal national interest determinations.

THE EMERGENCE OF INTERNATIONAL GUIDANCE MECHANISMS

A possible way out of this dilemma has evolved, perhaps as much by default as by design. Precluded from achieving binding international regulation of MNC activity, yet needing some device to ameliorate growing international conflicts over MNC issues, global policy-makers discovered the use of voluntary codes of conduct, directed primarily at non-governmental entities. This mechanism essentially joins two preexisting strands—the intergovernmental search for international investment law, as described above, and an evolving body of voluntary international investment statements developed primarily within the MNC business community. The union of these two developments was achieved in the 1976 OECD Guidelines for Multinational Enterprises, a landmark document that has set the standard for a whole new body of diplomatic instruments based on the use of voluntary codes of conduct that favor guidance over regulation in international business dealings.

Business Discussions of International Codes

The origins of the international business community's concern with foreign investment codes dates back to the late 1940s, when the International Chamber of Commerce (ICC) issued its "International Code of Fair Treatment for Foreign Investments." This code was directed at governments and intended to establish their responsibilities toward foreign investors. In the early 1950s a proposal was made by the U.S. Council to the ICC for a counterpart code of "foreign investment standards" that would briefly outline in eight paragraphs the responsibilities of international businesses. After some discussion and draft revisions in committees of the ICC, the U.S. proposal was abandoned. Among the reasons cited for this action were the difficulty of drafting general provisions that were applicable to varied business situations and the possible inappropriate use of voluntary guidelines as leverage against international companies.[17]

The idea of a general voluntary international business code of conduct then entered an incubation period. Some stirrings were felt in the late 1960s when a joint U.S. and Canadian Chamber of Commerce committee sponsored a set of "precepts" that largely paralleled the Canadian government's guidelines for external investors. The concept also gained impetus from an extensive list of "recommendations" addressed to MNCs, governments, and international organizations, contained in a 1968 study, known as the "Stikker Report," commissioned by the United Nations Conference on Trade and Development (UNCTAD).[18]

In 1969 the ICC again took up the idea of an international business code, despite the reservations expressed by the author of the background paper on international corporations, prepared for the twenty-second ICC Congress in Istanbul.[19] Following further committee consideration and deliberations in various ICC sessions, the organization adopted their ICC Guidelines for International Investment in 1972. This document contained recommendations directed to foreign investors as well as home and host governments. The code sought to offer practical guidance for improving the dialogue between MNCs and governments across a series of issues including ownership and management, finance, employment, technology, and commercial policies. A parallel exercise with a specific regional focus resulted in a similar but somewhat less comprehensive set of guidelines, the Pacific Basin Charter, adopted just prior to the ICC action in 1972 by the Pacific Basin Economic Council.[20]

At roughly this same time some individual corporations were beginning to develop their own codes of conduct, as will be discussed in detail in Chapter 6. The movement toward individual corporate codes of conduct did not develop significantly until after the intergovernmental efforts at investment law and the business community's discussions of international codes merged in the OECD negotiations of the mid–1970s.

The OECD negotiations and resultant Guidelines for Multinational Enterprises served as the conjunction of two trends. Previously the government and business discussions had progressed along largely distinct and highly partisan tracks. Intergovernmental efforts focused on how to extend regulatory powers over MNC activities to bring these enterprises under governmental control without creating or exacerbating jurisdictional conflicts between nations. This approach sought to develop enough common ground in governmental policy positions to define international investment law standards.

On the other hand, while the business community also favored harmonized government policy to minimize conflicts and uncertainty, support for legally binding instruments was largely confined to areas that would constrain possible government discrimination against foreign investors rather than actual regulation of business activity. Business documents recommended how governments could adopt a regulatory framework that would attract foreign investment, while suggesting that only voluntary standards were needed to guide MNC behavior in international business operations. Indeed, a strong rationale used by voluntary business code supporters was that such self-directed initiatives might help avoid mandatory government regulation of business activity.

Discovery of a Voluntary Code Instrument

The two strands of intergovernmental investment negotiations and international business code discussions came together when government negotiators in the OECD settled on a combined approach that met short-term OECD needs and set a precedent for the evolution of a new mechanism for international diplomacy to deal with troublesome MNC issues. The claim that this OECD action evolved a new diplomatic instrument rests on the unique combination of four elements involving private addressees, voluntary adherence, interpretation needs, and a pliant implementation process.

To begin with, both the OECD Guidelines and many subsequent code mechanisms are intergovernmental documents adopted by political authorities that address primarily, if not exclusively, private international actors. Many standard bilateral or multilateral agreements of the past have certainly affected private corporations, but these agreements typically express themselves in terms of governmental rights and duties. These agreements might regulate the flow of business between nations or prescribe certain governmental treatment of enterprises, but the intergovernmental document is clearly addressing itself to public authorities who will in turn regulate private actors as appropriate and necessary. Past international agreements thus affected enterprises indirectly through the intermediaries of national political authority.

On the other hand, the new codes address themselves directly to private parties, setting forth the conditions not just for intergovernmental transactions, but also for private business operations. To be sure, various public authorities (and publicly owned enterprises) are also addressed in most codes, a condition that is a central demand of MNCs and many developed country governments. This dual addressee function nevertheless should not obscure the novelty of an international document on investment issues, negotiated between governmental authorities, that specifically directs itself to the responsibilities of individual private enterprises. Indeed, it is clear that this private sector element, not the sections directed to governmental responsibilities, is the real *raison d'être* for the code; that is, the key component that sets the code apart from other instruments.

The element of voluntary adherence to these new codes is also an important, if not completely novel factor. Many developing nations and socialist-oriented countries favor binding international accords, at least in negotiating rhetoric, but they have been willing to compromise on a voluntary instrument to achieve a code agreement, as with the UNCTAD Code on Restrictive Business Practices. Acceptance of the voluntary mode has been essential to secure participation in the code by most Western governments as well as the acquiescence of many corporations. The 1976 OECD Guidelines actually came wrapped in a four-part package, including two binding OECD Council Decisions on government investment policies, but the MNC guidelines addressed to corporate activity were fully voluntary. In general, the principle of voluntary adherence to the MNC codes has been a compromise position necessary to overcome the many roadblocks that have prevented agreements on international investment law.

Having recognized the key role of voluntary adherence, two equally important caveats must be added that make such a compromise acceptable to proponents of mandatory accords, and that help give these new codes their distinctive character. The first qualification concerns the broad and sometimes ambiguous formulation of standards outlined in the codes, leading to a need for interpretation. This approach helps overcome innumerable drafting difficulties, but it also opens the door to later revision of the document.

While most international negotiations are based upon political compromise, international code negotiations raise diplomatic language drafting to a high art form. Having been freed from the need for legal precision by acceptance of a voluntary adherence mode, code provisions reach levels of generality and ambiguity clearly unacceptable in more binding instruments. This relative freedom in drafting can help overcome many differences of opinion on substantive issues, and grants to corporations a seemingly wide latitude for applying broad standards as best fits localized conditions. In return for accepting generalized provisions, however, proponents of tighter regulations have gained a review and interpretation body.

Agreement on the need for interpretation of broad, voluntary code standards is significant for three reasons. As in the case of the precedent-setting OECD action, specific cases of alleged violations of voluntary standards can be brought before an interpretation body to seek clarification of how the code should be applied in given circumstances. Although the interpretation body is not to make any judgment on the merits of individual cases or serve in any type of quasi-judicial capacity, it provides an official location for airing charges against alleged code violators and a possible leverage point for further political pressures.

Interpretation needs also lead into the natural follow-up activity of code revision. If interpretation shows that the original code needs further clarification or elaboration in any significant areas, the door is opened to expand the scope or tighten the language of code provisions. Finally, interpretation needs can be important simply by leading to the establishment of a bureaucratic body that can serve as the organizational advocate for the code, perhaps undertaking various other types of activity that broaden into a larger implementation process.

A pliant implementation process is indeed the final element that distinguishes these new codes from past diplomatic instruments. Since the document was to be based on voluntary adherence, implementation procedures received little attention until the latter stages of the OECD discussion, when designation of an interpretation/revision body was generally perceived as the final step. Actual practice has revealed a much wider potential array of implementation activities and as a consequence provisions relating to implementation processes are now drawing much greater attention in other international code discussions.

Much of the implementation activity surrounding the OECD Guidelines has developed as an outgrowth of the interpretation function. The key intergovernmental Committee on International Investment and Multinational Enterprises (CIME) conducts reviews of the Guidelines and their acceptance by corporations, examines cases brought to it for interpretation of the Guidelines' application, and recommends certain changes and additions to the Guidelines. Officially recognized advisory groups for business and labor (Business and Industry Advisory Committee—BIAC; Trade Union Advisory Committee—TUAC) are very active in both the interpretation and implementation process. The TUAC has brought numerous cases of alleged corporate code violations before the CIME while the BIAC is the primary vehicle to encourage and demonstrate business support of and compliance with the Guidelines.

Other actors are also involved with the Guidelines' application from time to time. Several of TUAC's charges, sometimes backed by national government support, have generated widespread media attention that has added public image pressures to the voluntary adherence principle. Various institutes and academicians are involved in researching and documenting code compliance (or non-compliance) and several consumer and environmental groups are seeking more direct participation in OECD activities. The OECD itself moved beyond the CIME to promote establishment of "national contact points" in most member countries, to include government agencies or, as in the United States, public advisory mechanisms. These groups are prohibited from issuing clarifications of the Guidelines, but they do serve as a first stop in the interpretation process and can also function as promotion devices for the code's promulgation.

Finally, the CIME has set a precedent by undertaking information-gathering activities to inform their discussion of the 1976 investment accords. Surveys of government actions on national treatment policies and investment incentives and disincentives were matched by government and advisory group reports on the extent of voluntary corporate compliance with the code. More recently, the CIME in 1982 used survey devices to investigate the role of multinational enterprises in the structural adjustment process, an issue with obvious ties to many of the Guidelines' provisions, particularly in the sensitive employment and industrial relations section. Even though the results of this investigation reflected rather favorably upon MNC performance, this type of investigatory procedure must now be considered an acceptable part of the Guidelines' flexible implementation process.

The importance of this investigatory element is reflected in the effort to include such a procedure in the implementation process of other voluntary international codes, including the UNCTAD Code on Restrictive Business Practices and the ILO Tripartite Declaration of Principles Concerning Multinational Enterprises and Social Policy. Indeed, John Robinson sees implementation as this decade's "litmus test" for the ILO code. He points out that its implementation program, agreed to in 1980, includes not only periodic surveys on the Declaration, but also a disputes settlement mechanism. Unique to this code arrangement is the direct presence of labor and business representatives as well as government officials in the ILO body who would handle any complaints under the code.[21] Some dissatisfaction with the review action taken in 1983 will add to the pressures to show results from this process.

The implementation process, begun in most cases through an interpretation function, is thus an integral element of the new codes. In many instances the potential for flexibly expansive implementation has been the key to a compromise solution that allows progress on voluntary intergovernmental investment codes when international investment law efforts have failed. Evolving implementation actions also raise questions about the potential impact and importance of these codes for MNCs, especially as implementing mechanisms are constructed in organizations less likely than the OECD to respect rigorously the limitation of voluntarism, and more likely to pursue aggressively the policy interests of host developing countries.

A combination of four elements thus helps to distinguish the type of intergovernmental code of conduct referred to in this book as a new instrument of diplomacy—private addressees, voluntary adherence, interpretation needs, and a pliant implementation process. Being able to describe the general components of these new codes, however, does not yet provide a clear definition that will readily distinguish them from other close relatives. To aid further in this task of separating guidance from regulation, a brief discussion of code definitions, purposes, and political effects may prove useful.

Intergovernmental Codes as International Business Guidance

The discovery of international codes of conduct marks a new development that differs from past code terminology. In domestic usage codes usually refer to a compilation of laws in the public sector or non-legally binding statements of ethical principles in the private sector. On the international level code terminology normally implies some type of systematic ordering of agreements covering a subject area, where the binding nature of the rules can vary widely and the covered parties are usually subscribing governments. The new code of conduct hybrid thus introduces private parties into the agreement as direct addressees, specifies a voluntary adherence mode, but then adds compliance pressures through interpretation needs and a flexible implementation process. The UN Group of Eminent Persons' report came closest to identifying the nature of this code approach.

Finally, a code of conduct may be a consistent set of recommendations which are gradually evolved and which may be revised as experience or circumstances require. Although they are not compulsory in character, they act as an instrument of moral persuasion, strengthened by the authority of international organizations and the support of public opinion.[22]

Since few people remember long or complicated definitions, the characterization that has most popularly described these new codes is the term "soft law." This concept is identified by John Robinson as "politically-agreed behavior which cannot be directly legally enforced but cannot either be legitimately infringed." He goes on to point out the disturbing, untraditional nature of soft law for companies who find its "openendedness" disconcerting. While violations of soft law are not punishable by legal penalties, even alleged violations can exact a high public image cost, as has already occurred under the OECD Guidelines experience with a number of firms. This consideration will be particularly important for companies dependent on name recognition, personal services, or otherwise possessed of a high public profile. Thus, as Robinson puts it, "Soft law can have hard consequences."[23]

Along with a definition of soft law, however, the perceptive portrayal of these codes as "politically-agreed guidelines" should also be retained. The catchy reference to soft law and hard consequences focuses attention primarily on the corporate interest in such codes, while the concept of political compromise looks more directly at the codes' origin and *raison d'être*.

There are many possible formulations of a code's purpose that hold some validity. Raymond Waldmann identifies six potential objectives in his book *Regulating International Business Through Codes of Conduct* (1980). Most of his formulations deal with the codes' relationship to laws, especially the enhancement of national laws or the harmonization of national regulation between countries. These purposes are encompassed within the motivations leading to the discussion of international investment issues and can be furthered to limited degrees by voluntary code arrangements. It is his last point, however, that reaches the real essence of the new intergovernmental codes "providing alternative ways to subject private enterprise to public and governmental policies."[24]

Law-related purposes could be handled better by an international law solution, but it is the global community's very inability to reach such binding investment accords that makes necessary the search for other "alternative ways" of handling MNC issues. The new codes are a novel effort to develop a political answer to ordering MNC relationships that are not currently amenable to legally binding international standards. This emphasis on a political over a legal orientation is particularly important for understanding the emergence and likely continued proliferation of code instruments. Governments are struggling to ameliorate potential disputes over MNC activity without actually sacrificing tenets of national sovereignty in the process.

This ambiguous nature of intergovernmental code discussions bothers many legal analysts who feel that the purpose of such exercises is often left unclear. Do the documents exist to create minimum performance standards, guide extraordinary corporate efforts, promote global economic welfare, supplement national regulatory powers, recognize positive MNC benefits, or control negative MNC impacts? The answer, of course, is "yes" to all of these objectives and to a whole range of other ones that are both explicit and implicit in the various codes. In truth, the purpose(s) must remain ambiguously broad because the documents are essentially political and not legal in nature. Ambiguity is the basis for international political compromise where the precision of international law standards is unattainable.

GUIDANCE OVER REGULATION IN INTERNATIONAL BUSINESS DEALINGS

The new intergovernmental codes of conduct signify the emergence of a framework based on guidance over regulation in international business dealings. The traditional strength of national law remains largely unabated and indeed the increase of national regulations portends even more potential conflicts of overlapping jurisdiction where multinational enterprises are concerned. Bilateral treaties and regional economic agreements remain inherently limited in their scope and application, offering no effective resolution for the most contentious MNC issues. Efforts at direct international investment law negotiation have proven futile, as governments are unwilling to sacrifice effective sovereignty over key aspects of domestic economic life that are affected by the deep penetration of direct investment trends.

The pressures of international interdependence and the spread of MNC business activity have nevertheless combined to focus intergovernmental efforts into an expedient political compromise. Voluntary codes of conduct have evolved that directly address MNCs and encompass flexible interpretation and implementation mechanisms. These codes provide for formal intergovernmental agreement on many MNC issues, while retaining maximum national government prerogatives. In cases of alleged corporate wrong-doing, each government can choose between highlighting the transgression by emphasizing the agreed good conduct standards, protecting its own corporations by pointing to the voluntary adherence rule, or simply sitting on the fence, as individual case circumstances may dictate.

In the meantime, the burden is publicly shifted to MNCs to live up to the governmentally agreed standards of good corporate citizenship, while the precise definition of such behavior is often still lacking. Some of the resulting dilemmas and challenges for business are illustrated in the examples of early code applications, discussed in Chapter 5, on codes as law or levers, which directly follow the next chapter's brief summary of the specific intergovernmental code instruments already completed or in an advanced stage of negotiation.

NOTES

1. Raymond Vernon, *Sovereignty at Bay: The Multinational Spread of U.S. Enterprises* (New York: Basic Books, 1971), pp. 46–59.

2. *Multinational Corporations in World Development*, Department of Economic and Social Affairs (New York: United Nations, 1973).

3. *Transnational Corporations in World Development: A Re-Examination*, Economic and Social Council, Commission on Transnational Corporations (United Nations, 1978), p. 5. The growing confidence and competence of host country regulators has continued into the 1980s, even under changing economic circumstances. For an updated discussion of this development, see *Transnational Corporations in World Development: Third Survey*, United Nations Centre on Transnational Corporations (New York: United Nations, 1983), pp. 9–11, 55–58.

4. John M. Kline, *State Government Influence in U.S. International Economic Policy* (Lexington, Mass.: Lexington Books, D.C. Heath, 1983), pp. 127–155.

5. For a general discussion of Andean Pact history and recent developments related to investment issues, see Robert Black, Stephen Blank, and Elizabeth C. Hanson, *Multinationals in Contention* (New York: The Conference Board, 1978), pp. 174–184, and *The International Organizations Regulatory Guidebook*, International Business-Government Counsellors, Inc. (Washington, D.C.: International Organizations Monitoring Service, 1984), pp. 59–64.

6. See C. Fred Bergsten, Thomas Horst, and Theodore H. Moran, *American Multinationals and American Interests* (Washington, D.C.: The Brookings Institution, 1978), pp. 415–416, 419–424; and Raymond Vernon, ed., *Big Business and the State* (Cambridge, Mass.: Harvard University Press, 1974), pp. 14–17.

7. Black, Blank, and Hanson, p. 160.

8. John Robinson, *Multinationals and Political Control* (New York: St. Martins Press, 1983), pp. 19–45.

9. Ibid., p. 37.

10. See Don Wallace, Jr., *International Regulation of Multinational Corporations* (New York: Praeger, 1976), pp. 16, 31; and *Multinational Public Affairs Briefing Seminar, Selected Proceedings* (Washington, D.C.: Public Affairs Council, February 25, 1976), pp. 72–73.

11. Ibid., p. 31.

12. See Paul M. Goldberg and Charles P. Kindleberger, "Toward a GATT for Investment," *Law and Policy in International Business*, vol. 2, no. 2, Summer 1970, pp. 295–325; and Charles P. Kindleberger, *A GATT for Foreign Investment: Further Reflections* (New York: The Carnegie Center for Transnational Studies, 1980), p. 5.

13. Don Wallace, Jr., ed., *International Control of Investment: The Dusseldorf Conference on Multinational Corporations*, Institute for International and Foreign Trade Law, Georgetown University (New York: Praeger, 1974), pp. vii–x.

14. *Multinational Corporations in World Development*, pp. 92–93.

15. Cynthia Day Wallace, *Legal Control of the Multinational Enterprise* (The Hague: Martinus Nijhoff Publishers, 1983), p. 304.

16. See Ibid., p. 305; and Don Wallace, Jr., *International Regulation of Multinational Corporations*, pp. 85–88, 143, 168–169.

17. *The Search for Common Ground: A Survey of Efforts to Develop Codes of Behavior in International Investment*, a special report to the United States Committee, Pacific Basin Council (New York: The Conference Board, 1971), pp. 10–11.

18. Ibid., p. 13.

19. Sidney Rolfe, *The International Corporation* (Paris: International Chamber of Commerce, 1969), p. 141 and Epilogue.

20. *International Business Principles: Codes* (Stanford Research Institute International, no. 24, Menlo Park, Calif., 1975), pp. 9–16.

21. Robinson, p. 175.

22. *The Impact of Multinational Corporations on Development and on International Relations*, Department of Economic and Social Affairs (New York: United Nations, 1974), p. 55.

23. Robinson, p. 111. For an excellent discussion of this new "soft law" concept applied to both trade and investment topics, see Seymour J. Rubin and Gary Clyde Hufbauer, eds., *Emerging Standards of International Trade and Investment*, published under the auspices of The American Society of International Law (Totowa, N.J.: Rowman & Allanheld, 1984).

24. Raymond J. Waldmann, *Regulating International Business Through Codes of Conduct* (Washington, D.C.: American Enterprise Institute, 1980), pp. 21–23.

4

The Intergovernmental Code Movement

This chapter outlines major organizational activities relevant to the negotiation and adoption of intergovernmental codes of conduct. The focus is on those institutions, discussions, and resulting documents and programs that are related to the new type of voluntary code instrument described in Chapter 3. Primary attention is paid to activities in the Organization for Economic Cooperation and Development (OECD), the UN Economic and Social Council (ECOSOC), and several other specialized agencies.

No attempt is made to detail actual provisions of the various codes, although the OECD Guidelines are reprinted in the appendix for reference purposes. Similarly, the capsule descriptions of these activities are time-dependent, drafted to reflect the circumstances prevailing in mid–1984. Readers interested in obtaining more detail on the content of specific codes or in learning the current status of a particular activity will find a number of good information sources available to them. Among the best resources, from which much of this chapter's summary is compiled, are:

- UN Centre for Transnational Corporations, publisher of *The CTC Reporter* and a source for various UN documents relating to MNC issues.

- U.S. Department of State/Office of Investment Affairs, which serves as secretariat to the public Advisory Committee on International Investment, Technology, and Development. For the last several years the Office has updated annually an informative *Current Status Report on Selected International Organization Activities Relating to Transnational Enterprises*.

- U.S. Council for International Business, the U.S. arm of the International Chamber of Commerce. Utilizing its status as a non-governmental organization at the UN as well as advisory channels to the OECD, the Council publishes periodic issue studies as well as several timely newsletters, including *UN Report, EC Update, OECD Update*, and *International Information Flows*.

- International Organizations Monitoring Service, a client service of International Business Government Counsellors, Inc. A particularly useful summary document is the annual *International Organizations Regulatory Guidebook.*

ORGANIZATION FOR ECONOMIC COOPERATION AND DEVELOPMENT

The OECD is central to the intergovernmental code movement. This Paris-based group of twenty-four industrialized countries represents the nations that are both home and host to the vast majority of the world's MNCs. The 1976 OECD Guidelines for Multinational Enterprises was the first significant intergovernmental code directed at voluntary compliance by industry. Work continues in the organization, both on follow-up to the Guidelines and on more specific MNC issues. The OECD is an important forum for discussions among industrialized countries and a focal point for testing MNC responsiveness to a voluntary code approach.

OECD Guidelines for Multinational Enterprises

Largely at U.S. initiative, the OECD Council of Ministers established in January 1975 a Committee on International Investment and Multinational Enterprises (CIME) to improve cooperation among member countries on international investment issues. The United States was concerned about growing pressures in Western Europe that threatened to erode a liberal international investment climate. Many European nations, on the other hand, were increasingly concerned about MNC policies and actions, particularly as they affect national employment. The CIME's work agenda reflected both these concerns as it negotiated concurrently on standards for MNC conduct as well as on government policies covering national treatment for foreign investment and official investment incentives and disincentives.

After eighteen months of negotiations, the OECD Council of Ministers on June 21, 1976 adopted a Declaration on International Investment and Multinational Enterprises. The Declaration itself is very short, but it contains in an appendix the MNE Guidelines and three Decisions (binding on signatory governments) on intergovernmental consultation procedures, national treatment, and investment incentives and disincentives. Since the Declaration and Guidelines are reprinted in the appendix of this book, only a brief outline is offered here to highlight a few key points.

An introduction to the MNE Guidelines acknowledges the substantial benefits MNCs can bring to countries, offering the Guidelines as a way to encourage these positive contributions while minimizing difficulties that can arise from MNC operations. Although no precise definition is offered, MNCs are clearly described as including state-owned or mixed enterprises along with private companies. The Guidelines are explicitly stated to be voluntary and not legally enforceable. Finally, brief reference is made to governmental responsibilities to treat enterprises equitably and in accordance with international law, agreements, and contractual obligations.

Standards for corporate conduct are enumerated under the headings General Policies, Disclosure of Information, Competition, Financing, Taxation, Employment and Industrial Relations, and Science and Technology. Within these areas, the most contentious negotiating issues arose with regard to competition, information disclosure, and employee relations. The latter two areas are also the center of most follow-up attention on the Guidelines' implementation.

A related intergovernmental consultation agreement requires periodic CIME meetings on the Guidelines' implementation. BIAC and TUAC are invited to make presentations on the Guidelines. Individual enterprises may also be invited to present their views on Guidelines' implementation, but no conclusions can be reached as to their conduct in specific cases. Governmental consultation is encouraged where MNCs are subject to conflicting national requirements and a three-year period is set for a review of the Guidelines.

The OECD Council Decision on National Treatment pledges governments to notify the OECD of existing or new exceptions from a standard that would treat MNCs in accord with international law and no less favorably than domestic enterprises. The CIME is designated to act as a consultation forum on this issue and periodically to review compliance with the standard, with a view to extending its application. This nondiscrimination standard does not, however, apply to the entry of new foreign investment and it leaves open the use of national security and other rationales for maintaining exceptions to the general standard.

The Decision on International Investment Incentives and Disincentives is an even weaker intergovernmental agreement. The CIME is again designated as a consultation body to which governments can turn if they feel adversely affected by a member nation's incentive or disincentive measures. The objective is to reduce to a minimum such adverse impacts on other countries, but the Decision does not set any additional governmental obligations in this regard. As with the other parts of the Declaration, an initial three-year review period was specified.

Several working groups were established by the CIME to carry out its responsibilities under the 1976 Declaration. One working group focuses on international investment policies, essentially handling implementation of the two relevant Council Decisions. In 1982 this group also began studying trade related investment measures (TRIMs), or trade performance requirements, in both OECD nations and developing countries. Another working group concentrates on accounting standards, seeking to improve international comparability of financial information. This group works on technical clarifications of accounting terms contained in the Guidelines and considers such issues as foreign currency translation, consolidation, and the Guidelines' application to financial reporting by banks and insurance companies.

56 International Codes and Multinational Business

The third CIME working group is charged with reviewing the Guidelines' acceptance, discussing clarifications, and proposing any needed changes. The Guidelines underwent an official review in 1979 three years after its initial adoption. Subsequently, the working group undertook a number of projects leading up to a mid-term report in 1982 and another full review, conducted in 1984. The group's activities included a survey on experience with the Guidelines, promotion of national contact points for matters concerning the Guidelines, and sponsorship of a study on MNCs and structural adjustment.

In addition, the group considered a number of specific cases of alleged MNC violations of the Guidelines in order to clarify their application (without reaching judgments in any individual case). One proposed change was accepted and incorporated into the Guidelines to cover an unforeseen issue about the transport of workers across national boundaries during a strike, bringing the OECD standard into line with an ILO principle. Some additional explanatory comments on the scope and meaning of Guidelines' provisions were offered in a report on the review.

During the most recent 1984 review, the Guidelines were amended to add a brief new reference to consumer interests. The review report also called on MNCs to cooperate with host government policies on technological innovation. Other major items centered on labor relations issues, as MNCs were also asked to negotiate with a subsidiary's employees in the workers' national language, to adopt a positive approach toward employee organizing activities, and to cooperate more fully with labor on mitigating adverse effects of management decisions. Another full review is not scheduled until 1990, but the CIME will continue to issue clarifications or even recommend amendments to the Guidelines as needed in the interim. The review report indicated that further work will be done to apply the information and disclosure section to banking and insurance companies, new surveys may be undertaken on other Guidelines' sections, and environmental protection issues will be given especially close attention, perhaps warranting a new addition to the Guidelines.

The significance of the OECD Guidelines and its implementation activities will be considered in Chapter 5. Substantively the document sets a common core of standards covering important areas of corporate conduct. Still, the principal authority of national law is recognized at the outset, while politically negotiated wording leaves much deliberate ambiguity in areas where harmonization of national policy is unattainable. This ambiguity, combined with the Guidelines' voluntary nature, allows some room for flexible corporate implementation under individual circumstances.

Corporations are thus left to use this flexibility to apply the Guidelines' standards in areas where national policies and approaches may differ. The relative success of MNCs in meeting this challenge then becomes the subject of governmental and, at times, general public scrutiny as review sessions test experience under the Guidelines.

OECD Privacy Protection Guidelines

On September 22, 1980 the OECD adopted a set of Guidelines on the Protection of Privacy and Transborder Flows of Personal Data. This document, in both background and content, mixes the traditional approach to intergovernmental agreements with the voluntary MNC code concept. The most interesting aspect of this example is that MNCs strongly supported negotiation of the Guidelines and vigorously promote their voluntary endorsement of it as a rationale for avoiding tighter national regulation of transborder data flows (TBDFs).

The Privacy Protection Guidelines originated from a concern that the evolution of data banks and data processing equipment could lead to electronic transmission of personal information across national boundaries in ways that violate personal privacy. Governments objected to the loss of control over information on their citizens once such data were transmitted outside their territorial jurisdiction. In Europe this concern led to a proliferation of national laws establishing new regulatory bodies. Registration and/or licensing was required for data that would be stored, processed or otherwise used outside the country of origin. For MNCs this procedure means extra time and expense as well as the possible denial of planned transmission or a need for maintaining duplicative facilities in several countries.

The Council of Europe negotiated a convention, completed in 1980, that attempted to harmonize the evolving national procedures among European countries. The convention provides that personal data flows among signatory countries will not require special authorization. For nations outside the Council, such as the United States, there is no guarantee against the imposition of special requirements.

The OECD Privacy Protection Guidelines were negotiated from the U.S. side to achieve a set of minimum common standards that, if observed voluntarily by companies, might mitigate the need for national government regulations. The guidelines set forth provisions concerning the collection, accuracy, disclosure, and other related treatment of personal data. At the urging of U.S. government officials and some business organizations, many U.S. MNCs quickly endorsed the guidelines. By the first OECD follow-up meeting in 1981, U.S. officials presented a list of over one hundred corporate and association endorsements, a number that has now nearly doubled. The U.S. argument is that voluntary adherence to the guidelines by these corporations means that at least these firms do not require tight regulation by national data protection authorities. Critics contend that endorsement does not constitute implementation and that some of the MNCs do not follow the guidelines in their actual business operations.

The Guidelines provide for compliance through either voluntary actions or national legislation. These Guidelines are addressed more directly to governments than is the case in the general OECD Guidelines for MNEs, but the negotiating background and U.S. use of the document's voluntary approach makes it a close relative of the new intergovernmental code form described in Chapter 3.

In the OECD the issue of transborder data flows now has moved to an examination of broader trade, economic, and legal aspects of the problem. A Group of Experts on TBDFs helps guide public and private discussions on these subjects, encouraging studies that were considered at a symposium on TBDFs in late 1983. Slower progress is being made on the U.S. request for an OECD statement of general intent by member governments to support free dataflows across borders. Other studies on TBDFs are now also underway in the United Nations.

Other OECD Activities

The OECD sponsors intergovernmental discussions on a growing range of important topics relating to economic relations between the industrialized countries. Much of the work is technical in nature and aims at harmonization or at least coordination of government policies in areas where a common approach can be defined. While most of these activities take the form of traditional intergovernmental accords, a few discussions seem to be leading a bit closer to the code approach discussed in this book.

Relevant to the subject of MNC codes is the OECD "Code of Liberalization of Capital Movements," adopted in 1961. Despite its code designation, this document remains an example of a traditional intergovernmental accord in the international investment area. Member nations agree to progressively eliminate restrictions on capital movements between their countries, with certain exceptions. A Committee for Capital Movements and Invisible Transactions oversees issues relating to the Code and in 1981 began work on a proposed amendment dealing with the right of establishment. As adopted at the 1984 OECD Ministerial Meeting, this amendment complements the investment policy standards in the 1976 Decision on National Treatment, which covered only existing investment rather than new entry conditions. Pending a demonstration of increased effectiveness, however, the code and its many reservations still exemplify the limited success of traditional international investment agreements rather than real movement toward binding international policy harmonization.

Restrictive business practices and the control of transfer pricing for tax evasion are two other areas where limited but important technical work is occurring within the OECD. For both these subjects, the emphasis has been on designing consultation, coordination, and information-sharing procedures. A similar approach is being followed in the OECD's Committee on Consumer Policy, first formed in 1969. While concentrating mainly on information exchange and consumer education, the Committee also drafted a section on MNC obligations to consumer protection for incorporation into the OECD Guidelines on MNCs. (The CIME opted instead to include consumer protection among a list of items on which MNCs should consider national goals.) Most recently the Committee began a cost-benefit study to compare voluntary versus mandatory standards on product safety. The study's outcome, combined with rapid movement toward written standards in some other international forums, may push the OECD closer to developing voluntary guidelines for MNCs in this area to go with the procedural aid being given to intergovernmental coordination efforts.

In a somewhat similar vein the OECD's work on environmental protection evolved several sets of guidelines to improve coordination between member countries' policies, particularly in the areas of hazardous waste and chemicals. These guidelines deal with such subjects as notification of hazardous exports, responsibility for waste management, submission of premarketing data to regulatory agencies, product testing and laboratory practices, and the availability of information to the public. These guidelines are again aimed at affecting government procedures first and corporate conduct indirectly. Several topics relate to broader international code concerns, however, and could lead to discussions on voluntary MNC codes if intergovernmental coordination fails to develop fully or if it becomes necessary to address the issues on a global basis rather than just within the more relatively homogeneous OECD environment.

UNITED NATIONS

The United Nations is the seat of diverse intergovernmental code discussions, as befits its role as the most fully representative global organization. These activities display a remarkable range, from an all-inclusive MNC code to specific sectoral marketing guidelines. Despite the tendency in some quarters to dismiss UN debates as exercises in eternal futility, code activities are proving to be remarkably adaptive to political realities and potentially effective under flexible implementation procedures. The best way to examine these activities is to begin with the broadest code discussions and then briefly survey related developments in other UN agencies.

Economic and Social Council

The UN Economic and Social Council (ECOSOC) operates to coordinate and set priorities for the activities of many specialized agencies and institutions. In 1972, the ECOSOC initiated actions leading to the Group of Eminent Persons' study of MNCs and later followed up its recommendations by creating the UN Commission on Transnational Corporations (TNCs) and the UN Centre on TNCs. While the ECOSOC oversees many other activities as well, the work of the TNC Commission encompasses the most comprehensive code effort.

Commission on Transnational Corporations

Formulation of a code of conduct for MNCs was given the highest priority among the various tasks undertaken by the TNC Commission. Through its first four years, this effort was guided by a special intergovernmental working group that identified major issues, debated their application, and in 1980 began drafting actual code paragraphs. By 1982, over sixty draft provisions existed when ECOSOC decided to convene a special TNC Commission session to conclude the code.

While some further progress was made on the code at this 1983 special session, most of the major problem areas remained. Agreement has been largely achieved on provisions dealing with MNC conduct covering:

* respect for national sovereignty and developmental objectives
* contract negotiation and renegotiation
* human rights
* balance of payments
* ownership and control
* transfer pricing and taxation
* consumer and environmental protection
* information disclosure
* cross-referencing of the ILO "Tripartite Declaration on MNEs and Social Policy"
* intergovernmental cooperation and code implementation, assessment, and review procedures.

Disagreements remain on both broad and specific issues. The most difficult areas appear to be (1) definition of TNC—whether state-owned and mixed public–private enterprises should be included, a position opposed by socialist countries; (2) jurisdiction—the exclusive local authority (Calvo doctrine) view of developing countries versus international arbitration procedures supported by developed nations; (3) nationalization/compensation—related to the jurisdiction question regarding whether national authority or international law and practice should determine settlements; (4) code status—legally binding versus voluntary code adherence. Several other issues still lacking agreement relate to technology transfer, capital repatriation, national treatment for TNCs, and transparency of national laws and regulations.

In 1983 it appeared that this code exercise might finally break down when first the TNC Commission and then the ECOSOC failed to renew a mandate to continue code negotiations. Finally late in the year, the General Assembly called for another session in 1984, which took place in June after a January preparatory meeting.

While there was some initial movement on the TNC definition issue, little progress was made during the three-week meeting. Higher-level political decisions are now required, particularly among the developing countries, before next steps are taken regarding the timing and nature of future discussions.

International Agreement on Illicit Payments

The ECOSOC in 1976 established an Intergovernmental Working Group on Corrupt Practices to negotiate an international agreement to prevent and eliminate bribery and extortion in international commercial transactions. This action stemmed from a strong U.S. initiative connected to overseas bribery scandals and passage of the FCPA. Reversing its position on other aspects of code of conduct discussions in the UN and elsewhere, the U.S. government called for a legally binding agreement on illicit payments.

After several years of negotiations, a nearly completed and unbracketed (agreedto) text was ready by early 1979. The few remaining issues could probably be resolved at a diplomatic conference, which was proposed by the United States. The developing countries agreed to this action only if it was linked to a similar diplomatic conference to conclude the overall MNC code, a position rejected by the United States. This deadlock over differing interests and priorities has left the largely completed illicit payments text to wait until further progress is made on the general MNC code. The mandate for the committee working on illicit payments expired and no further action has been taken or is likely until the question of linkage to the full code is resolved.

International Standards of Accounting and Reporting

Another code-related exercise under ECOSOC's jurisdiction is the work of an intergovernmental group of experts in the area of international standards of accounting and reporting. An early group operating under the TNC Commission produced a report in 1977 that contained an extensive list of items that should be disclosed by MNCs. Developed nation representatives objected that this group had exceeded its mandate, and they insisted a new group replace it.

The new group of experts was to concentrate on more technical harmonization issues, but it also discussed and drafted a text on accounting provisions for consideration as part of the overall UN Code on TNCs. Some observers point to the agreement achieved on certain issues in these and other group discussions as evidence that further progress might be possible on the same issues in the general MNC code. For instance, there was general agreement on the principle of nondiscrimination between MNCs and national enterprises in terms of reporting requirements; a call for financial statements giving a "true and fair view" (a standard accounting practice in developed nations) rather than the use of "accurate and honest" terminology favored by many developing nations; and the generally voluntary implementation approach assumed by the group's recommendations.

Consumer Protection

Beginning with a 1979 request for a report on the subject, the UN rapidly evolved draft guidelines for consumer protection, formally proposed to ECO-

SOC in mid–1983 and referred for further negotiation the following year. The general UN Code on TNCs already has a draft provision on consumer protection, but these guidelines offer more extensive treatment of standards for areas such as physical safety and quality, information programs, redress measures, and specific guidelines for food, water, and pharmaceutical products. Significant U.S. opposition to the guidelines claimed that the standards assumed too much government regulation and not enough voluntary business action.

After some compromises, the UN General Assembly adopted by consensus in April, 1985, revised consumer protection guidelines as a set of principles to assist countries in establishing consumer protection policies. Some provisions are weaker than desired by consumer interest groups, but several issues were decided against the U.S. position. For example, the document retained references to some specific industries, such as pharmaceuticals, and did not use the qualifying term "unreasonable" in discussing risks and hazards.

The UN Centre on TNCs

The UN Centre on Transnational Corporations (TNCs) does not exactly fit the nature of the previously discussed ECOSOC code activities, but it is integrally related to all of them. Created by ECOSOC in 1975, the Centre is part of the UN Secretariat that serves as a focal point for MNC-related activities. Three functions comprise the Centre's work in this area: staffing code of conduct discussions, conducting research and gathering information on MNCs, and providing technical assistance to developing countries.

The Centre supplies staff resources needed by the UN Commission on TNCs in its work on a code of conduct. This responsibility then involves the Centre in related discussions as well, since the Commission has used specialized working groups or other forums to work on specific issues. The Centre's staff function has often supplied a needed capability for independent review and the suggestion of alternatives when political negotiations between government representatives hit an impasse.

Much of the Centre's research and information-gathering activity is related to the code work, providing documentation for the discussion of particular issues. Studies have covered the impact of MNCs in specific industry sectors, the status of national laws and regulation affecting MNCs, the relationship of MNCs to particular issues such as transborder data flows or the environment, and an effort to develop corporate profiles by collecting data on individual MNCs.

The Centre's technical cooperation program is designed to aid developing countries by strengthening their capability to negotiate with MNCs. This assistance includes training sessions on negotiation and regulation techniques, an advisory service on regulations or contractual arrangements, an information clearinghouse on MNCs, and a roster of international experts who can consult with governments on specific aspects of MNC operations.

Other Intergovernmental Code Activities

Lying outside the ECOSOC are a number of other UN-related agencies and programs that have a direct bearing upon the code of conduct exercise. Discussions in several specialized agencies are examining MNC standards on particular issues and a few completed codes have been adopted. Other activities, sometimes in organizations less directly connected to the UN exercise, also bear upon the current evolution of the intergovernmental code movement.

International Labor Organization

The International Labor Organization (ILO) is a unique tripartite body (including representatives of governments, employers, and workers) that is establishing important precedents in the international code area. Created in 1919 by the Treaty of Versailles as an agency of the League of Nations, the ILO survived the League's demise when it became affiliated with the new United Nations, agreeing to accept UN member states into its organization. The ILO's tripartite governance makes it an important center for discussions of MNC issues, resulting already in standards covering MNCs and social policy, as well as an evolving implementation process for that code.

In 1976 a group was formed by the ILO's Tripartite Advisory Committee on the Relationship of Multinational Enterprises and Social Policy to draft a set of principles that would cover the impact of MNCs on employment, training, industrial relations, and other aspects of work and life. A completed draft was adopted by the ILO in November 1977 as the Tripartite Declaration of Principles Concerning Multinational Enterprises and Social Policy. While the United States had temporarily withdrawn from the ILO at that time, the U.S. government had participated in drafting the code and has since supported the document.

The ILO Declaration contains several important principles that are relevant to international code discussions. Within the labor area, the document addresses freedom of association, MNC working conditions in host countries, notification and provision of information to governments and unions on MNC operational changes (such as takeovers or production transfers), and collective bargaining practices, such as threatening production shifts to influence unfairly the labor-management negotiations. On more general issues, the ILO Declaration is a voluntary code. Consistent with its tripartite nature, it addresses firms and labor organizations as well as governments. State-owned as well as private firms are included in its definition of MNCs, and it supports nondiscriminatory national treatment between domestic enterprises and MNCs.

A year after the ILO Declaration was adopted, the UN group that was drafting the code of conduct for MNCs agreed to use the ILO document as the UN code's section on employment and labor relations. The Declaration will be cross-referenced in the code and printed in its annex, thus helping to resolve code

negotiation difficulties in the sensitive labor relations area. This cross-referencing solution was reached by formally agreeing that some positions taken in the
ILO document would not prejudice decisions still to be taken in the code negotiation, such as the voluntary adherence principle and the definition of an MNC.
Despite this caveat, the ILO Declaration sets an important political precedent,
similar in many respects to the UNCTAD Code on Restrictive Business Practices (to be discussed next), that points the way toward a resolution of problems
that have thus far prevented agreement on a full UN code on MNCs.

Action in the ILO is setting an important precedent as well in the area of
code implementation. When the Declaration was adopted, the issue of its implementation procedures was left unresolved. After reviewing several alternatives, the ILO Director General recommended that governments periodically report on experience with the Declaration. Responses to a first survey questionnaire
were considered in 1980 by a special ILO committee. Subsequently the ILO
Governing Body approved another round of reports and established the Standing Committee on Multinational Enterprises to monitor implementation, guide
research, and deal with disputes concerning the Declaration.

Following a 1983 review of the second survey, the new committee considered additional implementation steps. In order to insure better reporting from
labor and business, future ILO surveys may be sent directly to these groups
rather than just to governments, or may otherwise seek government assurances
that their replies reflect direct consultations. Some discussion of making the
Declaration mandatory was turned aside vigorously by representatives from the
industrialized countries. The stage appears set, however, for the new committee
to function in a more direct dispute settlement role.

Under the ILO Declaration, complaints about an MNC's noncompliance with
the code's principles should be raised first with the company and then with the
host government. If the dispute remains unresolved, the government can raise
this issue to the intergovernmental level by asking the ILO for an interpretation
of the Declaration. If the government chooses not to raise the issue or does so
unsatisfactorily, the labor union may then directly raise the issue with the ILO.

The new ILO committee would handle such complaints in much the same
way as the OECD's CIME discusses clarification of its Guidelines for MNC's.
The major difference is that the tripartite nature of the ILO committee gives
labor unions direct participation in the interpretative body. Although no cases
have yet been brought to the ILO in this manner, the International Confederation of Free Trade Unions (ICFTU) publishes a handbook explaining how this
ILO procedure can be used in the bargaining process with MNCs. The ILO
Declaration thus demonstrates the potential for a flexible code implementation
process, evolving from no agreement on procedures at the time of adoption to
a standing tripartite committee that oversees implementation reports, directs study
projects, and can hear disputes over noncompliance with the Declaration's voluntary principles.

Another recent ILO action was the 1982 adoption of the Convention and Recommendation on Termination of Employment at the Initiative of the Employer. The Convention will become law in countries ratifying it, while the Recommendation is a non-binding guideline often referenced in business–labor negotiations. These documents list invalid reasons for termination of employees, implying a rejection of the ''fire at will'' doctrine used in the United States. Procedural steps are outlined that include information disclosure, consultations, and right of appeal. While more radical proposals were modified before the documents were adopted by the ILO, the U.S. business and government representatives voted against the Convention and abstained in voting on the Recommendation. These new labor standards will become important reference points for MNCs, particularly in cases involving mass dismissals.

Discussion has begun on another proposed recommendation that would establish non-binding principles on employment policy with particular relevance to MNC actions. This proposal seeks to control MNC investments as well as the introduction of new technologies in order to minimize adverse effects on employment. Consultations are called for between government, business, and labor, while the role of collective bargaining is also emphasized.

Finally, the ILO has completed the drafting of a Code of Practices on the Safe Use of Asbestos. The code is intended as a guide to both government and industry, containing scientific and technical information regarding safe use of the material. Discussion is continuing on the possibility of a different international instrument that would establish binding fundamental principles for worker protection against industrial risks, such as work with asbestos.

UN Conference on Trade and Development

The UN Conference on Trade and Development (UNCTAD) includes all UN members as well as a few nations that are only members of some specialized agencies. Originally focused on trade issues between developing nations and the industrialized countries, UNCTAD has evolved into the main UN body for a range of developing country problems, including work on MNC issues and calls to implement a New International Economic Order. Two major code of conduct exercises are centered in UNCTAD covering restrictive business practices and technology transfer issues, while the organization could serve as a catalyst for action on the other MNC-related issues in the future.

Successful conclusion of the UNCTAD Code on Restrictive Business Practices (RBPs) stands in contrast to the pessimistic views voiced by many observers who see UN code discussions as hopelessly deadlocked over irresolvable issues. This viewpoint was expressed concerning the RBP code as late as the year before its approval. After more than a decade of UN deliberations, UNCTAD activities culminated with two diplomatic negotiating conferences on RBPs in 1979 and 1980, leading to General Assembly adoption of the code in December 1980. Officially named The Set of Multilaterally Agreed Equitable

Principles and Rules for the Control of Restrictive Business Practices, this document exhibits many of the characteristics of a new intergovernmental code of conduct for MNCs.

In subject-specific content, the RBP code contains numerous important provisions, but seemingly deferred to the industrialized (primarily U.S.) positions on many major issues. Among such areas are the code's use of a "rule of reason" test; treatment of parent-subsidiary relationships in a way that minimizes challenges to intracorporate transactions; and avoidance of a shared monopoly provision in defining dominant position, so companies in an oligopolistic industry are not judged to hold a dominant position unless they are acting together to restrain trade.

On more general code issues, the RBP agreement establishes a significant pattern for possible compromises. The code addresses recommendations both to governments and, particularly in one chapter, directly to enterprises. The definition of MNCs is established in a way that includes state-owned firms. National treatment is addressed by including nondiscrimination language in applying RBP standards to all enterprises. The code is voluntary, but implementation devices and a five-year review period are established. A permanent Intergovernmental Group of Experts is created by the code. Although forbidden to pass judgment in specific disputes, the Group monitors implementation, exchanges information, facilitates consultations, provides technical assistance to developing countries, conducts research studies, and acts as an on-going forum for discussion of RBP issues. Annual reports on the code's effectiveness will culminate in a conference in 1985 that will conduct a major review of the code and its implementation.

The UNCTAD also is negotiating, but has not yet completed a code on technology transfer. These discussions date back to 1975, when contrasting code drafts were offered by the developing and industrialized nations. Periodic talks continued until a major obstacle was seemingly removed in 1979. That year agreement was reached that the code could be voluntary as long as appropriate implementation procedures were established. In practice, this issue has evolved into a discussion over whether a review conference, to be held about four to six years after the code's adoption, will have the ability to make the code into a binding instrument.

Nearly two-thirds of the draft text is agreed upon, but significant problems remain. Developing countries perceive that they compromised too much on the RBP code, so there are major disputes over how RBPs will be applied to technology transfer activities. Disagreement exists on how to treat intracorporate transfers of technology and actions by local companies on behalf of an MNC. Another compromise is needed on provisions concerning the relationship between national law and dispute settlement agreements.

The UNCTAD is also active in a number of other areas that are relevant to MNC issues. Major actions are underway in shipping, where the UNCTAD Convention on a Code of Conduct for Liner Conferences has been ratified by enough countries to enter into force. This instrument is more a traditional international convention establishing agreement between governments rather than the new type of intergovernmental code aimed at MNCs. Other UNCTAD discussions are proceeding on registration of ships, essentially aimed at phasing out flags of convenience sometimes used by MNCs. There are efforts to get UNCTAD more involved in the discussion of standards in pharmaceuticals and in the regulation of patents, but thus far the organization is only studying these issues while major negotiations on the subjects are conducted in the World Health Organization (WHO) and the World Intellectual Property Organization (WIPO), respectively.

World Health Organization

The WHO is another intergovernmental body whose membership is open to any UN member countries. For many years the organization has coordinated global health activities, providing medical training and technical assistance, promoting medical research, and exchanging information on communicable diseases and the substances used for their control. Recently the WHO became involved more directly in MNC issues, most notably on standards for the marketing of infant formula, but also with regard to essential drug distribution and the control of hazardous or unsafe products.

In 1981, the annual meeting of the World Health Assembly, WHO's governing body, adopted an *International Code of Marketing of Breast-milk Substitutes*, with only the United States casting a negative vote. This code, originated jointly with the UN Children's Fund (UNICEF), suggests restrictions on promotional activities for infant formula covering such activities as advertising, samples, and sales incentives. The code itself is not legally binding, but governments are encouraged to pass national legislation to implement it.

When WHO reviewed the code's implementation in 1983, the results were mixed, as many nations had taken some steps to change their policies but the code was not being fully enforced. No changes were made in the code itself since more time seemed necessary to concentrate on follow-up measures. In addition to governmental policy actions, many MNCs directly endorsed the code and stated that they would voluntarily bring their practices into line with its provisions, whether or not required to do so by local law. Reviews of the code will take place regularly every two years, beginning in 1984. A Secretariat report requested for 1986 could open the door to discussion of extending the code to other infant foods.

The WHO has also developed an Essential Drug List and is seeking to work cooperatively with pharmaceutical firms and others to make these drugs available to meet the most critical health needs of developing countries. Another initiative, undertaken jointly with the ILO and United Nations Environment Program (UNEP), focuses on the collection and exchange of information on hazardous chemicals, pesticides, and pharmaceuticals. A related exercise is the WHO's work with the Food and Agriculture Organization (FAO) in administering the *Codex Alimentarius* regarding international safety and quality standards for foods, as well as some new research specifically on pesticide residue in food. Future WHO activity may lead it toward international guidelines involving alcohol and tobacco, since it has already begun health-oriented activities with regard to both products.

UN Environment Program

Created by the General Assembly in 1972, the UNEP coordinates a series of activities, several of which affect MNCs, with one area evolving into a guideline-drafting exercise. A meeting on environmental law in 1981 recommended development of an international code, convention, or guidelines to address such issues as marine pollution, transport of hazardous wastes, and international trade in harmful chemicals. Follow-up sessions of governmental experts in 1983 and 1984 resulted in first drafts on some guidelines in these areas, with the nature and content of the standards now subject to further negotiations and the solicitation of technical advice.

Intergovernmental Bureau for Informatics

The Intergovernmental Bureau for Informatics (IBI), composed primarily of developing countries, has since 1978 focused on transborder data flow issues, including the formulation of draft guidelines on the subject. Originally created in 1951 as a part of the UN Educational, Science, and Cultural Organization (UNESCO), the IBI became independent in 1974 and has gained prominence through several conferences, beginning with a 1978 meeting on Strategies and Policies for Informatics (SPIN). While France, Italy, and Spain are IBI members, most developed countries including the United States have not joined the organization, although some send observer delegations to its meetings.

The IBI created three working groups on TBDFs in 1981, covering economic, legal, and technical issues. These groups carry on various studies within their areas and help frame issues for further deliberations at upcoming conferences. The IBI additionally provides training and technical assistance to some national government programs on informatics. The scope and nature of the draft TBDF code is still to be resolved at future IBI conferences, but the organization's activities have stimulated more attention and activity on the issue among governments, business, and other international forums.

Organization of American States

In 1975 the Organization of American States (OAS) undertook a study of MNCs designed to culminate in a code of conduct. A list of ten principles was constructed, but the United States offered a list of reservations, principally to application of the Calvo doctrine on exclusive local jurisdiction and to the idea of a binding code. The ten principles were ultimately passed over U.S. objections by the OAS General Assembly in 1978. This action had no real impact, however, since all parties deferred to UN efforts to negotiate a global code. It is doubtful that a regional OAS code for MNCs could be meaningfully implemented if the UN code, blocked by many of the same arguments, cannot be successfully negotiated.

EVALUATING INTERGOVERNMENTAL CODE PROGRESS

An evaluation of the intergovernmental code movement depends largely on one's perspective and initial expectations. Nevertheless, for a concept that is only about a decade old, intergovernmental codes have generated an enormous amount of activity and a surprising record of concluded agreements. Only tentative judgments can be ventured on the movement's ultimate impact, since the real effects from codes will be measured in their implementation, which is just beginning, and in the response of MNCs to this new form of international guidance.

Previous chapters traced the evolution of international codes and identified their origins in the failure of multilateral diplomacy to achieve more traditional agreements in the international investment area. Obstacles to an international law solution were circumvented by the use of non-binding code instruments directed largely at corporations, where the standards' voluntary nature and flexible implementation process allow governments to agree on guidelines while still maintaining maximum sovereign authority over their application in individual circumstances.

The United Nations and the OECD provide the main focus for this chapter's summary, reflecting the nature of developing country and labor union criticism of MNC operations and the attempt by industrialized country governments to fashion a common response among themselves. If developments had been restricted to just two general code instruments, the OECD Guidelines and the UN Code on TNCs, the issue would be relatively simple to dissect and probably not as significant. Instead, the multifaceted nature of MNC operations, combined with the particular interests of diverse intergovernmental agencies, caused a proliferation of code activities. Theoretically, these separate discussions might be squeezed under the umbrella of a general UN code, such as in cross-referencing of the ILO Declaration. In fact, the other activities have taken on a life of their own, with different specific interests, implementation procedures, and bureaucratic involvement all expanding the reach of the intergovernmental code movement.

Despite substantive obstacles and diplomatic wrangling, a series of new diplomatic instruments have been negotiated in just over a decade. The OECD Guidelines are well established and their implementation process is becoming progressively more sophisticated. The ILO Declaration has set forth agreed standards in a particularly contentious subject area and the document's implementation process is now entering a crucial testing phase. The UNCTAD Restrictive Business Practices Code demonstrates how quickly negotiations can move from deadlock to agreement, although some developing countries now feel they compromised too much on the document and will try to recover lost ground through implementation procedures and negotiations on the technology transfer code. The WHO code on marketing of infant formula is evidence that the intergovernmental code movement can evolve instruments affecting operational business procedures in specific product areas. Even large parts of the general UN code have been agreed upon, although the remaining areas of disagreement are still very significant.

A broad potential also exists for code expansion into new areas and issues that reach into other aspects of multinational business dealings. Some discussion is already occurring on a sectoral basis, as with pharmaceuticals and chemicals, while other activities focus on general issues like consumer protection or specific issues such as collusive tendering of bids.

Another potentially important stimulus to code activity is the work of some European institutions. The Council of Europe (CoE) has already passed a Convention on transborder data flows that helped generate the OECD Privacy Guidelines. A follow-up, non-binding Recommendation allows room for possible industry codes to apply data protection standards to direct marketing. In 1984, a CoE Recommendation on broadcast advertising drew heavily on voluntary industry self-regulation codes on that subject. More controversial work is being considered on pharmaceutical marketing, as will be discussed in Chapter 6. Actions in the EEC Commission could also lead to code-related activity, particularly where Community-wide industry policy proposals lack the political consensus for adoption as a binding Directive, but could be passed in a non-binding Recommendation form.

With all of this past, current, and potential activity on codes of conduct, what significance should be attributed to these voluntary instruments? Even if the intergovernmental code movement is not a transient aberration that will go away if ignored long enough, is it really worthy of serious attention? A proper evaluation of the likely impact of these codes, and the argument that appropriate corporate action is indeed necessary, depends on an appreciation of their use as law or levers, which is the subject of the next chapter.

5

Intergovernmental Codes as Law or Levers

Proliferating discussions on international codes of conduct leave many people feeling uneasy as they try to grasp more firmly the deliberately vague nature of these documents. The code label has been attached to a variety of devices in the past and does not itself denote any single sure meaning, particularly when applied at the international level. Traditionally codes agreed upon between governments were at least related to legal instruments, as either a compilation of preexisting standards or a separate new document. These types of accords still exist, but a new form of voluntary intergovernmental code, directed primarily at MNCs, has been added.

Voluntary intergovernmental codes are often associated with laws despite their proclaimed non-binding nature. This tendency stems primarily from three sources. First, any set of standards developed, issued, and endorsed by governments is by virtue of authorship associated with legal authority. A related second reason is that current voluntary standards can become the forerunner of later mandatory regulations. Finally, the spectre of possible binding standards is used by both proponents and opponents of these codes to gain wider attention and to argue their different points of view.

The concept of intergovernmental codes as a lever derives mainly from their use by organized labor in early experience with the OECD Guidelines. Labor unions consciously exploited public pressure aspects of the voluntary code to gain advantages in confrontations with individual MNCs. This use of code standards as a public pressure lever confirmed one of the fears expressed by some business executives, but closer examination of this experience shows that such leveraged outcomes are highly dependent on case circumstances and particularly on the role played by national government actors.

These two dimensions of intergovernmental codes as law or levers have dominated most analyses of their impact. Business executives fear the unfair use of codes in either way and thereby approach code development and endorsement from a very defensive posture. Unions and other MNC-critic groups, including many developing country governments, purposefully seek to design and use code instruments as new law, or at least as additional leverage, to alter the outcome of specific bargaining situations. Unfortunately, this focus on law and levers obscures the guidance nature of these documents. Greater attention to a guidance role could actually help avoid many of the difficulties inherent in a law or in a political leverage approach to using codes in resolving MNC problems.

This chapter builds on the theme of intergovernmental codes as a new diplomatic instrument as outlined and illustrated in Chapters 3 and 4. In order to assess the codes' significance and potential, strands of past perceptions, expectations, and factual experience are separated to clarify the actions now being taken by governments, labor unions, and MNCs. This examination should help show how new intergovernmental codes relate to the subject of individual corporate codes of conduct, which will be the focus of the next three chapters.

CODES AND LAW

Traditional intergovernmental accords focused on legally binding commitments in the form of treaties, conventions, or other such documents. When properly ratified and entered into force, these agreements achieve the status of national and/or international law. Certain agreements establish binding commitments between governments where the effects of the commitments are less specific and direct. Several such intergovernmental accords are associated with voluntary MNC codes: for example, the OECD Code of Liberalization of Capital Movements and the OECD Council Decisions on National Treatment and on International Investment Incentives and Disincentives. These types of commitments are to principles or procedures rather than to the specification of direct law.

The OECD Council Decisions are, of course, part of the 1976 Declaration on International Investment and Multinational Enterprises that contains the Guidelines for MNCs. The Guidelines are specifically voluntary and, being addressed directly to corporations, introduce the novelty of a governmentally adopted, non-binding MNC code. The Decision on intergovernmental consultation, however, sets out binding procedures for governments on their talks about the Guidelines' implementation. This packaged approach combines the traditional with the new, binding with voluntary, and intergovernmental with corporate, setting a precedent for similarly mixed patterns in other MNC codes.

For example, the OECD's Privacy Guidelines establish agreed standards, not law, but leave open to national implementation whether voluntary or mandatory follow-up procedures are used. The UNCTAD Restrictive Business Practices Code is a voluntary document where governments agree on general antitrust standards, but it also directly addresses issues of appropriate MNC actions. The

WHO *International Code of Marketing of Breast-milk Substitutes* is not legally binding, but governments are encouraged to implement it as national legislation, while corporations are voluntarily adopting its standards.

This strange mixture of binding and non-binding provisions, combined with different enforcement applications at the national and international levels creates a confusing legal picture. Such a result is inevitable, however, given the objectives of the major government, labor, and business participants in the code development process.

Governments are torn between the desire to achieve international investment law in the areas that serve their interests and the determination to maintain sovereign authority over vital spheres of unilateral national regulation. The U.S. government wants binding international commitments to a liberal investment climate, but not at the expense of losing its extraterritorial jurisdiction claims or generating tighter international regulation of its free enterprise firms. Other OECD nations jealously guard their right to take national interest actions in foreign investment matters. Many of these nations favor increased regulatory powers over MNCs, but differ over the specific application of more controls, as is evident in debates over proposed European Community company directives. Developing countries promote binding international controls over MNCs, backed by home country enforcement commitments, but are unwilling to sacrifice any of their own national jurisdiction claims, such as in the Calvo doctrine, to international law standards.

Labor unions' objectives are clearer since their current powers are not placed in any jeopardy by the proposed codes. The unions generally favor binding agreements that place MNCs under tighter government regulation, thereby expanding union leverage at the national level and creating new labor rights regarding consultation and bargaining at the international level. If a fully binding international accord cannot be reached, unions consider a lesser commitment a first step and concentrate on extending available implementation procedures to their own advantage.

Even the business community's position enhances the connection between intergovernmental codes and legal commitments. A fundamental corporate demand is that any code document must be balanced; that is, it must recognize governmental as well as corporate obligations and responsibilities. Confusion arises because corporations insist that the document should be voluntary vis-à-vis business conduct standards, but undertake binding commitments regarding government responsibilities to business. The composite package of binding and non-binding documents in the OECD Declaration is a good reflection of this position, except that business would have preferred tighter standards for governmental conduct.

Paradoxically, the business community's greatest fear is that voluntary intergovernmental codes for MNCs will evolve into binding international standards, or will stimulate new national law patterned on voluntary international codes. This fear is hardly groundless since such a development is the explicit desire and intention of both organized labor and many developing countries. Statements by TUAC with regard to the OECD Guidelines clearly state a preference for binding standards as well as an intention to press for tougher EEC or national laws. Similarly, the developing countries' position regarding a review period for UNCTAD codes is designed to allow for a modification of the voluntary codes into legally binding commitments.

This mixed set of objectives and perceptions thus assures that voluntary intergovernmental codes addressing MNC conduct is strongly associated with the notion of international law and the regulation of multinational business. In practice, however, the link between voluntary codes and law appears much more tenuous. The very reason for new intergovernmental codes is that voluntary standards are needed on international investment issues where international law accords cannot be reached. The vagueness and ambiguity of voluntary code provisions are a testimony to the serious policy differences that exist between national states on the regulation and distribution of benefits from MNC operations.

The connection between international law and voluntary codes is perhaps closest in the area of restrictive business practices (RBPs). The draft ITO charter contained a provision on the subject early in 1947 and ECOSOC held debates on it in the 1950s. Extraterritorial application of U.S. antitrust law to MNCs has caused numerous diplomatic controversies and the European Community applies regional antitrust rules. The first UN report on MNCs in world development identified RBPs as good candidates for international policy harmonization.[1] Both the OECD and the UNCTAD have created voluntary standards on the subject and UNCTAD is considering a model law on RBPs for use by developing countries.

An examination of the two voluntary documents on RBPs does not give much support to the notion that these codes are an important breakthrough in policy harmonization on the way to international antitrust law. A report issued by USA-BIAC to help explain the competition section of the OECD Guidelines to the business community concludes that the Guidelines do not achieve a common standard of policy harmonization. Instead, ambiguity in language is used to bridge differences among national policies. The major significance attributed to the competition guideline is the encouragement of further cooperation among national enforcement authorities and the development of a common OECD position for political negotiations in the United Nations on RBP policy.[2]

The UNCTAD Code on RBPs is also not a meaningful step toward international antitrust law. It is not clear what even the developing countries have in mind when they press for a binding RBP code, since their notions seem to reject international enforcement or arbitration on the document and fall back instead on national enforcement devices and decisions.[3] In fact, the UNCTAD RBP Code has not even provided an acceptable common standard for application to the draft UNCTAD Technology Transfer Code, where the RBP section is one of the most contentious in the document.

The influence of these codes on specific national law standards also appears limited. In OECD nations a prolonged pattern of cooperation between antitrust enforcement authorities might eventually lead to somewhat more common approaches, but the OECD Guidelines will make a minor contribution to this effort compared to more bilaterally inspired consultation arrangements, such as those the United States has worked out with Canada, West Germany and Australia. Similarly, the UNCTAD RBP Code does not provide a specific enough standard to serve as a real basis for developing national laws on the subject, although some actions in Argentina and elsewhere have purportedly drawn on the code. Indeed, UNCTAD's model law effort is designed to provide a better guide for drafting national law, but its attempts to elaborate more specific provisions preclude international consensus on the document. At a meeting of the State Department's Advisory Committee on International Investment, Technology, and Development, Joel Davidow, a U.S. Justice Department official who was a delegate to the UNCTAD conferences, concluded that the UNCTAD Code is not related to antitrust law in any immediately meaningful way. As Committee minutes record:

Mr. Davidow responded that lawyers prefer to start legal systems with the best set of rules possible. Clearly, nothing contained in a voluntary UN code is going to become law anywhere anytime soon in anyplace meaningful. But the code will be read, studied, and quoted. It could be used in arbitration. It could create an appropriate climate.[4]

International policy harmonization efforts will continue and progress is possible on some specific issues and procedures, particularly in the fields of accounting and taxation. In most other areas, however, harmonization will be very slow and the incremental contribution of voluntary MNC codes to this progress is likely to be minimal. In one way, the codes may even inhibit progress, since their ambiguity and voluntary format allow nations to conclude a formal intergovernmental agreement that may relieve some of the diplomatic pressure to resolve real policy differences. The primary obstacles that in the past have blocked attempts to formulate international investment law are circumvented, not overcome, by voluntary MNC codes.

An association of voluntary codes with international law concepts nevertheless exerts a powerful influence on the perception of these documents. Most analyses of voluntary codes use the evolutionary law idea to cast them into a general category of international business regulation. This approach lends a certain air of inevitability to the process and implicitly disparages the importance of instruments that are not at least on their way to becoming binding regulations. The most unfortunate result of this international law preoccupation is that it distorts the perception and response of businesses to voluntary MNC codes.

Corporations approach the negotiation and implementation of intergovernmental codes behind a phalanx of lawyers. Draft provisions are reviewed and specific terminology scrutinized for its import as a legal precedent. Corporate evaluation of final code documents is often dominated by a law department orientation. Public statements on the voluntary codes are carefully drafted so that no undue corporate commitments are implied.

Certainly MNCs should be concerned about the stated intentions of some groups to seek binding regulations, and the close involvement of legal counsel is both necessary and prudent. An excessive preoccupation with the legal aspects of code discussions, however, can create misimpressions and missed opportunities.

In the OECD Guidelines exercise, the legalistic orientation of corporate involvement obscured important public affairs implications, particularly regarding the elaboration and use of implementation procedures. Little attention was given to the follow-up process until the very end of the negotiations on the Guidelines and corporations were slow to react to organized labor's use of the Guidelines in public pressure tactics, as described in the next section on codes as levers. A fear of legal commitments also restrained many companies in their endorsement of the OECD Guidelines, thereby compromising the voluntary nature of the most favorable MNC code likely to emerge from intergovernmental organizations in the near future. This corporate reticence was evident in discussions that took place at an early U.S. business conference called to promote the OECD Guidelines. Even the U.S. business community's best examples of corporate support for the Guidelines are a study in carefully worded comments that carry a heavier imprint from law department concerns than from a public affairs evaluation of the code exercise.[5]

The new intergovernmental codes directed to MNCs are not law, nor are they likely to become law in the foreseeable future. The documents do have legal implications, but these aspects must be appropriately placed within a broader context that better recognizes the more immediate use of the codes as non-binding political levers.

CODES AS LEVERS

The use of voluntary intergovernmental codes as levers on MNC conduct is a more factually supported measure of these documents' significance. Most of the evidence for this approach comes from some early successful attempts by labor unions to use the OECD Guidelines in confrontations with MNCs in Europe. The concept of codes as levers is neither as simple nor as one-sided as may first appear, however. National governments use non-binding codes partly to maintain independence of action in individual cases and it is the governmental role that appears crucial in most instances where codes are successfully employed as levers. Additionally, MNCs have invoked voluntary intergovernmental codes to advance their own interests, thereby making the device a more neutral lever in terms of its potential application.

The most prominent leverage cases originated soon after the OECD Guidelines were adopted. Through the TUAC organized labor collected information on cases where they felt MNCs were not adhering to the Guidelines. The first set of about a dozen cases was transmitted by the TUAC to the OECD Secretary-General on March 24, 1977 and forwarded to the OECD's Committee on International Investment and Multinational Enterprises (CIME). The cases were then discussed during an exchange of views between the TUAC and the CIME according to the Guidelines' implementation procedures, a pattern repeated the following year when more cases were added. By the time of the first official Guidelines' review in 1979, around twenty MNCs had been the subject of specific labor union accusations of noncompliance.[6]

The TUAC strategy used the Guidelines as a lever in several interrelated ways. First, in direct bargaining with firms, unions would seek a corporate statement of compliance and, if possible, even insert this commitment into collective bargaining contracts. Specific language is suggested in a handbook for labor negotiators put out by the International Confederation of Free Trade Unions.[7] Particular Guidelines provisions could be cited to seek greater information disclosure, to gain access to higher, perhaps foreign management levels, or to meet other such union objectives. An ultimate union goal was to seek corporate acceptance of international collective bargaining, a position vigorously resisted by most MNCs.

Failing to achieve a satisfactory result by referencing the Guidelines in a direct bargaining approach, the unions could up the ante by appealing to outside parties. At this point unions usually approached government officials and sometimes the media. Such a practice is not uncommon in labor-management disputes, but the involvement of an MNC and reference to new ''good corporate citizenship'' guidelines added greater interest, and thereby greater potential leverage, in these cases.

A third step could be added by channeling the case through the TUAC, or through a cooperative national government if possible, to the OECD for clarification in discussions of experience under the Guidelines. While the CIME is prohibited from making judgments in individual cases, a discussion involving specific allegations adds to the pressure on a firm and on governments that are either home or host parties in the dispute. Naturally the TUAC could inform the media of the proceedings as well, focusing attention on specific cases as a test of whether the voluntary Guidelines procedures would have any practical effects.

Finally, the labor strategy positioned the unions to argue for mandatory measures if the voluntary Guidelines were not working. In a speech to the CIME in 1978, TUAC's president complained about MNC activities and about CIME's silence on interpreting the Guidelines application in specific cases. He reported growing worker disenchantment with voluntary standards and increasing pressure for more binding rules,[8] a position reiterated in later years as well. This approach seemed to promise maximum gains for the union position, either in implementation successes or movement toward tighter MNC regulations.

The most celebrated case of union success in using the OECD Guidelines as a lever concerns the Badger Company in Belgium, a subsidiary through other EC connections of the Raytheon Company in the United States. This case is well analyzed and documented elsewhere for anyone wanting full detail on the specific charges and events.[9] Suffice it here to say that Badger's bankruptcy led to severance pay claims under Belgian law that exceeded the firm's liquidated assets. Under the principle of limited legal liability the parent corporation had no enforceable responsibility to cover the remaining liabilities of its Belgian subsidiary, nor did the OECD Guidelines specifically cite any such obligation. The labor unions nevertheless claimed that the MNC had a duty to meet the obligations of its subsidiary and that its failure to do so violated the spirit of the Guidelines. TUAC's submissions to the OECD characterized the Badger case as a direct challenge to the OECD and its member governments, stating that public opinion would interpret a failure to resolve the case as an instance where loopholes in the OECD Guidelines helped an MNC to evade Belgian labor practices.[10]

A critical element in the Badger case is that the Belgian government supported the labor position and vigorously intervened on its behalf. The government bilaterally approached the U.S. State Department, as well as Great Britain and the Netherlands where other subsidiary corporations were located.[11] The Belgian government then took the case directly to the CIME, supporting TUAC's submission. The government noted that under the Guidelines, MNCs have a responsibility to provide reasonable notice and to help mitigate the effects of plant closures, as well as to take national policy objectives into account. In this case the government argued that the parent company's actions and decision-making powers gave it the responsibility to cover its subsidiary's debts.

The Belgian government's presentation acknowledged that the CIME could not pass judgment on the case, but noted the great importance attached to its outcome by unions, business, public opinion, the press, and the Belgian Parliament. The government suggested that other bodies would quickly pursue more binding regulations if the Guidelines proved ineffective. The presentation closed by expressing a view that the parent company must be compelled to meet its obligations.[12]

The CIME formally responded to questions raised by the Badger case in its 1979 report on the three-year review of the Guidelines. In a particularly long and complicated paragraph, the Committee noted that the Guidelines had no effect on legal parent-subsidiary obligations, but could introduce non-legal supplementary standards of behavior. In the end the application of these standards was left to individual circumstances, which of course left all parties free to act as they willed in each case.[13]

In actual practice, the Badger case had already been settled, with the company agreeing to terms more favorable to the workers than was legally required, transferring at least an additional twenty million Belgian francs to the subsidiary's account to meet compensation costs. As part of the settlement the unions agreed that the company's action brought it into full compliance with the OECD Guidelines.[14]

Much of the credit for the settlement was attributed to leverage provided by the OECD and its Guidelines. Perhaps overstating the impact a bit, a widely circulated article in *The Economist* concluded that the voluntary Guidelines were given some real effect when "the OECD leaned hard" on the company, leading to a settlement portrayed as a labor union victory. It should be noted that, in a parenthetical aside, the article also credited the Belgian government's role as the key to the union's success.[15]

The second major example associated with the Guideline's use as a lever concerns a labor dispute involving Hertz Rent-a-car in Denmark. In this case the union charged that the company temporarily transferred workers from other European countries to undermine a lawful strike in Denmark. A similar allegation was made about a Hertz action in Belgium.[16] The case presented an issue of MNC action contrary to a Guidelines' article about unfairly influencing labor negotiations, although the article's language referred to the transfer of an operating unit. The unions asked that the Guidelines be altered to state clearly that a transfer of workers in such circumstances was unacceptable and suggested that binding rules might be needed.

This case also gained wide publicity and attracted direct governmental involvement. The Danish government submitted the issue directly to the OECD for clarification under the Guidelines and asked the EEC Council of Ministers to consider whether the Community's policy on free movement of labor was abused by such a practice. The European Parliament also debated and passed a resolution condemning the matter and inviting the EEC Commission to draw up rules that would prevent similar cases.[17]

The CIME did not rule the company had violated the Guidelines, but it did state that such behavior by a company would not be in conformance with "the general spirit and approach" of labor relations provisions as they had been drafted.[18] Under similar union pressure the ILO included language in its Declaration of Principles that explicitly covered the transfer of workers to undermine negotiations. Specific language was drafted by the CIME and incorporated into the OECD Guidelines to cover such actions as well, constituting the only change made in the document's text after the 1979 review. This action reinforced the notion of a labor victory in using the OECD Guidelines and its follow-up procedures.

Another result of the 1979 review was the establishment of a system of national contact points in member countries that created a more formal and layered implementation procedure. These bodies operate as the second step in consultations on the Guidelines if a case cannot be satisfactorily resolved in direct labor-management discussion. The change interposed a more formal additional step into the process before specific cases are brought before the CIME. Combined with the rather lengthy five-year hiatus between the first and second formal Guidelines' review sessions, this action seemed to restrain the initial pressure put on OECD institutions to respond to specific case allegations, thereby limiting somewhat the available leverage such a forum might provide.

On the other hand, this action responded to union calls for more specific national government action on the Guidelines. Formal national contact points could increase the possibility of gaining national government attention and involvement in a case, which seemed a prerequisite to success on the OECD level anyway. Looking at the record, national governments had only brought three cases to the CIME prior to the procedural changes made in the 1979 review, compared to nearly two dozen cases advanced by the TUAC. The two biggest labor successes were scored in cases where governments brought the issue before the OECD (Badger and Hertz). The third government-submitted case involved British American Tobacco Company (BATCO) in the Netherlands, but the Dutch government made it clear in its OECD submission that the government was remaining explicitly neutral. Citing problems in determining the case's factual information, the government presented the views of both labor and management and asked the CIME only to consider the general issue of how the Guidelines relate to the closure of a profitable subsidiary.[19]

Experience under the national contact point system has proven a mixed success for labor union initiatives, while providing further evidence on the important role of national governments in determining how the OECD Guidelines' lever can be used. John Robinson surveyed this uneven experience in *Multinationals and Political Control* (1983).[20] In the Nordic and Benelux countries the contact points have been active, with strong labor unions pressing their case before receptive national governments. Many of these governments were among the proponents of stronger or even mandatory MNC standards when the OECD Guidelines were being drafted. On the other hand, trade union protests have had little success in Great Britain, while activities in most other countries seem directed only at urging general corporate compliance with the Guidelines. The U.S. contact point is cited by Robinson as an active group due to its monitoring of the employee relations of foreign (particularly Japanese) MNCs in the United States, but this activity has been very limited and the government has not brought special pressures to bear in these cases.

Labor unions and governments are thus the primary users of intergovernmental codes as levers, with governments employing the devices to introduce supplementary, non-legal obligations on MNCs in selected case circumstances. Corporations can also use such codes for their own purposes, particularly to forestall mandatory legislation or even to influence the administration of existing regulations. General business support for voluntary MNC codes has always been partly based on a desire to avoid more binding regulation, but action on the recent OECD Privacy Guidelines shows the direct use of a code lever to influence the administration of current, as well as the consideration of future, government regulations. As with labor union actions, this business strategy appears most successful where national government support is also present.

Chapter 4 outlines the response in many European nations to fears that personal privacy could be compromised by the transfer of information across national boundaries. National legislation as well as activity in the Council of Europe sought to prevent possible abuses, primarily through the creation of administrative bodies to regulate and perhaps license transborder data flows (TBDF). These developments threatened U.S.-based MNCs who feared unnecessary or discriminatory restrictions on their information activities. This fear was exacerbated since the United States was not covered by the Council of Europe's nondiscrimination provision prohibiting special regulatory requirements for companies from member states. Primarily at U.S. instigation, discussion began in the OECD to seek common policy standards on TBDFs.

The resulting OECD Guidelines on the Protection of Privacy and Transborder Flows of Personal Data established some general standards for the collection and treatment of personal information. The Privacy Guidelines allowed for either voluntary or binding implementation of its principles through action at the national level. The United States viewed the document as a set of standards for corporate conduct, endorsed by the European governments, that would mitigate the need for mandatory regulations if followed voluntarily by corporations.

The Privacy Guidelines were seen as a lever to influence the adoption and administration of European national legislation. This objective is reflected in a newsletter report from the U.S. Council for International Business to its corporate membership concerning the evolution of European regulation on TBDFs.

There is no doubt that the legal instruments being adopted by European governments will take precedence over voluntary instruments, such as the OECD Guidelines. However, those U.S. companies which are seen as acting more responsibly will certainly come under less scrutiny under the national laws. Endorsements of the OECD Guidelines and consistent application of the principles enunciated therein will provide a solid basis for a responsible corporate approach to privacy protection.[21]

This business use of the OECD Privacy Guidelines as a lever, and the support given it by the U.S. government, is evident in follow-up activities concerning the code's implementation. A concerted effort was made to promote business endorsement of the voluntary code and to offer this support as evidence that further European national regulation was unnecessary. A letter from U.S. Secretary of Commerce Malcolm Baldridge to U.S. business leaders (1981) made clear the need for prompt and public endorsement of the voluntary standards as a way to forestall further foreign legislation.

Successfully implementing these voluntary guidelines and thus possibly forestalling more foreign legislation requires affirmative steps by firms such as yours. In October 1981, the OECD will review steps taken to implement the Guidelines. Secretary Haig and Ambassador Brock join with me to stress the prompt need for strong industry support.

I urge you and executives of firms with a stake in assuring the international free flow

of information to endorse publicly the OECD Guidelines and our national policy of relying on voluntary private sector compliance to safeguard privacy.[22]

A similar but far less forceful approach had been taken with the general OECD
Guidelines for MNEs. In that case the strongest portion of the U.S. government
letter communicating the Guidelines to U.S. firms simply stated that the government would "commend" the Guidelines to the companies. Within the business community there were serious objections to any idea of a sign-up list for
companies who would endorse the MNE Guidelines. In fact, USA-BIAC was
criticized during a 1977 conference for its plan to serve as a clearinghouse for
information on the business community's response, even in ways that could cloak
the identity of individual enterprises.[23] While a few companies did respond directly to the government's letter, progress was made very slowly beyond the
firms that had been directly involved in USA-BIAC's advisory role in drafting
the MNE Guidelines. Some two years after the Guidelines' adoption, a BIAC
report to the OECD cited a figure of only about fifty U.S. corporations having
indicated support for the Guidelines.[24]

By contrast, the U.S. business community showed much less reticence on
questions of endorsement and individual identification with regard to the OECD
Privacy Guidelines. The business response was rapid, more direct, and much
more enthusiastic. At an OECD meeting only one year after the code was adopted,
a State Department document reported that "the U.S. delegation was able to
table an impressive list of U.S. firms and trade associations who support the
Guidelines."[25] The first year's roster of around one hundred supporting companies has since nearly doubled (almost four times the initial response for the
MNE Guidelines). This type of showing was important, of course, to the argument that European regulators could relax their enforcement scrutiny, at least
for the firms who were listed as Privacy Guidelines supporters.

Voluntary intergovernmental codes can be used as levers in several ways by
several different parties. The primary beneficiary of the code as lever has been,
and probably will continue to be, organized labor. Other MNC-critic groups
should also be expected to make progressively greater use of these instruments
as the codes multiply through more intergovernmental organizations. Certainly
part of the pressure for codes in areas such as consumer protection and environmental matters comes from organized lobby groups on these subjects. The
WHO marketing code on infant formula was used in both its adoption and follow-up monitoring as a lever to change corporate operations in that area.

National governments must be considered as other principal beneficiaries of
these codes as well. The negotiation of voluntary intergovernmental codes helps
governments to circumvent costly political deadlocks when they cannot harmonize investment policies through traditional diplomatic measures. Additionally, the non-binding codes provide governments with great flexibility to press
supplemental standards on MNCs, remain neutral, or defend business interests

as may be called for in individual circumstances. Even MNCs can use these codes as a lever to influence or avoid more binding regulation.

The outlook for the future is that the use of codes as levers will grow. More intergovernmental codes are being concluded under compromise arrangements where supporters of a mandatory standard settle for a non-binding instrument if it is combined with a pliable implementation process. The evolution of an implementation process need not ever reach the stage of a legal commitment as long as the potential exists for using the codes for flexible political leverage beyond what is available without their existence. This objective can be reached through a combination of follow-up procedures involving international secretariats, implementation surveys, study and research reports, formal reviews, and clarification or modification possibilities.

Being the first new intergovernmental code directed at MNCs, the OECD Guidelines provides the most supportive evidence for the use of voluntary codes as levers. Other code exercises are rapidly approaching a test stage for their use as well. The ILO Declaration of Principles was adopted in 1977 without a clear decision on its implementation process, but procedures have since been established and John Robinson suggests that it is now about to enter its operational phase. The ILO document is more detailed than the OECD Guidelines and the tripartite composition of its implementing body makes it a potentially more receptive leverage point for labor views.[26] Certainly the handbook put out by the International Confederation of Free Trade Unions sees the ILO as an appropriate leverage point along with the OECD. The chapter "A Check-list for Trade Unions" describes how union negotiators can employ the voluntary standards and procedures from both organizations to gain more favorable recognition of union viewpoints.[27]

Some of the other intergovernmental code efforts are in even earlier stages of development, but monitoring and implementation procedures in the UNCTAD, WHO, and other bodies offer a range of possibilities for eventual leverage actions. Further proliferation of code standards into some of the subject areas mentioned in Chapter 4 would expand these possibilities further. Codes as levers seem more important than codes as law, but an analysis should not stop there.

CODES AS GUIDANCE

An examination of intergovernmental codes as law or levers tends to obscure their more fundamental role as guides for multinational business conduct. More than anything else these codes are expressions of public concern about areas involving MNC operations that must be addressed voluntarily by individual corporations if pressure for a law and/or political lever solution is to be avoided. Problem areas cited in a code may be caused by the nature of MNC operations or they may result from the inability of national governments to agree on policy harmonization or benefit distribution measures. In either case a voluntary code shifts much of the burden for potential conflict resolution onto the companies. Corporations must either conduct business in such a way as to avoid conflict situations or else clearly demonstrate that the resolution of a problem lies beyond their resources or appropriate sphere of action.

In order to meet this challenge, business must be more sensitive to the concerns expressed in intergovernmental codes and position themselves individually to make an effective response to problems that may arise in those areas. These codes can help guide voluntary corporate conduct so that the more contentious use of codes as either law or political levers in individual case situations can be largely avoided. Such a corporate orientation to codes will require active public affairs efforts to align internal policy with societal demands as well as to communicate with interested constituencies regarding the basis for corporate actions.

The guidance function of intergovernmental codes has been recognized by several commentators. For example, in a review of the legalistic competition section of the OECD Guidelines on MNEs, Barry Hawk, a law professor at Fordham University, told a conference of U.S. businesspeople:

Because of the generality of language, the competition guideline is not intended to be applied so as to judge or evaluate particular business practices of specific multinationals. In other words, multinationals should view the competition guidelines not as a code or statute applicable to a particular arrangement or business practice, but rather as an expression of areas of antitrust concern to OECD member countries.[28]

This view of code provisions focuses attention on the broader business-government relations aspects of MNC dealings rather than on the legal precision of the code's language. A similar approach is called for in areas such as labor relations and information disclosure. Code provisions are drafted to indicate the major items where serious concerns exist. National law directives are clearly the more explicit and paramount requirements. Supplemental international code standards purposefully leave rather wide latitude for voluntary implementation in individual corporate situations.

This implementation flexibility means that firms must consciously evaluate and be prepared to explain the basis for their policies and actions. The decision to use general codes or guidelines acknowledges that the standards may not be strictly applicable in all circumstances. Corporations must, however, be able to explain their interpretation and application of code standards, or other alternative bases for their operational conduct.

This burden may appear unfair to many executives and the use of codes as political levers by MNC critics only adds to this perception of unfairness. One business fear is that public criticism focusing on a very small item can blot out recognition of a firm's excellent voluntary compliance with the vast majority of a code's standards. Another difficulty arises when allegations of code violations pertain to actions not specifically called for by the standards. These concerns drive businesspeople back toward the refuge of carefully worded endorsements and strict interpretation of code provisions in the belief that such a position is more defensible.

At this point, the real dangers of a legal orientation to codes emerge. MNCs cannot escape the impact of proliferating intergovernmental codes by relying upon legal interpretations and defenses. Corporations can point out that carefully drafted, legally precise code provisions do not require them to take certain actions, but such an approach misses the whole point of a code exercise and is likely to increase the use of codes as effective political levers. A corporate defense that would win in a court of law may provide very little support when defending corporate actions vis-à-vis non-legal guidelines in a court of public opinion.

Explanations of MNC conduct must be based primarily upon a clear and persuasive exposition of the reasons for business actions rather than on arguments that such an issue does not fall under the precise coverage of code provisions. MNCs must adopt a strategy that uses codes to guide corporate adaptation to societal concerns, preferably positioning the firm correctly before it could receive a specific public challenge. This approach should actively seek to draw on the "spirit" of code standards to guide corporate policy rather than clinging to the "letter" of code provisions to defend corporate actions after the fact.

Executives fearful of becoming locked into compliance with some ambiguous but at least written voluntary standard will undoubtedly recoil at the notion that their operations should be guided by the "spirit" of an intergovernmental code. Yet this approach is in accord with the political reality of the use of codes as levers and with the business objective of avoiding expanding regulatory nets that trap MNCs in legal conflicts between national sovereigns. The corporation is inherently more capable of adjusting its operations individually to meet situational needs than are governmental regulations that impose cumbersome and inflexible common requirements across-the-board on everyone. An effective corporate response to expressed concern about MNC conduct also stands a better chance of defusing the political pressures that can turn codes into useful levers for anti-MNC groups.

In responding to the Hertz case, the CIME found that the transfer of workers "would not be in conformity with the general spirit and approach underlying the drafting of the Employment and Industrial Relations chapter."[29] This reference to the spirit of the code exercise is also found in a booklet published by USA-BIAC (1978) on the employee relations section of the Guidelines. In discussing the Hertz case, the commentary seems to recognize the need for a more flexible corporate approach to using code standards to guide their actions.

There no doubt will be other cases where unions and others will claim that the spirit of the Guidelines prohibit practices not specifically interdicted and employers need to keep this in mind in deciding on a course of action. Standing firm on the precise terminology of the Guidelines is at times called for, but there may be instances when a given action not specifically prohibited might better be avoided because of the political and other forces that may be marshalled against it.[30]

Similar sentiments came out at a business conference on the OECD Guidelines during discussion of the problems likely to emerge under the employee relations section. Commentators recognized that labor unions would seize every opportunity to use the Guidelines for leverage in negotiations and that, in a way, the absence of a court system for code interpretation could actually work to the firm's disadvantage. On the other hand, labor pressures and a resort to media involvement would be likely in any case, at home or abroad, particularly when a company could not or would not explain the rationale for actions such as plant closures. The expressions of concern in the Guidelines exercise should at least help alert MNCs to the need to anticipate and defuse in advance possible pressure points in those areas.[31]

In addition, corporate self-initiative in being guided by the spirit as well as the letter of voluntary code standards can help avoid more restrictive and inflexible measures. At the same conference, George McCullough, Manager of Employee Relations for Exxon Corporation, discussed labor union leveraging action in the Hertz case, warning that the OECD Guidelines could be put to similar use in the future. He also recognized from a longer-range perspective that, "It may be in our common interest to operate within the letter and spirit of the Guidelines, because anything less will probably invite much more restrictive control," in either national legislation or more unfavorable code actions in other international organizations.[32]

Disagreements will certainly emerge about what constitutes the spirit of a code, just as there are differences over the meaning of actual written standards. The important objective, however, is to stimulate a change in corporate orientation toward these codes from a defensive posture based on the precision of language to an activist mode that uses codes as guidance to direct corporate policies and actions. Corporations need to demonstrate a good faith effort to voluntarily meet the concerns identified by code activities on an individual firm level as best fits the company's particular circumstances.

Would this different orientation actually bring any changes in corporate operations as they are presently conducted? Probably. Corporate policy is usually inherited, so current management may not have a clear idea about its real rationale. Other times policy or its application is not regularly reviewed despite changes in factual circumstances, particularly relative to globe-straddling MNC operations. Codes can guide corporations in examining those areas where public concerns are the greatest. The company needs to consider whether the basis for corporate actions in these areas can be effectively explained in a public forum. If not, the company should probably consider changing its policy. MNC policies must not only be internally rational, but also externally understandable and acceptable, taking into account the diverse locations and constituencies that MNCs must face. This corporate self-evaluation process is especially necessary in those areas where intergovernmental codes indicate an active public concern about the impact of MNC operations.

Using codes as guidance places a very large burden on corporations, a load that is in many ways more demanding than if the company complied only with specific legal directives. Yet the fact remains that law in the international investment area is very difficult to achieve, and most corporations want to avoid the constraints of a regulatory approach to controlling corporate operations. This reality leaves MNCs facing societal demands for more corporate responsiveness, with governments as well as special interest groups ready to employ political levers to influence corporate activity to meet their objectives. The business community has taken some steps toward developing more flexible self-regulation in the face of this challenge, both collectively and at the individual corporate level. The nature and direction of this business response is the subject of the next chapter.

NOTES

1. *Multinational Corporations in World Development*, Department of Economic and Social Affairs (New York: United Nations, 1973), pp. 91–92.

2. USA-BIAC Committee on International Investment and Multinational Enterprises, *A Review of the OECD Guidelines for Multinational Enterprises: Competition*, prepared by Barry E. Hawk, New York, 1977, p. 32.

3. Joel Davidow, "Multinationals, Host Governments and Regulation of Restrictive Business Practices," *The Columbia Journal of World Business*, Summer 1980, p. 17.

4. U.S. State Department, Advisory Committee on International Investment, Technology and Development, minutes from a meeting held in Washington, D.C., November 13, 1980, p. 23. See also Joel Davidow, "The Implementation of International Antitrust Principles," in Seymour J. Rubin and Gary Clyde Hufbauer, eds., *Emerging Standards of International Trade and Investment*, published under the auspices of The American Society of International Law (Totowa, N.J.: Rowman & Allanheld, 1984), pp. 119–138.

5. See Phillip Coolidge, George C. Spina, and Don Wallace, Jr., eds., *OECD Guidelines for Multinational Enterprises: A Business Appraisal* (Washington, D.C.: Institute for International and Foreign Trade Law, Georgetown University, 1977), pp. 198–228; and USA-BIAC Committee on International Investment and Multinational Enterprises, *U.S. Corporate Response to OECD Guidelines: Examples of Voluntary Cooperation*, New York, April 1978.

6. See Organization for Economic Cooperation and Development, Note from the General Secretary of the TUAC to the Chairman and Members of the Committee on International Investment and Multinational Enterprises, Paris, March 25, 1977; John Robinson, *Multinationals and Political Control* (New York: St. Martin's Press, 1983), pp. 122–140; and Roger Blanpain, *The OECD Guidelines for Multinational Enterprises and Labor Relations 1976–1979* (Hingham, Mass.: Klower Law and Taxation Publishers, 1979), pp. 123–124.

7. International Confederation of Free Trade Unions, *Trade Unions and the Transnationals: A Handbook for Negotiators*, Madrid, November 1979, pp. 53–59.

8. Trade Union Advisory Committee to the OECD, speech by TUAC President at the Occasion of the Consultation with the CIME Committee on April 11, 1978.

9. Blanpain, pp. 125–146.

10. OECD, Note from the General Secretary of the TUAC, pp. 6–7.

11. Robinson, p. 126.

12. Organization for Economic Cooperation and Development, communication by the Belgian Delegation to the Committee on International Investment and Multinational Enterprises, Paris, March 23, 1977.

13. Organization for Economic Cooperation and Development, Review of the 1976 Declaration on International Investment and Multinational Enterprises, documentation for meeting of Council at Ministerial Level, Paris, June 13 and 14, 1979, pp. 28–29.

14. Blanpain, pp. 125–146.

15. "Chasing the Multinationals: The OECD guidelines for multinationals are, after all, being given some real effect," *The Economist*, June 4, 1977, pp. 93–94.

16. OECD, Note from the General Secretary of the TUAC, pp. 9–11.

17. Blanpain, pp. 219–228.

18. OECD, Review of the 1976 Declaration, pp. 37–38.

19. Blanpain, pp. 123, 161–173.

20. Robinson, pp. 142–146. For a detailed study of cases involving labor union complaints under the OECD Guidelines, see Duncan C. Campbell and Richard L. Rowan, *Multinational Enterprises and the OECD Industrial Relations Guidelines*, Multinational Industrial Relations Series no. 11 (Philadelphia: University of Pennsylvania, 1983).

21. U.S. Council for International Business, *International Information Flows*, newsletter, no. 2, April 1983, p. 3.

22. Malcolm Baldrige, Secretary of Commerce, letter to American business leaders concerning the OECD Privacy Guidelines, July 20, 1981.

23. Coolidge, Spina, and Wallace, pp. 215–222.

24. Blanpain, p. 84.

25. U.S. State Department, *Current Status Report: Selected International Organization Activities Relating to Transnational Enterprises* (Washington, D.C.: Office of Investment Affairs, July 1982), p. 23.

26. Robinson, pp. 171–176.

27. International Confederation of Free Trade Unions, pp. 53–59.

28. Coolidge, Spina, and Wallace, p. 152.

29. OECD, Review of the 1976 Declaration, p. 37.

30. USA-BIAC Committee on International Investment and Multinational Enterprises, *A Review of the OECD Guidelines for Multinational Enterprises: Employment and Industrial Relations*, prepared by Vernon O'Rourke, New York, May 1978, p. 29.

31. Coolidge, Spina, and Wallace, pp. 127–129, 134–135.

32. Ibid., pp. 109–110.

6

The Private Business Code Movement

International corporations spent much of the 1970s defending themselves from a wide range of charges concerning corporate misconduct. On the international level, companies commented on intergovernmental code activities while formulating a few private sector documents that addressed MNC issues. The International Chamber of Commerce (ICC) developed a general set of guidelines as well as one that addressed the issue of bribery in international commercial transactions. Some specific industries also discussed, and in a few cases adopted, international standards that apply to issues of particular concern in their own product area. Despite these actions, progress toward aggregate international business codes has been slow and limited in scope and application.

A more extensive response occurred within the U.S. business community when a large number of corporations developed and issued individual codes of conduct. These codes were largely a response to the overseas bribery scandals and were meant as both corrective actions and preventive measures against future abuses. Most corporate codes proved to be seriously limited in purpose and perspective, however, since their reactive nature did not address questions of real corporate identity or individual operating policy.

Two dominant findings appeared from a survey of the policy codes issued by over one hundred leading international companies. First, the corporate policy statements did not reflect well the real international character of these firms. This finding ran counter to expectations, given the international origin of many corporate misconduct charges and the multinational nature of the surveyed enterprises. Second, most corporations drafted documents that simply codified internal employee directives rather than constructing a broader policy instrument that could guide operations and frame a global corporate identity. This narrowly focused, reactive approach to code drafting prevented most MNCs from recognizing the code mechanism's potential as a means for addressing the needs of both internal and external constituency groups.

On the other hand, an important minority of surveyed corporations has pioneered an alternative approach, characterized in this chapter as a self-identity code. This type of code addresses a broader range of issues confronting contemporary global enterprises and could help bridge the misunderstanding and distrust that often mark relations between MNCs and their various domestic and foreign constituencies. An international self-identity code could help MNCs meet the challenge of properly guiding their conduct in international business dealings.

INTERNATIONAL BUSINESS CODES

The first promulgation of voluntary international codes by the business community is discussed briefly toward the end of Chapter 3. The historical roots of this movement trace back to the late 1940s when the ICC developed a proposal that represented the business community's ideas for a postwar international agreement on foreign investment issues. This International Code of Fair Treatment for Foreign Investment was, as the name implied, a standard for government treatment of business rather than a code of conduct for the investors. A U.S. business proposal for a counterpart document on company standards was discussed in the ICC, but the group decided that drafting such a general code applying to all businesses was too difficult and any voluntary standards might be used improperly as levers against the companies.

ICC Codes of Conduct

Discussions on an international business code began again in the ICC toward the end of the 1960s. After several years of consideration, the organization adopted in 1972 the ICC Guidelines for International Investment. These standards represented a departure from the earlier ICC Code since actions of companies as well as home and host governments were addressed. As recorded in the Foreword to the ICC Guidelines:

Today, the ICC presents its Guidelines for International Investment. These reflect a new approach—instead of the international convention concept focused on the conditions to be fulfilled in a country seeking to attract foreign investments, the Guidelines define the responsibilities which have to be accepted by all parties concerned. Instead of being specifically concerned with the relations between foreign investors and developing countries, they are universal in character. In short, the Guidelines demonstrate the essential interdependence of investors, of governments in the investor's as well as in the host countries, and they underline the need for goodwill and cooperation between them in the interest of the fulfillment of common objectives.[1]

Despite taking the major step of addressing corporate as well as governmental responsibilities, the ICC Guidelines were perceived as too general and self-serving to make a real difference within the context of the times. The standards were expressly designed to facilitate consultations and a better understanding of the needs and objectives of all governments and investors. By the early 1970s, however, foreign investment was under increasingly specific attack for conduct symbolized by the ITT/Chile incident and labor-related runaway plant charges.

Developing nations pressed for recognition of more specific rights as detailed in the New International Economic Order. Home governments worried about tax evasion through transfer pricing and other operational control problems. Special interest groups, headed by organized labor, vocally expressed their own concerns about MNC conduct. A business document aimed at creating a climate for general business-government discussions to encourage greater foreign investment had missed its target in the rapidly changing environment of the 1970s.

The ICC Guidelines remain of interest today less for their substantive content or effect than for their mark as the only set of general, self-formulated international business standards, issued by the most globally representative business organization. Other more limited business efforts, such as the Declaration of Basic Principles contained in the regionally adopted Pacific Basin Charter on International Investment, have essentially been eclipsed by ongoing events.

The ICC has also issued some interesting, more functionally specific types of international business standards. In 1937 the organization developed a Code of Standards of Advertising Practice. This code attempted to recognize the social responsibility of business by designing rules that could help safeguard consumer interests. Implementation procedures were to operate on the national business community level, although an ICC committee was assigned general oversight tasks. The code has been updated in each decade since it was first issued. The rationale for this approach to voluntary self-regulation was described in a 1973 ICC resolution.

Further, the ICC maintains that professional regulations voluntarily applied can ensure more speedily than government regulations the elimination of any malpractice, and offer also the advantage over the legal process of being more easily adaptable to changing economic and social conditions.[2]

The ICC published an International Code of Marketing Research Practice in 1971. Two years later, in conjunction with the updated 1973 edition of the Advertising Practices Code, the organization also issued a new International Code of Sales Promotion Practice. This document set forth general standards for all forms of sales promotion, going beyond the focus of the advertising code. Interestingly, in its introduction the Sales Promotion Code is expressly offered for legal as well as self-regulation purposes.

The Code is designed primarily as an instrument of self-discipline but it is also intended for use by the Courts as a reference document within the framework of any appropriate national laws in countries where sales promotions are governed by law. The Code being the unique international guide to sales promotion ethics may also serve as a pointer to the direction in which any international harmonization of the laws on sales promotions might be guided.[3]

In 1974 these three functional ICC codes were combined into one publication, the International Code of Marketing Practice. Subsequently the marketing research part of the code was replaced by a new set of standards, prepared jointly with the European Society for Opinion and Marketing Research, entitled The International Code of Marketing and Social Research Practice. Other relevant ICC standards are the 1974 Environmental Guidelines for World Industry and two 1978 efforts, the International Code of Direct Mail and Mail Order Practice, and the International Code of Direct Sales Practice.

Most immediately related to the MNC controversies of the 1970s was another ICC initiative in the area of international commercial bribery. A commission of business leaders was set up in 1975 to investigate the bribery issue and the extent to which national laws control such practices. Finding great diversity in the enforcement of national standards, the ICC adopted in 1977 a report on Extortion and Bribery in Business Transactions that concluded ''complementary and mutually reinforcing action by both governments and the business community is essential.'' Recommendations were made for both governments and the business community, the former suggested actions at the national and international level while the latter contained basic rules of corporate conduct and guidelines for implementation.[4]

The ICC emphasized the relationship between bribery and extortion, pointing out that much bribery is not initiated by companies but results from extortion pressures. The ICC report therefore urged governments to negotiate and adopt a binding treaty, pass and enforce national measures, and establish procedures for international cooperation and judicial assistance—all aimed at creating the legal means and the political will to eliminate extortion and bribery from commercial transactions. The self-regulatory business rules are short and general, directed at controlling larger transgressions rather than settling questions related to so-called facilitating payments. Greater attention is paid to setting up implementation procedures, including a somewhat unusual set of by-laws for an international panel to interpret, promote, and oversee the rules.

Creation of this implementation panel was seen at the time as a potentially significant move. Under its procedures any enterprise or public authority with a legitimate interest in a case could request an examination of an alleged infringement of the rules, even if an accused firm was not an ICC member. This panel could mediate or conciliate with the consent of the parties. While deliberations and any decision were to remain confidential, the panel could recommend to the ICC Executive Board that the allegations' general nature be made public along with any replies or comments by the respondent. Firms that suffered commercially could thus generate international pressures through a board of peers and possible general publicity against a firm that violated the anti-bribery code. In reality this device has not been used.

Two other aspects of this ICC effort are important for the current debate over MNC codes. First, the Basic Principle of the ICC document on extortion and bribery clearly recognized a corporate responsibility to meet the spirit as well as the letter of these voluntary standards: "All enterprises should conform to the relevant laws and regulations of the countries in which they are established and in which they operate, and should observe both the letter and the spirit of these Rules of Conduct."[5] A similar principle is contained in other ICC standards, such as in the International Code of Sales Promotion Practice, which states, "The Code is to be applied in the spirit as well as the letter, bearing in mind the varying degrees of knowledge, experience and discriminatory ability of those to whom promotions are directed."[6] These international business codes accept a corporate ability and responsibility to conduct operations in a way that looks to a code's spirit, applying standards in a flexible and positive manner rather than clinging to a strict interpretation of a standard's exact language. This position seems to diminish somewhat the strength of business protests discussed in Chapter 5 that corporations should not be expected to operate beyond the letter of voluntary international conduct standards.

Second, the ICC extortion and bribery guidelines recognized in the implementation section that action in the form of individual company codes would help give more specific application to the general business community's rules. Article 10 of the ICC document states:

These Rules of Conduct being of a general nature, enterprises should, where appropriate, draw up their own codes consistent with the ICC Rules and apply them to the particular circumstances in which their business is carried out. Such codes may usefully include examples and should enjoin employees or agents who find themselves subjected to any form of extortion or bribery immediately to report the same to senior management.[7]

Before turning to an examination of individual company codes, it is necessary to consider another type of international business code. Since the ICC represents all types of businesses, its code efforts are approached from a functional perspective, attempting to define general standards of business practice appropriate for all enterprises. A somewhat different approach can be used by focusing on a sectoral basis, designing business practice standards that are more specific to the nature and problems of a particular industry.

Industry Codes of Conduct

The most important and currently relevant example of an industry-based international code is the Code of Marketing Practices developed by the International Federation of Pharmaceutical Manufacturers Associations (IFPMA). The obvious direct impact of pharmaceuticals on individual health and welfare makes the involvement of foreign companies in such a product sector an especially sensitive matter politically. The IFPMA code contains a set of permissible marketing practices, but recognizes the difficulty of establishing a simple standard that will be applicable under differing worldwide conditions. The code is therefore offered as a model for member associations who bear the major burden for adopting and monitoring the industry-wide standards.[8]

This industry's self-regulation effort is particularly significant because of the pressure in several intergovernmental forums to establish additional control standards for the marketing of pharmaceuticals. A resolution adopted by the Council of Europe's Parliamentary Assembly in 1983 welcomed the IFPMA code, but called on member governments to help extend their own safeguards to pharmaceuticals traded to developing countries and suggested that the Council develop a code of conduct for European pharmaceutical firms. The resolution also recommended support for efforts to develop a pharmaceutical marketing code in the World Health Organization (WHO). A move was made by several countries in the UNCTAD to seek member governments' comments on the IFPMA code, as well as on a very different draft code drawn up by Health Action International (HAI), a voluntary consumer lobby group that has gathered and disseminated information critical of the industry's self-regulation efforts. Protests from the developed nations blocked this UNCTAD action, however, deferring instead to WHO consideration of pharmaceutical industry issues.[9]

The WHO has thus far decided not to embark on a code-drafting exercise, but is considering a 1985 meeting on drug marketing and use. The IFPMA reportedly offered to provide WHO with copies of monitoring reports on its own code, presumably to argue that intergovernmental action was not needed. Cooperation between the industry and WHO is important to WHO's main initiative in the field, an Action Program for Essential Drugs, that aims at making critically needed drugs available to developing countries at affordable prices. Some pharmaceutical companies have offered favorably priced products and management services for use in these efforts. The WHO will also draw on other organizations and look to generic substitutes in some areas to assist national programs in member states. While the code issue can be viewed as a diversion from more pressing WHO concerns, efforts by some countries and groups such as HAI will likely keep attention on the intergovernmental code option, including in upcoming international conferences in the WHO and elsewhere.

An interesting parallel exists, of course, with the already adopted WHO *International Code of Marketing of Breast-milk Substitutes*. This 1981 code is another example of a sectorally based standard on functional marketing issues, albeit an intergovernmental one. In this sector an industry-sponsored code also had existed, first promulgated in 1975 by the International Council of Infant Food Industries (ICIFI) as the Code of Ethics and Professional Standards for Advertising, Product Information and Advisory Services for Breast-Milk Substitutes.

The infant formula controversy and the evolution of these industry standards is a subject unto itself that would require far more time and attention than can be devoted to it in this study. In light of the recent settlement ending the boycott action against the Nestlé Company, it seems likely that someone will undertake a full case-study review of this topic. For purposes of this analysis, however, the conclusion to this complicated story bears directly on the potential significance of international industry codes.

Corporate adherence to international business standards, even when applied to industry-specific problems, will be measured by performance at the individual company level. Whether the industry endorses an ICIFI standard or the WHO code, an IFPMA guideline or even an OECD Privacy Code, the success of voluntary corporate compliance will be measured by how well individual corporate operations translate these standards into practice. The essential link in the chain of voluntary standards, no matter how long that chain might be, must rest at the level of individual company codes, policies, and operational implementation.

Other International Business Codes

Before turning to the issue of individual company codes, two other variations of international business codes should be acknowledged. The first type is country and issue-specific, relating to corporations that do business in South Africa. The foundation for this effort is the so-called Sullivan Principles, a set of standards aimed at the goal of equal treatment of workers of all races in South Africa. Initially endorsed voluntarily by twelve companies in 1977, the code was eventually signed by over 120 American firms representing nearly three-fourths of the employment by U.S.-based MNCs in that country. Implementation reports are evaluated by an independent firm and the principles have been progressively expanded since their inception. Proposals before the Congress seek to make this voluntary code mandatory for all U.S. companies, while other pressures are being exerted to force divestment of corporate holdings in that country.

In related developments, the governments of Great Britain, Holland, and Canada all adopted codes of conduct for their MNCs operating in South Africa. While voluntary, these measures called for corporate reports on their actions. In 1977 the European Community's Foreign Ministers also agreed to a similar code for all EC companies. There is disagreement over the importance and impact of these codes, especially when viewed within the gravity of the South African apartheid issue, but at least the Sullivan Principles appear to have encouraged meaningful improvements for workers at the signatory companies. This type of code appears to be a unique undertaking, however. Few if any other situations are likely to match the specific and narrowly directed condemnation that South Africa's apartheid system has generated.

The other code variation is represented by two examples: The Code of Behavior for Japanese Investors Overseas, first issued by the Japan Foreign Trade Council in 1973; and Precepts for Successful Business Operations Procedures in Canada and the United States, issued by a joint committee of the U.S. and the Canadian Chambers of Commerce. The latter document followed the Canadian Government's publication in 1967 of *Some Guiding Principles of Good Corporate Behavior for Subsidiaries in Canada of Foreign Companies.*

These examples also seem to incorporate unique situations that would limit their general applicability as approaches to international business codes. The Japanese business community's late rush into the ranks of overseas investors and the homogeneous strength of their relatively centralized business associations provided the occasion and ability to attempt a common national business code aimed at guiding the conduct of Japanese investors overseas. The U.S.-Canadian investment relationship appears equally unique regarding the magnitude of corporate involvement across the common border, coupled with the existence of the Canadian Government's formal investment review procedure. Few other binational circumstances seem likely to generate a similar attempt at developing business conduct standards.

From the General to the Specific

These various forms of international business codes do not seem a fully adequate answer to guide MNC actions. As with voluntary intergovernmental codes, such standards can provide important guidance, but meaningful MNC standards must be applied and operationalized at the individual company level. A 1975 booklet, *A Review of Standards and Guidelines for International Business Conduct*, published by USA-BIAC, surveyed many of the approaches taken to that point in time. The conclusion recognized that:

Attempts by business organizations to formulate a set of guidelines applicable to all companies and industries, however, run into the problem of the great diversity of enterprises. MNCs cover a wide spectrum of countries and include industry sectors, ranging from extractive to manufacturing to service industries. They use various kinds and levels of technology and have complex requirements, quite apart from the differences in their business practices and corporate philosophies. Guidelines stated in terms broad enough to accommodate the great variety of the business community are apt to be much too general to serve a useful purpose.[10]

While suggesting that general guidelines could help "create a desirable atmosphere," the report seemed to favor individual company codes.

One approach is to recognize that "self-policing" by MNCs will in most cases be the most effective procedure. They can set for themselves standards of responsible conduct. Such guidelines for conduct could be publicly available and serve as a guide for self auditing. In addition, many international companies believe that voluntary guidelines addressing both governments and companies could assist both host governments and MNCs in conducting bilateral negotiations. Furthermore, individual corporate guidelines for behavior might serve as a useful introduction of a company and its beliefs to a prospective host government. In several recent cases, individual companies have formalized guidelines for their conduct in host countries and have published them in the public interest.[11]

The Business Roundtable seemed to reach a similar conclusion in a report that stated, ''While the growth and diversity of companies make it difficult, if not impossible, to develop a universal code for all business,'' the best approach is ''to encourage individual companies to develop their own guidelines.''[12] The U.S. Chamber of Commerce leaned in this same direction when a special task force of the organization's Multinational Corporations Panel developed a working document entitled ''Elements of Global Business Conduct for Possible Inclusion in Individual Company Statements.'' The document included a section on public policies that would help enhance an MNC's contribution to a host country, but the major emphasis was on providing a checklist of issues that companies could use in developing their own individual codes of conduct. The paper stated:

The experience of several companies which have developed their own public statements on principles of global business behavior has shown that statements of this kind can serve many purposes and many audiences. Such statements can be useful expressions of existing practices of operating principles to which a corporation and its affiliates would adhere and upon which it would be willing to be judged by governments and by the public at large. In addition to facilitating negotiations on terms of entry, they can also play a stabilizing role once an investment project is in operation. Moreover, the very process of internally developing such a statement can be useful to multinational corporations seeking to define a coherent set of management policies for worldwide operations.[13]

This apparent coalescing of opinion in the U.S. business community behind the need and desirability of individual corporate codes seemed to stimulate a growing response. Many corporations did undertake efforts to develop their own code of conduct, often drawing on the ICC documents, the U.S. Chamber's ''Elements,'' and a few examples of earlier company codes. This development bears closer examination, however, as to its origin, content, and impact, particularly regarding whether these corporate documents can meet the international challenges that must be addressed in an MNC code of conduct.

INDIVIDUAL CORPORATE CODES OF CONDUCT

Individual codes of conduct proliferated rapidly among U.S. corporations in the late 1970s, but the majority of these documents are limited in both scope and purpose. Most corporate codes are internally oriented manuals that seek to direct employee activities along prescribed lines of behavior. The code itself often comprises little more than a composite statement of individual policies on questionable payments, conflict of interest, and antitrust regulations. A survey of over one hundred international corporations thought to be in the forefront of code development found that the international dimension of corporate activities was particularly understated, or was missing altogether from individual code documents.

International corporations must relate to a wide range of cross-cultural groups that often have competing and sometimes conflicting needs and goals. The very nature of transnational business also obscures corporate motives and operating methods in a way that leads to even greater suspicion. During the 1970s, this concern increased when a number of corporations were found to have engaged in improper activities, ranging from isolated interference in national political affairs to more widespread overseas payments which were, at best, often "questionable" business practices.

One common response in the United States to political and media charges of improper business practices was the formulation of individual corporate codes of conduct. While a small number of firms had developed their own codes earlier, a major impetus toward corporate code building came with the U.S. Securities and Exchange Commission's (SEC) "voluntary disclosure" program, particularly its requirement for specific corporate policies to prevent future improper payments. Passage in 1977 of the Foreign Corrupt Practices Act (FCPA) and moves in various intergovernmental organizations to develop international codes of conduct added further legal and public relations stimulus to this effort.

Despite the international origins of this corporate code movement, little attention has been paid to the actual international content or utility of the resulting documents. Early analyses dealt primarily with the problems of initial code formulation. Later writings either focused on domestic issues when analyzing corporate codes or provided isolated individual case studies. By contrast, this discussion is based on research that attempted to investigate how well corporate codes meet specifically international concerns about multinational business activity by comparing over one hundred individual corporate documents.

Since the primary research interest was the codes' relationship with international corporate activity, a composite target list of 180 companies thought most likely to possess an internationally relevant code was compiled with the advice of executives in several U.S. business organizations. Materials were solicited directly from the corporations, 132 of whom responded, including 12 firms that replied their corporations did not have a published code or submitted material which clearly did not fall within a code definition, as described below.

No claim is made that this survey constitutes a comprehensive sampling of the international business community since the target list was not specifically balanced by industry or other relevant factors and the respondents were over 90 percent U.S.-based firms. Nevertheless, the sample was specifically designed to reach those companies expected to be in the vanguard of the international corporate code movement, so the findings have been used to develop and inform a tentative evaluation of corporate performance in this area.

Defining Codes by Objective

In its most general sense, a corporate code of conduct is a statement of policy regarding how an enterprise does or should act on a range of relevant issues. The label "code of conduct" has no common operational meaning across individual corporations, however, as was shown by the wide range of documents and materials submitted by companies responding to the survey. Thus the first result to emerge from an examination of submitted code material was the need for a classification system. Documents were divided into three functional categories according to purpose: employee guidance, public relations, and corporate identity. These distinctions were used in order to help measure a code's relationship to the debate over guidance versus regulation of MNC activities; that is, a code's relevance, utility, and credibility as a means for responding to societal questions about business dealings, including particularly their international aspects.

Employee Guidance Codes

One approach to corporate codes centers around a concern for employee guidance and consists of a set of internally directed documents that essentially function as a mini-policy manual for the employees. The main purpose of these devices is to alert employees to potential problem areas that they might encounter in work-related activity, to state corporate policy on these issues, and to indicate how such situations should be handled or where counsel should be sought. This form of code was the most prevalent of those surveyed, encompassing over 56 percent of the cases. Individual examples include full policy manuals (up to eighty pages); shortened editions thereof (about twenty pages); annotated codes, with page references to a full policy manual; packages of brief statements on specific issues (such as bribery, conflict of interest, and antitrust); and a variety of short pamphlets and chief executive correspondence intended for wide, but internal, distribution.

Employee guidance codes are useful but limited documents that usually are of little relevance or utility in meeting broad political and social concerns. These codes seem particularly inappropriate to the diverse cross-cultural demands of the international marketplace. It is not that such an instruction booklet for employees causes any real harm, since standard policy manuals are used to good effect as internal guidance mechanisms within most corporations. The problem with employee codes is more that the opportunity for a creative use of the code device is lost when a firm stops the exercise after simply issuing a mini-policy manual for internal use only.

Public Relations Codes

The public relations code, by contrast, is externally directed, aimed primarily at social critics, the government, and the media. The documents generally respond to broad public issues in a similarly broad manner, with few operational business topics addressed within usually "glossy" publications or corporate executive speeches. Reports on corporate philanthropy or "good citizenship" activity in local communities and beyond are usually prevalent in these documents. Under 10 percent of survey responses to the request for a corporate code fall exclusively into this category, but companies often include such publications as a supplement to a code classified in one of the other categories.

Like much general public relations material, these code documents attempt to engage critic groups in a public debate on a rather high level of abstraction. Unfortunately, this type of code approach lacks the operational specificity or credibility that could aid the debate's proper resolution. If presented as the corporation's sole response, a public relations document can generate increased public cynicism, especially overseas where firms are seen to be evading issues by simply touting their "good citizenship deeds" as a response to serious questions concerning the compatibility of corporate operations and objectives in differing foreign circumstances.

Corporate Identity Codes

The third functional classification—a corporate identity code—strikes a middle ground between addressing internal and external audiences. Emphasis is placed primarily on communicating to any interested parties the role the enterprise sees for itself in society, its responsibilities to various constituencies, and the standards upon which its operations will be conducted.[14] These codes often cover many of the same functional standards that are the core of employee guidance documents, but do so in a manner that also relates the employees' activities to the firm's broader societal role so that both internal and external observers can understand the basis for corporate policies and actions. Public policy issues are often addressed, but these issues are generally dealt with in an applied fashion, responding to the specific nature of the individual firm's products and operations, rather than couched in the ideology of free enterprise and general business community goals. The discussion of corporate policies and operations in this type of code is also more likely to include a specific application to international business concerns.

Just over one-third of the submitted codes were functionally classified as corporate identity documents. The essential nature of codes taking this approach is not that they simply combine areas addressed by codes in the other two categories, but that they integrate those areas into an applied and, therefore, more credible identification of the corporation's own role, responsibilities, and standards of operation, including the firm's international business commitment.

A corporate identity code provides the most effective approach that individual companies can use in responding to societal concerns and promoting self-guidance over regulation in international business dealings. This type of code helps link corporate management, not only with its general workforce, but also with concerned segments of the public at large, at home and abroad. In order to illustrate this assertion, the following two sections compare the two major types of corporate code approaches, the employee guidance and the corporate identity document. The submissions of 110 companies falling into these two categories were examined in terms of their relevance, utility, and credibility as a response to international concerns about multinational enterprises.

Comparing Code Content

Examination of code survey material showed that a common core of general business topics was contained in both the employee guidance and corporate identity codes. This similarity is probably due to the shared motivational origin of most code efforts and the fact that several early corporate codes were used in the later drafting of other firms' documents. The identity and guidance codes exhibited somewhat different patterns, however, in terms of how constituency relationships were defined, the substance of the corporate message, and the route chosen to assure code implementation within the company. A marked difference also appeared between the two types of codes regarding their reference to specific ethical concepts and their treatment of international business issues. See Chart 1.

Constituency Relationships

In defining relevant constituencies toward which the enterprise acknowledged some responsibilities, the surveyed codes showed general agreement on a set of commonly cited constituency groups, but the corporate identity codes were more likely than the employee guidance approach to acknowledge and explain this responsibility relationship. For example, all codes addressed employees more than any other group, usually detailing a set of employee job responsibilities. The differences between the two documents emerge more clearly when a "responsibilities to" dimension of the corporate relationship is distinguished from the "responsibilities of" nature of employee work directives. Over 90 percent of the corporate identity codes recognized and elaborated on corporate "responsibilities to" employees in a worker/management relationship, while only about 42 percent of the employee guidance codes discussed specific "responsibilities to" their employees as an important constituency group.

In a similar fashion, other commonly identified constituency elements were addressed more often and in greater depth by corporate identity codes. Consumers/customers were the second most frequently cited group, followed by suppliers, the community, competitors, and shareholders. Government was also discussed by many codes, rating a separate section in sixteen documents while being incorporated within the code body in over one-half of the others. Interestingly, only five codes chose to balance their definition of corporate responsibilities to government with a discussion of government responsibilities to business.

Chart 1
Summary Comparison of Code Types

Employee Guidance Codes   Corporate Identity Codes

APPROACH AND SCOPE

Primarily internal documents directed   Addresses internal and external audiences,
at employee performance. Useful as   acting as a bridge between corporate
mini-policy manuals but generally   operating procedures and broader consti-
less relevant to external social con-   tuency responsibilities.
cerns or cross-cultural business re-
quirements.

INTERNATIONAL BUSINESS IDENTITY

Where expressed, international   Corporate international commitment defined
business coverage focuses on corpor-   with greater breadth and depth. Employee
rate payments policies and FCPA regu-   guidance concerns such as payments policy
lations. Occasional reference to   addressed within context of broader
antitrust, conflict of interest, or   issues, including:
other employee performance regula-   --technology transfer
tions.   --environmental concerns
                                            --consumer product quality standards
                                            --economic development in host countries
                                            --international trade regulations
                                            --intercompany pricing or currency specu-
                                              lation

ETHICS

Usually brief ethical references   Ethical precepts generally given more
contained in introduction, forward   extensive treatment, many times in
or conclusion. Ethics usually de-   separate section. Ethical corporate
fined in terms of general corporate   activity often coupled with an "above the
activity, e.g. "highest standards of   law" standard, elevating the firm's
business conduct."   operations beyond a legal requirement
                                            level.

CONSTITUENCY RELATIONSHIPS

Common core of acknowledged consti-   Commonly identified constituency groups
tuency relationships include employ-   addressed in greater depth, providing both
ees, consumers, suppliers, community,   an acknowledgment and explanation of the
competitors, and shareholders. Little   responsibility relationship. A balanced
detail specified on corporate respon-   "responsibilities to" dimension is added
sibilities to such groups; employee   to the worker/management relationship.
relationship generally emphasizes
"responsibilities of" workers.

CORE TOPICS AND IMPLEMENTATION PROCEDURES

Most codes cover employee policy   Most employee guidance topics covered, but
directives on: usually with more extensive treatment
 --payment or gifts   geared to the firm's nature and its
 --accounting standards   defined constituency relationships,
 --conflicts of interest   including international business concerns.
 --antitrust regulations   Implementation procedures generally adopt
Other common topics include internal   a chain-of-command procedure, often
corporate relations, environmental   providing additional resource personnel
concerns, and marketing practices.   to aid code interpretation by employee.
Code implementation procedures
generally rely on a formal certification
of employee compliance, while providing
varying degrees of policy interpretation
assistance.

Core Topics and Implementation Procedures

A certain core of topics appeared in nearly every individual corporate code of conduct. Most prominent among these topics were code sections on payments or gifts, accounting standards, conflicts of interest, and antitrust regulations. The first two topics reflect the immediate stimulus of the mid–1970s' revelations concerning overseas payments and off-the-books accounts, while the latter two subjects appear to be drawn from previously existing standards contained in the policy manuals of most large corporations. A manager charged with the task of designing a code of conduct for his company after the SEC began investigating improper payments in 1973, would usually start with at least this policy base of easily identifiable topics. Around 90 percent of the examined codes were not formulated until after the payments controversy had broken out.

Other subjects that received extensive treatment in many corporate codes included trade secrets, marketing practices, use of agents and consultants, environmental standards, and internal corporate relations. These types of topics generally reflected an employee guidance concern that was prevalent in both types of code categories, but the corporate identity codes often went well beyond the internal guidance perspective.

The major differences between the two code approaches' treatment of these core policy topics revolved around the constituencies being addressed and the detailed application of code topics to particular industrial sectors. Employee guidance codes focused on enunciating clear directives that would assure an employee's actions complied with legal regulations or other requirements placed on corporate activity in areas such as antitrust and product safety. Corporate identity codes, on the other hand, addressed employee performance responsibilities within a discussion of broader corporate responsibilities to other groups, tying a recognition of the basis for performance standards to their operational application.

For example, antitrust policy might be addressed in terms of the cost to consumers and competitors as well as simple compliance with legal enforcement standards. Product safety statements typically went beyond a commitment to physical product safety and internal production methods to a positive responsibility for more general consumer information and education as well. With regard to providing applied industrial detail, marketing practices were related to the particular problems faced by pharmaceuticals, foodstuffs, or other such consumer goods, while environmental measures were geared to the specific capabilities of an industry, such as in energy conservation, resource recycling, or the compatibility of new plant construction with surrounding community standards.

While sometimes ill-defined, sixty codes specified follow-up implementation procedures for employees to assure compliance with code standards, provide interpretations of stated policies, or answer questions regarding specific application of the code to real work situations. These implementation procedures tended to become more formal or legalistic (such as requiring the return of signed employee statements certifying the reading of and compliance with certain policy statements) where codes contained little more than narrow employee performance directives. Codes dealing with broader corporate identity concerns relied more on designating chain-of-command procedures or identifying specialized guidance personnel as resources for employees to use in seeking to understand or apply the code. The use of specialized training programs or specific review boards on ethics or social responsibility occurred in less than one-fifth of all the companies.

Ethical Concepts as a Business Guide

Specific references to ethical concepts were made by over three-fourths of the codes, but the nature of the references varied widely. The most popular approach, used by well over one-half of the firms that specifically discussed ethics, defined it in relation to corporate activity, talking of ethics as "the highest standard of business conduct" or "integrity and honesty in all business dealings." Nearly 14 percent of the codes referenced corporate ethics by relating business procedures to legal requirements as business standards which exist above the letter of the law. Around 28 percent of the codes chose to deal with the subject in an individual rather than corporate way, discussing personal ethics as the relevant standard.

In comparing types of codes, the corporate identity model was much more likely to give ethical precepts extensive treatment, devoting a separate section to their elaboration as compared to the more prevalent practice in employee guidance codes of placing a brief ethical reference in the foreword, introduction, or conclusion of the document. The corporate identity code was also more than twice as likely as an employee guidance code to utilize the less frequent "above the law" standard for business practices. This notion of conduct above the law is important to set a credible standard for corporate operations; that is, something more than that which a firm is required to do anyway by political enforcement authorities.

Defining an International Business Identity

One assumption supporting this research was the expectation that many corporate codes of conduct would contain a significant discussion of international business operations. A survey by the Business Roundtable[15] in 1975 which elicited materials from some 100 of its member companies reported that a number of them included international operating standards among the concerns they addressed. A study in 1978 by Robert Chatov for the California Roundtable[16] reported in the Summer 1980 *California Management Review*, covered a diverse sample of nearly 300 firms nationwide, about one-third of them multinational in character. Among the conclusions of his code analysis was a finding that, compared to the earlier Business Roundtable study, corporations were placing an increased emphasis on discussing their international operations.

The target list of companies selected for this survey comprised those firms thought most likely to have a well developed international business code. While a direct comparison with other previous surveys is not possible without analysis of unavailable data concerniing the overlap of sample respondents, the survey's results provide further evidence concerning the specific international content of corporate codes.

One of the most striking findings is the greater likelihood of corporate identity codes to deal more frequently and in greater depth with the international dimension of corporate operations compared to the treatment it receives in employee guidance documents. From the 110 codes analyzed in this regard, 78 of them specifically dealt to some degree with international concerns. Fully 38 of the 42 classified corporate identity codes (90 percent) addressed international issues compared to 40 of 68 employee guidance codes (58.8 percent). In addition, virtually all of the corporate identity documents attempted to deal with international issues in a substantial way, either devoting a separate section to their discussion or clearly integrating international concerns into operational sections spread throughout the document. Less than one-half of the employee guidance codes that incorporated any mention of international aspects showed a comparable measure of significance.

The greater depth of the corporate identity documents' treatment of international business relationships was further reflected in the range of issues discussed. As might be expected from the nature of employee guidance directives, most of these codes focused on corporate payments policies and FCPA regulations, but went little beyond this subject into other overseas business activities. This concentration of corporate codes on foreign legal/political relationships, and on the issue of questionable payments specifically, had been suggested by a broad-based survey conducted in 1978 by the Foundation of the Southwestern Graduate School of Banking.[17] Over one-half of 174 corporate codes examined in that study covered questionable payments, while 14 percent discussed social aspects of international relationships and only 9 percent covered types of investment policy decisions.

This current survey of more specifically international business codes suggests that the corporate statements most likely to deal substantively and comprehensively with international business subjects are those codes adopting an integrated corporate identity approach. Only one corporate identity code singled out the FCPA as the focal point of its international business section. While corporate identity codes usually dealt with such a payments policy somewhere within the document, this code type handled the issue in a way that allowed a broader discussion of international business issues that was not dominated by a response to the foreign payments controversy. Often included in the range of international concerns addressed by corporate identity codes were such topics as technology transfer, economic growth or development in host countries, restrictive business practices, intercompany pricing and currency speculation, international labor relations, international organization activities, and export control or international boycott regulations.

For example, several corporations pledged themselves to a continuous effort both to encourage innovation internationally and to respect the need to transfer appropriate technology within a national or regional context. Advertising, labeling, and packaging standards of honesty and accuracy were taken further in their international application by a recognition of multilingual communication needs and a corporate commitment to be sensitive to the differing mores and practices of host nations. Most corporate identity codes stated their policy to follow standard "arms-length" pricing practices in intercompany transactions and many added a specific pledge not to engage in currency dealings to obtain speculative profits.

THE CASE FOR A CORPORATE IDENTITY CODE

A clear preference for a corporate identity code of conduct emerges from the above comparison of corporate code content. This type of document is the most effective, responsive approach to both internal and external individuals or groups, including a global audience, that are concerned about the role of MNCs in relation to societal needs. A corporate identity code is the most relevant as it addresses more appropriate issues of interest to a range of constituency groups, including international business operations; it possesses effective utility in that code standards can serve practical internal guidance functions as well as responding to public interest questions; and it is a credible policy instrument, particularly because its internal guidance dimension can provide some standards against which the company's position on public policy issues can be measured.

This preference for a corporate identity approach does not mean that either employee guidance or public relations documents are without value. Both types of efforts can serve their own worthwhile functions. Virtually all firms need an employee guidance manual that addresses in sufficient detail practical questions of work rules and regulations. Public affairs activities and publications are also essential corporate tools that can address needs ranging from worthwhile philanthropic efforts to legitimate government relations representation on specific public issues. But to stretch the use of either of these traditional approaches in an attempt to meet new code of conduct purposes as well is to miss the mark, perhaps denigrating or damaging their original central function and certainly losing the opportunity to fashion the most effective type of code instrument. What is needed instead is an integration of elements from both areas into an internally applied but externally understandable and relevant document that will functionally outline the firm's identity and role within society.

While the exact formulation of a corporation's code of conduct must be an individualized exercise, some outlines for constructing an effective corporate identity approach can be drawn from the analysis of aggregate code content. The code should contain employee guidance topics with functional descriptions of operational corporate policy, perhaps keyed to the corporate policy manual for more detailed regulations and appropriate follow-up procedures. "Responsibilities to" as well as "responsibilities of" employees should be elaborated upon so that internal and external audiences will understand both sides of the worker-management relationship.

The corporation's functional relationship and responsibilities toward other constituency groups should also be outlined, probably including at least the ones mentioned earlier as they are relevant to a particular firm's situation (for example, general shareholders where the corporation is publicly held). The issue content of a code should be determined by the composition of these constituency relationships, with an attempt made to cover at least the most common concerns that can be identified. For instance, a corporation's policy with regard to plant closures (process or criteria for decision-making; timing of notification; approach to prior or subsequent discussion) would be a legitimate and common question regarding corporate operations that directly concerns employee and community groups, as well as other constituencies more indirectly.

No standard list of topics can be enumerated in advance that is applicable to all corporations. A code will be most credible if it seeks to address real issues in a way that relates to the actual nature of the firm's operations and its particular relationships and role in society.

Two topics, however, merit additional attention. To the extent that a corporate code of conduct addresses the specific question of ethical concepts, as this author believes it should appropriately do, the corporate identity approach is best suited to a discussion of ethical standards in business dealings (as opposed to strictly personal ethics). Even more appropriate would be the identification of these ethical standards as lying above the minimum required by law, giving an added measurement dimension to abstract ethical precepts that can give them practical meaning as actions taken beyond those required by legal enforcement authority.

International business operations is a second topic that deserves greater emphasis. One conclusion emerging from this research is that if these firms do indeed represent the companies most likely to possess international corporate codes, then the U.S. business community still has a long way to go in fully incorporating international concerns into their code instruments. With firms becoming ever more global in nature, often relying on international activities for between 30 to 60 percent or more of corporate income, an explicit recognition and elaboration of this international dimension is an essential part of any effective code of conduct.

The actual approach to addressing international business concerns can and should vary depending on the nature of the enterprise and its engagement abroad. For example, there was an evident distinction between the codes examined of those defining international positions in terms of special responsibilities and obligations (usually in relation to developing countries and often in natural resource areas) as compared to firms that approached international operations on the basis of a harmonization or integration of foreign activities with those in the domestic headquarters (for instance, a standardization of product quality, measured by maximum interchangeability of parts; or fair and nondiscriminatory treatment of employees, including advancement and training opportunities). The key point in formulating an effective code outline is simply to include a clear identification of the corporation's international interests and responsibilities while defining the functional expression of these aspects as best fits actual corporate positions and operations.

When selecting the code approach and outlining its content, four important points should be kept in mind:

1. A corporate identity code should be constructed to do exactly what the name states; that is, the code should identify the corporation's basic values, objectives, relationships, positions, and procedures. A document that seeks to portray the corporation as it is, not necessarily equivalent to a public relations department portrait, would be most beneficial to all parties concerned, including the corporation. All too often business evokes undue cynicism or skepticism through offering narrative description which it believes the public would like to hear, even though it may be obviously unconnected with operational reality.

2. It is not the length of a corporate code that is crucial, but its relevance, utility, and credibility. A code cannot and should not attempt to address all issues, detail all procedures, or anticipate all questions. A code formulation that identifies the most common concerns of the major internal and external constituency groups in a way that relates to the specific firm's actual policies and modes of operation will best meet the tests of relevance, utility, and credibility.

3. A self-evaluation exercise, which must be the first step in a good code-building effort, will likely yield additional and unforeseen benefits. Often corporate management is helped to identify and understand more clearly the basis for inherited and previously unanalyzed corporate positions and procedures. This process should be repeated through review and possible code revision efforts, either periodically undertaken by designated departments or more continuously applied by a specific code committee or board.

4. The role of top management, and particularly the chief executive officer, is crucial to the origination and maintenance of an effective corporate code. Without active and visible backing from the firm's top leadership, code development attempts are unlikely to achieve a meaningful evaluation of operating principles and precepts or to set forth policies that can guide future corporate actions in an applied, realistic fashion.

THE CHALLENGE OF CORPORATE CODE DEVELOPMENT

A legitimate and perhaps inevitable question for executives considering an individual corporate code of conduct is—why bother? Certainly the immediate public pressure for their adoption has decreased and management attention to such a task is not cost-free. While corporate codes can serve many worthwhile domestic purposes, particularly in helping to improve worker relations and avoid unnecessary government regulations, an important part of the answer to this question rests with the cross-country adaptation needs of contemporary international business. These documents can provide a mechanism for rationalizing the basis for comparative operating methods across national boundaries in a way that could aid timely, self-informed adjustments, while minimizing the likelihood of later misunderstandings regarding a company's operating modes and objectives.

For example, where a firm maintains significant subsidiary operations in several countries, questions are likely to arise regarding such issues as its comparative practices in labor relations or the location of research and development efforts. There are many, very legitimate reasons for differences to exist based on industry characteristics, country endowments, national cultures, and other considerations. Without a forthright corporate standard explaining how such factors are considered in corporate decision-making, however, firms present all-too-easy targets for vague charges of corporate exploitation. These charges will be especially hard to counteract in public forums if the company cannot cite a previous public statement setting forth the basis for its operating methods.

International corporations can, of course, ignore such issues in the interests of "letting sleeping dogs lie" as long as their firm has not yet come under such an attack. A realistic look at the global environment, however, argues against such a late, reactive approach—whether it be recognition of proliferating intergovernmental codes, the push for stricter labor regulations in Europe, or the increasingly sophisticated bargaining of developing nations for a greater share of the benefits associated with MNC activities. Such policy debates and negotiating sessions will be demanding enough on their own merits without the corporation presenting itself as an easy target for increased pressures due to perceptions of it as secretive, exploitive, and essentially uncontrolled in its operations. A good corporate identity code could help avoid such external image handicaps while at the same time informing internal management goals as to the best basis for corporate policy decisions.

Many of the corporate codes examined in this research have made strides toward establishing a good basis for identifying the firm's character and objectives for relevant constituency groups. The next chapter takes a closer look at some selected provisions from many of these codes. These examples may help to fill in the rough outline that is suggested here for how other companies might select a corporate identity approach in their own code development. The challenge for a corporate code program will be to individualize such suggestions and examples in an applied manner that will provide a relevant, useful, and credible policy instrument for guiding the firm's role in society, at home and abroad, over the complex and demanding decades ahead.

NOTES

1. International Chamber of Commerce, *Guidelines for International Investment*, Paris, 1972.

2. "International Codes of Practice in Marketing," resolution adopted by the ICC Executive Committee, May 20, 1973.

3. International Chamber of Commerce, *International Code of Sales Promotion Practice*, Paris, 1973, pp. 3–4.

4. International Chamber of Commerce, *Extortion and Bribery in Business Transactions*, Paris, 1977.

5. Ibid., p. 13.

6. ICC, *International Code of Sales Promotion Practice*, p. 4.

7. ICC, *Extortion and Bribery*, p. 15.

8. *IFPMA Code of Pharmaceutical Marketing Practices* (Zurich: International Federation of Pharmaceutical Manufacturers Associations, 1981).

9. U.S. Council for International Business, *UN Report*, newsletter, Vol. 5, No. 4, May 8, 1984, pp. 4–5.

10. USA-BIAC Committee on International Investment and Multinational Enterprises, *A Review of Standards and Guidelines for International Business Conduct*, New York, September 1975, p. 19.

11. Ibid., pp. 18–19.

12. Clarence C. Walton, ed., *The Ethics of Corporate Conduct*, The American Assembly, Columbia University (Englewood Cliffs, N.J.: Prentice-Hall, 1977), p. 192.

13. Chamber of Commerce of the United States, Specialized Task Force of the National Chamber's Multinational Corporations Panel, "Elements of Global Business Conduct for Possible Inclusion in Individual Company Statements," Washington, D.C., January 1975.

14. The combined internal/external audience category is suggested by 1980 findings of an opinion survey of corporate executives on perceived benefits of a code. Internally executives most often cited legal protection and increased company pride and loyalty, while externally they pointed to setting a proper corporate tone. The corporate identity classification in this study is designed to encompass those corporate codes that are most explicitly directed at both internal and external audiences. For information on the executive opinion survey, see *Implementation and Enforcement of Codes of Ethics in Corporations and Associations*, a report prepared for the Ethics Resource Center by Opinion Research Corporation, Princeton, New Jersey, ORC Study #65334, August 1980. Also see the discussion on code purposes and objectives in Jack N. Behrman, *Discourses on Ethics and Business* (Cambridge, Mass.: Oelgeschlager, Gunn & Hain, 1981) pp. 138–139.

15. *A Survey of Business Roundtable Members on Business Conduct Guidelines*, The Business Roundtable, December 1975. A study by the Center for the Study of Applied Ethics conducted at about this same time found that most firms applied U.S. standards in their foreign business dealings, but a number of executives expressed a desire to use other country's standards. *Standards of Conduct in Business*, The Colgate Darden Graduate School of Business Administration, University of Virginia (Charlottesville, Va.: Center for the Study of Applied Ethics, 1977).

16. See Robert Chatov, *An Analysis of Corporate Statements on Ethics and Behavior*, prepared for the Standards of Performance Task Force, California Roundtable, June 1978; and "What Corporate Ethics Statements Say," *California Management Review*, Vol. 22, No. 4, Summer 1980, pp. 20–29.

17. *A Study of Corporate Ethical Policy Statements*, The Foundation of the Southwestern Graduate School of Banking (Dallas, Tex.: Southern Methodist University, 1980).

7

A Closer Look at Individual Corporate Codes

Executives faced with the challenge of developing a corporate code of conduct can find some assistance by examining a range of existing documents. Although the individual code movement is quite recent, enough corporations experimented with this device over the past decade to provide an initial inventory of examples. The key to designing an effective corporate code is its specific application to the individual company; code provisions are useful and credible only if they reflect the actual character of a firm's operations. Nevertheless, an examination of existing documents can suggest comparative ways to formulate codes and help identify some of the issues that must be addressed in order to respond to societal concerns about large international enterprises.

This chapter takes a closer look at individual corporate codes, building on the last chapter's comparison of aggregate code approaches. Priority is given to examining positive examples of how some corporations formulate policies to address particular international needs. It is beyond the scope of this work to investigate in case-study format the actual application of these codes within each of the corporations cited. While occasional examples are used to show the implications of different policy positions for corporate operations, no judgments are offered as to any particular firm's overall performance.

The examination of individual code examples is organized into three general areas related to concepts discussed in Chapter 6. A purpose and form section focuses on the corporate identity code approach, including a look at constituency group relationships and at how such documents deal with ethical norms. Next comes a series of illustrations showing how firms can adopt policy guidelines that relate business operations to international circumstances. Finally, the topic of code implementation is discussed, including the structuring of training, review, and revision functions within an enterprise.

CODE PURPOSE AND FORM

An effective corporate code of conduct integrally relates purpose and form so that corporate goals are reflected and supported by the code structure. Corporate codes will vary widely due to the innate diversity of business enterprises, but much of the specific variance is determined by the interaction of purpose and form. Existing codes differ particularly in their general or specific goal definitions and in the degree to which internal or external audiences are addressed. Purpose and form decisions also determine how a code deals with issues of constituency groups and with concepts of business ethics.

Many enterprises choose to develop a brief set of principles that embody general corporate objectives. These statements may be contained in a small fold-out pamphlet or enunciated in a chief-executive-officer letter. One such statement was issued by Borg-Warner Corporation in 1982 after an eight–month drafting effort involving about one hundred senior managers, headed by the firm's chief executive. A pamphlet, entitled " . . . to reach beyond the minimal," contained five paragraph-long statements that summarized the values and beliefs underlying company decisions. A preamble to the code, meant to reflect both the reason for drafting the statement as well as its goals, is reprinted in Exhibit 1. The document was based on a common premise for most corporate codes— that business performance can and should be guided by standards beyond the minimal formal constraints imposed on it by society.

Exhibit 1

Any business is a member of a social system, entitled to the rights and bound by the responsibilities of that membership. Its freedom to pursue economic goals is constrained by law and channeled by the forces of a free market. But these demands are minimal, requiring only that a business provide wanted goods and services, compete fairly, and cause no obvious harm. For some companies that is enough. It is not enough for Borg-Warner. We impose upon ourselves an obligation to reach beyond the minimal. We do so convinced that by making a larger contribution to the society that sustains us, we best assure not only its future vitality, but our own.

This is what we believe.

"...to reach beyond the minimal," The Beliefs of Borg-Warner, Borg-Warner Corporation, 1982.

Linking Purpose to Operations Through Form

Statements of purpose can be linked to functional corporate policies in a number of ways. The two key elements in this linkage appear to be the code's relationship to employee policy manuals, and the use of its goals in the corporate planning process. Both of these routes can add substantive content to general goal definitions, making a statement of purpose more credible by demonstrating its operational relevance.

For many corporations their code of conduct and their policy manual are synonymous. Traditional manager or employee manuals often took on the role of a broader code in the mid- to late–1970s when they were updated to reflect changed international circumstances that affected both political and market conditions. For example, the CPC International policy manual was revised in 1979 to pull together separate policy statements into a common format reflecting changed conditions. As noted in the manual's introduction:

> CPC International's business is conducted by many people in many countries throughout the world. The Company's success has traditionally depended in large part upon an ability to conduct its operations in diverse economic, political, and social environments in a manner consistent with its overall policies and objectives.
>
> In recent years, as the Company's operations have become larger and more complex and the business environment has evolved, many of the Company's policies have undergone change. This Manual has been prepared as a means of bringing together these basic policies in a common format, and providing ready reference to them.[1]

Other firms have designed code booklets that go beyond broad purpose statements to more focused goal objectives in specific policy areas. These documents usually summarize in guideline fashion the much more detailed rules and procedures spelled out in full policy manuals. While often directed to particular employee groups, as in the Ashland Oil brochure represented by the letter in Exhibit 2, these documents can also be made available to interested parties outside the company. Another example of this summary approach is the rather lengthy but effective IBM booklet, *Business Conduct Guidelines*, most recently revised and issued in 1983.[2]

A slight variation on the summary booklet form is represented by *General Foods Basic Policies*[3] and ITT's *Code of Corporate Conduct*.[4] These documents present brief explanations of corporate policies and goals under various topical areas, but also explicitly reference the exact corporate policy statement on that subject in the company's longer and more detailed policy manuals. This approach provides an accessible and readable summary document for employees as well as other individuals. Employees are more likely to familiarize themselves with overall corporate goals and philosophy in areas beyond their own immediate responsibilities if they are not overwhelmed by the size and detail of a full company-wide manual. On the other hand, the annotated references to

Exhibit 2

_____

                                                    March, 1977

To All Exempt Employees
Of Ashland Oil, Inc.:

        It is important for you to know and understand
the basic policies that guide the conduct of Ashland
Oil's various businesses.

        This brochure discusses a number of corporate
policies in brief, direct fashion. It is a summary of
the rules and guidelines set forth more
comprehensively and formally in the Ashland Corporate
Policy Manual, the company's Personnel Policy Manual,
and other documents. You are expected to follow them
carefully in making business decisions or determining
procedures to follow.

        Please read and keep this brochure. We hope it
will answer most questions that you may have on
Ashland's policy rulings and attitudes.

        If you encounter any situation in which you are
uncertain about the company's policies, contact your
supervisor immediately: it may be necessary for the
situation to be reviewed to determine a proper course
of action.

                              Chairman and
                              Chief Executive Officer

Corporate Policies: A Summary for Employees, Ashland
Oil, Inc., March, 1977.

_____

longer policy documents provide ready guidance in areas where more detail is
needed and make it clear to all concerned that corporate goal statements bear a
tangible relationship to operational business procedures.

Corporate code statements can also be linked directly to internal planning
processes to help translate general corporate purpose into specific performance
goals. One of the most comprehensive available examples of this approach is a
document entitled *TRW and the 80s: Statement of purpose, fundamental objectives and principal goals and strategies*. The drafting of this document resulted

from a reexamination of corporate objectives in light of rapid worldwide change. The "Introduction" portion is reprinted in Exhibit 3.

While most corporations regularly undergo evaluation and planning exercises, TRW used this process to develop for the first time a single, integrated statement of corporate purpose. Perhaps even more uniquely, the document is explicitly formulated to be used in three major ways: (1) to consider revised financial goals within a broader fabric of other corporate objectives, (2) to guide the development of operational strategies and programs, and (3) to serve as the basis for establishing detailed communications, both internally and externally, with interested constituent groups. The combination of these three functions embody the essence of a corporate identity approach to designing an individual company code of conduct.

The relationship of financial goals to a corporation's statement of purpose is crucial, both for internal and external purposes. The pursuit of profit is the driving engine of private, free enterprise and a statement of corporate goals that does not directly and specifically address this fact immediately risks its credibility. A statement of corporate purpose that ignores this financial concern will be seen internally to bear little resemblance to common financial yardsticks of performance that guide and measure operational programs. External credibility is similarly jeopardized by a document if it foregoes a discussion of measurable standards in favor of general pabulum or public relations wordsmithing.

On a more positive note, a corporate statement of purpose that relates stan-

Exhibit 3

```
Introduction

As TRW enters the 1980s, we face worldwide a rapidly
changing and increasingly complex social, economic,
technological and political environment.  The effects
of these changes and complexities on the societies in
which we function and their institutions, including
business, are and will continue to be profound and
pervasive.  TRW's success will depend in large part on
how well we understand these dynamic forces, influence
them in constructive ways and adapt to them in a
manner beneficial to the company and its constituents.

In this context, it has been our practice periodically
to reexamine and reevaluate our established
objectives, goals and strategies.  We make
modifications where called for, and where we believe
our present course is right, we reaffirm it.  As a
result we can be reasonably certain that our
objectives and goals are right for the times.  We have
regularly completed this process in the past and we
have recently completed it once again.
```

We have now decided for the first time, that we should
bring together in a single document a broad general
statement of these fundamental objectives and
principal goals and strategies. We have done this for
three reasons.

First, our planning process resulted in the revision
of our existing financial goals. In presenting these
revised financial goals, we want to be certain they
are considered in the context of all of our objectives
and principal goals, financial and nonfinancial,
quantitative and qualitative. For it is only in the
fabric of the integrated whole that they can be viewed
meaningfully.

Second, we intend to use this general statement in
developing programs designed to help achieve the
company-wide goals outlined here and as the basis for
developing goals, strategies and programs for
operating units and staff functions.

Third, we intend this statement to serve as the basis
for the development of additional documents which will
be used internally and externally in more detailed
communication with our constituent groups. These
documents will help explain what we stand for, what we
hope to achieve and how we feel about our
responsibilities. In the midst of the continuing
public discussion of the role of large corporations,
our communication of these points will permit public
scrutiny of the principles by which we operate. Such
disclosure will also encourage the kind of two-way
communication which is vital to the preservation of a
free political and economic system--the kind of
communication we seek and have been developing with
our principal constituent groups. This communication,
in turn, will help shape our actions and those of our
constituents.

This last point merits special explanation. We
believe that constitutional democracy and the free
market system are inextricably interwoven. Neither
can survive alone. Informed freedom of choice lies at
the heart of each and of their working together
successfully. In turn, informed choice requires free
and open communication between and among the groups
which form the societies in which all of us live and
work.

TRW and the 80s, TRW Inc., 1980, pp. 1-2.

dard financial objectives to other nonfinancial goals helps establish the importance and credibility of broader corporate standards by dealing with them in an integrated and operationally meaningful way. The clear linkage of these elements can give contextual substance to usual corporate claims that the pursuit of sales and financial results is constrained by broader considerations of proper business conduct.

A related benefit of dealing with financial goals in statements of corporate purpose may come from a more informed public. Businesspeople typically complain that opinion polls and other measures show that the public holds grossly inflated beliefs about corporate profitability, with presumed profit margins often running three to four times the actual rates. Yet despite these complaints surprisingly few corporations have chosen to define their financial goals in code statements to help correct this public misconception.

Certainly there are good, if not fully persuasive, reasons for not publicizing specific goals, including competitive considerations and the necessity for regular revision of objectives as economic conditions change. But does this difficulty preclude the possibility of providing any kind of financial goal statements? The TRW document, drafted for internal use, covers specific numerical goals for real internal rate of return, growth in real earnings and dividends per share, growth in real total assets, a debt leverage range, and a dividend payout range. Other firms grappled with financial goal definitions in their codes and other generally available documents, addressing such concepts as return on shareholders' equity, return on investment, return on capital, growth in sales, return on net worth, and sourcing of capital.[5]

The second envisioned use for TRW's statement of corporate purpose was to help formulate strategies and programs that would turn company-wide goals into more specific guidance for operating units and staff functions. Certainly the translation of financial goals into operating strategy is an important component of this step, but other implementational aspects also emerge that frame and influence financial performance measures. Among these additional considerations are product quality and reliability, research and development programs, market strategies that weigh international investment and exporting, technology transfer policy, diversification strategies, component sourcing decisions, management procedures, advanced training opportunities, and many other items. This translation of broad statements of corporate purpose into business strategies and operating programs is essential if the adopted goals are to guide internal actions and gain credibility with outside observers.

The final reason TRW adopted a single, integrated statement of purpose was to provide a basis for better communication with constituent groups, both internally and externally. Internally corporate goals touch most directly on employee standards such as hiring, advancement, compensation, privacy, career development, management responsibilities, and other such items. It is also important, however, to ensure that employees understand broader corporate goals and the vital role they play in the attainment of corporate objectives. Many studies have discussed the benefits of positive employee attitudes toward, and identification with, their enterprise. A basic step in building such ties and enhancing employee morale is to communicate an understanding of the corporation's purpose, operational goals, and societal role—in short, its corporate identity.

Communication of corporate identity is equally important with external groups. A variety of constituencies are affected and thereby concerned with corporate activity, beginning with close-in interests and ranging out to broader groups at home and abroad, including national governments. Effective communication of corporate standards is essential to the quality of a direct business relationship with many of these groups. A clear communication of purpose is necessary to fulfill the responsibilities of a corporate citizen operating for the benefit and at the discretion of different societies around the world.

Recognition and responsiveness to external constituencies is a central element in devising a corporate identity approach to individual codes of conduct. Employee guidance codes may cover many of the items discussed above regarding a statement of corporate purpose, linkage to operating programs, and internal communication. A corporate identity code, however, integrates into its definition of purpose and its communication efforts a recognition of responsibilities to broader constituencies ranging at times far outside its immediate employee group.

Defining a Standard for Measurement

The relevance of corporate codes to both internal and external constituencies is illustrated in several documents that directly address various groups and offer their codes as standards by which the corporation should be judged. This latter notion of measuring or evaluating corporate performance by code standards may also bind corporate responsibilities to a specific concept of business ethics. For example, an excerpt from the Boeing Company's *Business Conduct Guidelines* (Exhibit 4) ties together the elements of employee guidance, responsibilities to customers and competitors, and ethical standards anywhere in the world.

The actual constituencies listed in any individual corporation's code will vary, ranging across the many groups discussed in Chapter 6. It is not the specific enumeration of groups that is most relevant to a discussion of code purpose, but rather the clear recognition of a corporate responsibility to external constituencies. A corporate identity code acts as a bridge between internal and external parties and provides a standard by which corporate actions can be measured by both.

Union Carbide is another enterprise whose code explicitly recognizes its corporate responsibility to numerous constituencies, specifically including international relationships that date back over half a century. The company's chairman also acknowledged the measurement dimension of code standards, writing

Exhibit 4

Foreword
        As with most moral concepts, the principles of
proper ethics are often easy to state but difficult to
apply. This pamphlet is designed to answer some of
the questions Boeing employees may expect to encounter
in making ethical business decisions at a time when
the standards of business conduct are receiving
greater public scrutiny and attention. Corporations
today are being called upon as never before to explain
their business decisions. In answering this call,
corporations are compelled to speak out clearly in
defense of adopted standards of ethical behavior.
This pamphlet will allow our employees, customers and
competitors to know just where Boeing stands on the
more fundamental issues of business ethics. It is
intended that the following guidelines summarize
Boeing's ethical requirements for the conduct of its
business anywhere in the world.

Business Conduct Guidelines, The Boeing Company,
January 1981.

---

in the beginning of the firm's booklet, *The International Responsibilities of a Multinational Corporation*:

This booklet outlines nine business standards or policies that we believe are essential to assure the proper conduct of our corporation. These policies set forth our goals. While we continually strive to meet them, we realize that we may not always achieve them. However, it is by these standards, and the assumption of these responsibilities, that we must measure ourselves. Through this communication, I am asking all of our employees to rededicate themselves to these objectives and to their fulfillment.[6]

To this formulation must be added the realization that such standards function not only for self-measurement, but also as a basis for an evaluation by others. Union Carbide recognized this fact. The very first section of the booklet immediately after the chairman's introduction is entitled "A Standard to Follow and Be Judged By." That section concludes:

The responsibilities contained in this booklet constitute our definition of being a "good corporate citizen." It is upon this "code of conduct" that Union Carbide wishes to be judged.[7]

Views of Ethics and the Corporation

Several of the above code examples include a reference to ethics in linking statements of corporate purpose to operational programs and communications with constituent groups. A closer look at the ethics component of such codes reveals more clearly how a code's purpose and form are influenced by different notions of business ethics. Central to these differences are two related subjects—a view of the corporation as a unique individual entity as opposed to a collection of separate individuals, and the perceived relationship of business ethics and legal requirements. In corporate identity codes, these ethical concepts can help guide and support proper individual employee actions, while also providing standards of business conduct that rise above minimum legal norms.

A number of writers have suggested that business ethics may not exist much beyond the guarded confines of an academic classroom. According to this view, standards and norms do exist, but there is nothing separate or distinct about "business" ethics. In fact, many people believe that ethics can be defined and understood only in individual terms rather than as applied to organizations or institutions.[8]

One example of an individual-centered notion of business ethics is reflected in a 1976 letter from the chairman of the Koppers Company to the firm's managers. The company espouses a management philosophy that relies heavily on individual judgment, leading it to reject the use of detailed procedure manuals or organizational charts. Similarly, in responding to the public outcry against disclosures of improper overseas payments, the corporation rejected the use of written decrees or company codes. Stating that the corporate interest does not compel anyone to act against their own individual ethical beliefs, the letter points directly to the primacy of individual ethical standards.

Within each individual resides the will and the power to act in good faith, to uphold laws written and unwritten, and to understand the moral and ethical implications of our actions. The conduct of business does not take place between inanimate corporate entities but between individuals. We do not believe we can create moral conscience through the issuance of a "code of conduct" or by specific instructions for employee behavior.[9]

The Clow corporation also cites the central role of individual employee actions in determining the nature of corporate conduct. In a code of conduct policy statement, however, Clow states, "Further, external pressures and internal needs require the Company possess a conscious, analytical and systematic interest in ethical questions." The firm apparently interprets this conclusion to require the adoption of an active corporate role to influence individual employee behavior. Among the specific purposes of Clow's code of conduct is the intention "to make clear what is expected of employees and to serve as a basis for moral pressure."[10]

This Clow approach introduces the corporation itself as having both a vested interest and a role to play in determining individual employee actions on ethical questions. The position reverses Kopper's more passive approach, which had simply removed corporate interest as a justification for violating personal ethical standards, without trying to actively guide employee behavior. Instead, the Clow code is devised so that written corporate policy can actively guide and even "pressure" employee actions in an intended ethical direction.

Other companies and commentators accept much more directly the concept of business ethics. Conoco issued a booklet entitled *The Conoco Conscience* that explored moral principles relevant to its business operations. In a section, "The Living Corporation," partially reprinted in Exhibit 5, the company specifically accepts and endorses the notion of a collective as well as an individual ethic. Modern public opinion expects corporations to behave ethically, so it is incumbent on enterprises to structure policies and processes that promote a collective ethical standard.

One of the better philosophical presentations of the view that a corporation can be treated as a collective ethical entity is offered by Peter French. He ar-

Exhibit 5
The Living Corporation

In the first part of the 17th century, Sir Edward Coke, one of Great Britain's most eminent jurists, concluded that a corporation was but an impersonal creation of the law--not a being, just a product of written rules and government fiat. But the times have changed...

Although it may be true that Conoco remains an inanimate being for legalistic purposes, the company has a very personal existence for its shareholders, employees, officers, and directors...

No one can deny that in the public's mind a corporation can break the law and be guilty of unethical and amoral conduct. Events of the early 1970s, such as corporate violations of federal law and failure of full disclosure, confirmed that both our government and our citizenry expect corporations to act lawfully, ethically, and responsibly.

Perhaps it is then appropriate in today's context to think of Conoco as a living corporation; a sentient being whose conduct and personality are the collective effort and responsibility of its employees, officers, directors, and shareholders.

The Conoco Conscience, Conoco, Inc., 1976, p.2.

---

gues that every firm must have a "Corporate Internal Decision (CID) Structure" that handles decision-making chores. This CID Structure includes established corporate policy and the designated chain-of-command process that embodies the authority relationship between corporate employees. If an action is consistent with corporate policy and is properly ratified by established internal decision-making procedures, then the action can be considered a corporate action. Consistency with the CID Structure thus allows one to impute ethical responsibility for an action to a collective corporate entity. If the CID Structure has been breached, then implicitly there should be identifiable employees who would bear individual responsibility for the action, rather than the corporation.[11]

The concept of business ethics implies the need to address both policies and procedures within a corporation. Written codes of conduct can become an important statement of formal corporate standards, but attention must also be paid to the form of procedural implementation so that these standards are built into the operational decision-making structure.

The Cummins Engine Company has probably gone as far as any firm in attempting to integrate the notion of corporate ethics into an active guidance mechanism for employees in operational decision-making situations. The company's policy statement "Ethical Standards" makes it clear that ethics is a real-world concern and that the firm stands ready "to help any employee resolve a moral dilemma" and ensure that no career disadvantages will result from raising ethical questions or refusing to engage in questionable activities.[12] Furthermore, rather than relying solely on employee initiative to raise such issues, Cummins sought to build into its internal decision-making system some positive inducements to act ethically, particularly at those points where normal corporate performance pressures might incline someone toward more dubious actions. During a panel discussion of corporate ethics, Charles Powers, who served for several years as Director of Public Responsibility for Cummins Engine, described the firm's efforts to respond to the issue of questionable business activities.

We are attempting to go through the corporation and identify places and mechanisms where those activities might occur. We are beginning to talk to representative individuals who are likely to be pressured to violate company policy in an effort to discover what they believe would create the necessary countervailing pressures to stop these violations—in company policy, company compensation patterns, company auditing patterns, etcetera. We are trying to involve people in such company positions in order to understand how certain traditional short-term expectations of the company—increased sales, for example—can realistically be set aside enabling these employees to participate in a broader definition of a corporate purpose relying on integrity, not indiscretion.

In effect, we are saying to our employees that ethics is more than a formal statement, more than a simple question of honesty. It is a process of thinking through, in their own day to day practices, the impact of the entire corporate entity upon the society around it.[13]

Views on ethical concepts as they relate to a corporation and its individual employees help define the purpose and form of choices made in a code of conduct approach. The more ethical notions are tied to the corporation as an entity, the more code mechanisms can be used to state overall standards, guide individual action, and actively support operational decision-making that favors ethical conduct. To the extent that business ethics are not perceived to exist separately from each individual's personal ethics, the purpose and form of a code become much more restricted, if not entirely meaningless.

Distinguishing Ethics and Legal Requirements

Code purpose and form are also influenced by how a corporation views the relationship between ethical standards and legal requirements. Again the Koppers' letter is instructive of one common approach, making clear that it is corporate policy to obey all applicable laws.[14] A similar standard is adopted in Ashland Oil's policy on business ethics, which pledges the firm to observe "both the letter and spirit of applicable laws and regulations in all countries in which it operates."[15]

Operational difficulties exist for even a law-based corporate standard. The application of legal requirements to particular situations is not always clear, as evidenced by the complex trials filling ever-expanding court calendars. Furthermore, multinational corporations confront the challenging task of obeying different national laws that may compete or directly conflict with each other. Finally, an intention to comply with the spirit as well as the letter of laws and regulations introduces even more vagueness and uncertainty into a legal standards guideline.

The approach for most corporations facing circumstances of conflict or uncertainty in law, evident from both the Koppers and Ashland Oil pieces, is to rely on a policy of disclosure. If legal directives are unclear or conflicts cannot be resolved, ethical concepts come into play to dictate a course of action that would stand a test of full disclosure on television, before one's friends, and with one's family. This approach again tends to individualize ethical notions beyond the realm of legal standards, placing maximum responsibility on an individual's decisions and suggesting a minimal role for formal corporate policies or guidance mechanisms.

A somewhat different view of business ethics and legal requirements is suggested by the code approach adopted by some other firms. Many companies attempt to elaborate specific policies in areas that go beyond adherence to legal minimums, seeking to guide corporate actions through stated policy positions rather than relying solely on an individual-oriented disclosure standard. The essence for this type of view on the relationship between ethics and law is captured in the often quoted leadoff paragraph in the "Business Ethics" section of Caterpillar Tractor Co.'s, *A Code of Worldwide Business Conduct and Operating Principles*. It states: "The law is a floor. Ethical business conduct should normally exist at a level well above the minimum required by law."[16]

If one accepts this notion of business ethics, it is incumbent upon the corporation to then attempt to define those policies that should exist and guide corporate actions above the conduct dictated by law. A corporate code of conduct, keyed to meaningful operational standards, can serve this purpose.

The next section in this chapter will set forth numerous examples of how corporate codes define specific operational policies that can guide corporate conduct to standards beyond minimal or incomplete legal requirements. Exhibit 6 is offered now, however, to illustrate how a firm's statement on business ethics can lead to subject-specific policies that guide practical business operations.

Exhibit 6
Chase's Policy on South Africa

In the Chase Code of Ethics, adopted in 1977, we state:

"Strict attention should be given to the legal, moral and social implications of all loan and investment decisions on a global basis. We should seek to avoid business with identifiably harmful results and assure that we always carefully evaluate the long-term, as well as the short-term, meaning of our decisions."

In South Africa, this approach has resulted in a current lending policy which specifically excludes loans that, in our judgment, tend to support the apartheid policies of the South African Government or reinforce discriminatory business practices.

We recognize that our policy requires a high degree of subjective judgment when applied to specific instances. Our lending criteria are reviewed continually and are subject to change as circumstances may, in our judgment, warrant.

Currently, no new credit commitments are being extended to the Government of South Africa or its parastatal institutions. We continue our prohibition on loans to Namibia, the homelands and border industries. We continue to be willing to consider the financing of private sector needs of a productive nature and which we believe will result in social and economic benefits for all South Africans.

We believe that our involvement with the private sector is a constructive force for stimulating positive changes in that country.

"Chase's Policy on South Africa," The Chase Manhattan Corporation, April 18, 1978.

In this exhibit Chase Manhattan Bank sets forth a policy statement to apply its generalized policy on business ethics to the specific question of loans to South Africa. Ethical principles are given specific operational application to guide business decision-making in circumstances above and beyond the minimum requirements of law. This statement is also clearly an example of a policy action that seeks to provide corporate-wide guidance on ethical issues rather than relying on individual employee decision-making.

Perhaps the best way to conclude this section is to ask the reader to consider the opening paragraphs of *The Norton Policy on Business Ethics*, reprinted as Exhibit 7. This statement ties together many of the elements just discussed, including corporate purpose, constituency relationships, code form, ethics, and

Exhibit 7

To The People Of Norton:

The behavior of corporations, and particularly multinationals such as ourselves, is continually under searching public scrutiny. We welcome such scrutiny at Norton. Ours is a highly principled Company. Wherever we operate, Norton aims for a standard of conduct well above what the law demands--not just to keep us above reproach, but to nourish our self-respect and sharpen our sense of purpose.

While we have always had a commitment to moral conduct and to ethical behavior, it is important to restate our policy on business ethics and to put particulars down on paper. We do business in a fast changing world, and we acquire new employees, customers, suppliers and shareholders every day. All these people deserve from us a clear statement of our business ethics.

We must leave no doubt as to what Norton expects of its people and what people everywhere can expect of Norton. Over two years ago the Norton Board of Directors set forth our beliefs in a Policy on Business Ethics for our Company worldwide. It is our conviction that this document has been useful in focusing on an understandable and common set of values that govern our business operations. It is further our conviction that this is, and will continue to be, the single most important document issued by Norton Company.

The Norton Policy on Business Ethics, Norton Company, Revised February 22, 1979, p. 1.

---

the law. Norton's belief in their code's value comes through strongly, both as an operational guidance device and as a corporate identity statement.

OPERATIONAL LINKAGES AND INTERNATIONAL APPLICATION

One of the problems with developing a code of conduct for business is the tremendous variety of enterprises that exist in the modern world. While firms vary along many different dimensions, the most important for code purposes are probably size, location, and industry. In this book, the focus on multinational enterprises generally assumes a large size and an international scope. This particular section is designed to illustrate how individual MNC codes can link general policy statements with operations by focusing on industry-specific issues most directly related to their international business.

Codes of conduct can be written at such a high level of abstraction that the nature of a firm's product and the primary issues surrounding it remain unclear. Some codes rely on such unexceptionably general standards of business conduct that nothing is revealed about the individual corporation's identity. These code principles are virtually interchangeable between any enterprises. Other corporations use codes to confront particular issues facing their industry, applying business conduct standards to concerns specific to their own product and operations. Issues of central concern to one industry, for instance pollution controls, may naturally be less relevant to another firm that is more concerned about the privacy of information flows.

By addressing industry-specific issues, codes increase their relevance to societal concerns about the corporation and increase the code's credibility both for outside observers and for internal employees that need guidance on real operational problems. Given the wide range of possible corporate applications, the limited number of code examples cited in this section can only be illustrative of an approach rather than offering a drafting guide for each interested enterprise. Nevertheless, the cases illustrate some of the ways that general business conduct standards can be linked to specific industrial and international applications.

Industry-Based Standards

Not surprisingly, examples of the industry-specific code application appear most readily in those business sectors that present special or unusual issues. For instance, in the mid–1970s Bank of America developed and adopted a Voluntary Disclosure Code that attempted to reconcile the public's interest and right to know about bank operations with the enterprise's special obligations regarding the privacy of its transactions. Operating from the premise that a bank has a special need to maintain public trust, the disclosure code catalogued specific items relating to the different functional activities and services performed by the bank. Excerpts from the "President's Preamble" to the Voluntary Disclosure Code are reprinted as Exhibit 8.

Another example of industry-specific code application is the *Statement of Professional Policies and Practices* issued by Booz, Allen & Hamilton, Inc.[17] Due to the nature of the firm's service, this code focuses specifically on client relationships, discussing acceptance and performance of assignments, informa-

Exhibit 8
President's Preamble

Earlier this year a task force of our senior
executives undertook at my request a challenge unique
in the banking industry: the development of a
voluntary disclosure code for BankAmerica which would
open our operations to greater public scrutiny than
ever before.

Our reasoning was simple. We believe that our
business, within obvious constraints of
confidentiality and competitiveness, is the public's
business. We believe that openness as well as
truthfulness about what we do and how we do it is the
only way to maintain public confidence in business
ethics and competence...

Voluntary disclosure going beyond the minimum
requirements of law seems to us to be the proper
course...

The most perplexing problem was how to provide
maximum, meaningful information without violating the
rights of customer and employee privacy, or giving our
competitors needless advantage, or encouraging
speculative activity in our own stock or other
securities we buy and sell. Our challenge: to produce
a disclosure code which respects these constraints yet
permits outsiders to readily evaluate our operations
from any point of view...

We set out to develop a code which would establish the
basis for the fullest possible disclosure within
reasonable bounds. I believe we have achieved this.
It would be presumptuous to claim that we have created
a code that will work for everyone. But I am
convinced we have at least gone a long way in
advancing the public's right to know and our ability
to understand ourselves.

BankAmerica Corporation Voluntary Disclosure Code,
BankAmerica Corporation, November 17, 1976, pp. 1-3.

tion confidentiality, conflicts of interest, as well as firm-employee issues of a
more general nature. While this code does not extensively address corporate
relationships with broader constituencies, a short section on "corporate citizenship" does contain at least one surprisingly direct statement which is cited a bit
later in this chapter as a policy position responsive to a specifically international
business issue.

Other types of industries may find that certain issues warrant more specific
or detailed code standards due to concerns about their production process, product use, or the nature of their market. For example, AMF's *Principles of Conduct* recognizes the importance of advertising activity to their business and acknowledges the necessity for special sensitivity to audiences of children they
might reach and to possible impacts on societal groups where race, sex, age,
or ethnicity may be involved.[18] Johnson Wax commits itself to promoting safe
product use through actions involving labeling, information dissemination, and
other protections against product misuse.[19] Foremost McKesson's booklet *Corporate Public Policy* recognizes consumer interest in the issues of accurate and
informative labeling and packaging, along with broader concerns regarding the
relationship of corporate operations to land use needs, environmental protection, and energy conservation.[20]

Addressing International Concerns

Many corporate policies apply a common standard to all operations, domestic and foreign. This approach lays the foundation for an international identity
code of conduct and recognizes the enterprise's stake in the global community.
Further attention to the specifically international dimension of business operations is necessary, however, if corporate policy is to address effectively concerns about multinational business dealings. Corporate codes should respond to
at least two additional areas not addressed by an approach relying on a common
policy standard.

First, when policy standards are linked to corporate operations, such as labeling or safety issues, an effort should be made to address the often different
challenges posed by foreign as opposed to domestic operations: for example,
where language and educational levels may differ. Second, the code should also
address issues that may be raised only within the context of international operations, such as conflict of national law situations or requests for special consideration of developing country needs. Some examples of both these points
may help to clarify the special but usually overlooked needs of a code for international business conduct.

An example from the drug industry illustrates how corporate labeling and safety
policy can be linked to corporate operations and extended to encompass international business needs. In 1971, stimulated by a recent merger, Warner-Lambert began to standardize labeling of its ethical pharmaceuticals worldwide.[21]
Corporate policy statements committed the firm to provide all information, fa-

vorable or not, to government regulators responsible for making decisions regarding a drug's safety and efficacy. This commitment is similar to a common worldwide policy standard in the sense that it is undertaken for all countries, even where governments do not require the submission of adverse information on drug reactions occurring in other countries.

In applying this policy standard to international conditions, however, the company also recognizes a responsibility to submit labeling changes when appropriate to aid regulators in countries where understaffing or lack of full scientific expertise may constrain the regulatory process. The establishment of an internal management process requiring centralized approval for any new drugs abroad helps prepare the firm to evaluate, coordinate, and respond to the special challenge of applying standards of safety and efficacy under the varying circumstances of foreign government regulation. The company's policy statements also commit the firm to supply practicing physicians with the information necessary for the products's safe and effective use, including any needed precautions regarding adverse reactions.

In applying these policies to worldwide standardization of labeling, the firm reported its experience with one interesting international challenge. The company had selected a package insert approved by the U.S. Food and Drug Administration as the best labeling device to provide necessary information on the antibiotic Chloromycetin. Some eighty-eight package inserts used in different countries were to be standardized on this basic reference document in order to assure that the most complete information was available to physicians wherever the product was being used.

Difficulties arose when the process of attaining government approval in all the countries to change the official labeling insert proved exceedingly time-consuming. Rather than delay distribution of the new standardized information to physicians, the firm undertook a special campaign in order to meet its policy commitments. A document known as a monograph or expanded package insert was prepared as a separate, supplemental information piece to explain in detail how Chloromycetin could be used safely and effectively. The document was translated into fifteen languages to facilitate its use by physicians in foreign markets. In certain Latin American nations where package inserts are not permitted by local law (to discourage over-the-counter sale of drugs without proper medical supervision), the firm placed special warnings on the drug's bottle and carton.

This example is suggestive of some ways in which corporate codes can be responsive to international business issues when linkage is established between policy standards and operational application. To the extent that such international applications can be reflected directly in corporate codes of conduct, these instruments will become more responsive to global concerns about multinational enterprises and firms will be perceived as more sensitive to their own cross-national and cross-cultural character. Obviously there are constraints on how much specialized detail can be written into the code itself, but some explicit recognition of international applications would help develop and clarify the global commitment of MNC operations. The establishment of an international self-identity is not only important to the firm's own planning and operational processes, it is critical to a positive perception of the firm abroad by government officials and private citizens alike, who often view MNCs as ethnocentric entities that define themselves only in home-country terms.

A few other examples illustrate how companies can explicitly recognize their responsibilities to host countries by linking general policy standards to operational activities. For instance, PepsiCo's *Code of Conduct* sets a preference for purchasing products of the host country where such goods are fully competitive. In terms of employment objectives, the code states, "We also consider the staffing of host country operations with national personnel at every level to be an important objective which includes the providing of training programs to facilitate advancement."[22] Similar policies are set forth in the Johnson Wax code which encourages the use of local suppliers, commits the company to training programs, and pledges itself to "staffing and managing with host country nationals wherever practicable."[23]

Another type of special international role obligation arises for MNCs in the area of foreign currency transactions. Given the magnitude of interaffiliate trade between multiple MNC units located throughout the world, these firms possess the capability to act as potentially destabilizing factors in global exchange markets. The possibility of attaining profits through currency speculation might lead to MNC fund shifts that could undermine a country's monetary policies. Furthermore, internal transfer pricing mechanisms could be used to evade national currency controls and shift profits to escape high-tax jurisdictions. Suspicions about currency speculation and abuse of the transfer pricing mechanism have led to much public criticism of MNCs in both developed and developing countries.

In order to respond to such public concern and state clearly the company's operating standards, Caterpillar Tractor Co.'s *A Code of Worldwide Business Conduct and Operating Principles* includes a section on "Currency Transactions" that offers the narrative explanation contained in Exhibit 9. The firm also commits itself in the "Intercompany Pricing" section to an "arm's length" pricing standard that "assures to each country a fair valuation of goods and services transferred—for tariff and income tax purposes."[24] Johnson Wax makes similar commitments in its listing of standards that guide its practices in international trade and investment, including:

• adhering to an intercompany pricing policy that would exist between unrelated parties under similar circumstances.

• making royalty, licensing, and service agreements which are fair and reasonable, and which do not result in any hidden transfer of profits.

• limiting foreign exchange transactions to normal business requirements and for the protection of our assets.[25]

Exhibit 9
Currency Transactions

The main purpose of money is to facilitate trade. Any company involved in international trade is, therefore, obliged to deal in several of the world's currencies, and to exchange currencies on the basis of their relative values.

Our policy is to conduct such currency transactions only to the extent they may be necessary to operate the business and protect our interests.

We buy and sell currencies in amounts large enough to cover requirements for the business, and to protect our financial positions in those currencies whose relative values may change in foreign exchange markets. We manage currencies the way we manage materials inventories--attempting to have on hand the right amounts of the various kinds and specifications used in the business. We don't buy unneeded materials or currencies for the purpose of holding them for speculative resale.

A Code of Worldwide Business Conduct and Operating Principles, Caterpillar Tractor Co., Revised May 1, 1982, p. 10.

Bribery and Accommodation Payments

No discussion of linking corporate standards to international operations could ignore the overseas bribery issue that stimulated most MNC code development. Since so many corporate codes deal with this subject it provides an exceptional range of comparative examples. In a somewhat unexpected way the topic is also interesting as a measure of corporate sensitivity to somewhat broader foreign concerns about MNCs. Firms whose codes demonstrate the most developed international corporate identity often respond to the overseas bribery issue in a way that goes beyond simple legal compliance with the U.S. Foreign Corrupt Practices Act (FCPA). For instance, policies on the related issue of accommodation payments illustrate how corporations deal with practices that may fall outside the scope of the FCPA's bribery provisions but are still of concern to many foreign host nations.

In the immediate case of overseas bribery, most corporate codes contain explicit and often detailed, legalistic policies that are clearly designed to insure compliance with the FCPA. Such statements are desirable, but to the extent that they occurred only in response to the 1977 law, they are also unimpressive as a statement of corporate identity. Certainly most FCPA-inspired legal policies do nothing to suggest that the corporations are going beyond the minimum required by U.S. law.

As applied to an international corporate identity, codes that focus on FCPA compliance may actually suggest the opposite of an internationally oriented firm. For many corporate codes, FCPA-related policies and procedures are the only international issue that is dealt with in a way that is linked to real operational guidance. This type of code leaves an impression that the firm is responsive to the enforced minimum standards of U.S. law dealing with overseas business activities but says nothing about corporate responsiveness to foreign concerns.

An example of this impression is provided by the *Code of Worldwide Business Ethics* published by Levi Strauss and Company.[26] Issued in 1977, the document supersedes the earlier *Codes of Business Ethics* and applies corporate policy statements to global operations. Unfortunately, the only detailed references to specifically international issues arise in connection with policies on political contributions and improper payments. Broad statements about the application of general policies to worldwide operations provide some further recognition of the international realm; however, the document's emphasis on specific standards and operational procedures to assure FCPA compliance, with little counterbalancing discussion of other internationally relevant concerns, leaves a distorted impression of the firm's full international character. A similar impression is conveyed in the booklet *Corporate Mission and Philosophy of Management*, issued in 1978 by Dynalectron Corporation, where a section on "International Relationships" is also dominated by FCPA-related policies and control procedures.[27]

There are, of course, many ways in which a firm can progressively broaden its international identity away from strict FCPA-defined standards. Adopting operational policies on internationally relevant questions concerning host country suppliers, employment, financing, and other subjects is certainly one way. Even within the questionable payments area several approaches can show the international responsiveness of corporate policies in ways that reach beyond U.S. legal requirements.

One closely related step would be for corporations to extend prohibitions on bribery of foreign government officials (the focus of the FCPA) to similar prohibitions on commercial bribery. U.S. statutes seek to prevent commercial bribery in domestic transactions, but their extraterritorial application is much more problematic, while foreign legal coverage and enforcement of activities in this area vary widely. Some individuals will protest that such voluntary action on the part of corporations is an attempt to impose U.S. standards on other countries. On the other hand, an individual company should surely be free to devise a corporate standard on commercial bribery that would prohibit the practice anywhere, even if this action stands above the minimum required by local law. At least the firm would have defined its identity on a subject of undeniable relevance to international commercial activity, and other corporations and governments would be free to deal with the subject corporation, or not, as they so wished.

For example, Cummins Engine Company's policy on "Questionable Payments" explicitly goes beyond the FCPA standard, stating: "The Act does not prohibit corrupt payments to agents of private buyers. Cummins' standards do prohibit such payments." At the same time Cummins' policy offers explicit guidance on the question of so-called "facilitation" payments as well. These payments constitute the broadest gray areas under a questionable payments heading. The Cummins' policy sets criteria for permissible activity in certain circumstances, supplying detailed guidelines and using hypothetical examples to illustrate actual applications.[28]

While much has been written about the issue of facilitating payments, primarily because such payments are not generally covered under FCPA prohibitions, a related topic of accommodation payments offers an even more relevant test of an MNC's responsiveness to host country interests. Accommodation payments usually involve the transfer of funds to an agent, customer, or third party in a country other than the one in which the business is normally conducted. When properly recorded on corporate records, such payments would not usually contravene U.S. law, but these arrangements often help the foreign recipient to evade exchange controls or escape taxes at home. In short, accommodation payments raise the issue of an MNC's responsibilities to uphold foreign laws, perhaps even in countries where the MNC may not have a local affiliate to subject the enterprise directly to the foreign law in question.

Textron is one of the firms that has addressed this issue in a positive and forthright manner. In its *Business Conduct Guidelines*, the company describes accommodation payments in understandable terms, even to the extent of providing examples of the policy's application (Exhibit 10). The firm follows a similar policy standard in dealing with requests involving invoicing and overpayments, where improper practices could also serve to help customers evade foreign government controls. Although such practices might or might not involve illegal falsification of company records, Textron policy clearly prohibits questionable practices in either case.[29]

Two other good corporate examples that address such issues in an operationally linked manner are Allied Corporation's policy on "Proper Business Practices"[30] and Cummins Engine Company's standard on "International Distributor Accounts."[31] The Cummins case even sets up a procedure to handle specific exceptions to the general prohibition on these practices, such as for humanitarian reasons when extraordinary circumstances like a revolutionary change in government may occur.

Many corporations do not adopt policies that explicitly address these payments issues or they provide a much lower standard of guidance for employees in responding to actual operational situations. Where the topic is addressed, the most detailed treatment of corporate standards usually occurs, as is appropriate,

Exhibit 10
Accommodation Payments

ALL COMMISSIONS OR OTHER PAYMENTS DUE AN AGENT OR A
CUSTOMER SHALL BE (1) PAID DIRECTLY TO THE AGENT OR
CUSTOMER IN THE COUNTRY WHERE HE EARNED THE PAYMENT OR
IN THE PRINCIPAL COUNTRY WHERE HE NORMALLY CONDUCTS
BUSINESS OR (2) USED TO REDUCE EXISTING ACCOUNTS
RECEIVABLE FROM SUCH CUSTOMER.

Discussion

     In some businesses and some countries it has been
considered acceptable practice for a company such as
Textron to pay all or a part of a commission, discount
or other payment due to an agent or customer in a
country other than the one where the customer's head
office is located or where the payment was earned.   In
a variation of these arrangements the payment was made
to a third party designated by the payee or the funds
were held by the payor until instructions were
received from the party entitled to payment.   Since
these arrangements were usually made for the
convenience of the party entitled to the payment,
that is, "to accommodate" the payee, the arrangements
have been referred to as "accommodation payments" (or
"third country payments").

     Accommodation payments can be used by the payee
as part of a scheme to avoid taxes or exchange control
regulations.   These arrangements may also be used to
facilitate the payment of bribes or other improper
payments.   Accommodation payments are prohibited by
law in some countries.   Even where no such specific
prohibition exists, Textron shall not be a party to
such arrangements.

     To comply with this Guideline, every Textron
Division shall make certain that payments due to its
agents and customers are not allowed to accumulate but
are paid regularly and directly to such agents and
customers.   Such payments should be sent to the payee
in the principal country where he normally conducts
his business or in the country where the payment was
earned.   The only permissible alternative to such
payment would be to credit the amount due against an
outstanding account receivable of the payee or in the
case of a payee of doubtful credit standing, the
amount due may be held as an agreed upon credit
balance.   In such instances, Textron's records must
clearly show the offsetting transactions.

Examples

1.   An agent or customer located outside the U.S. requests that a payment due him be held and delivered to him during a visit in the U.S.   The request should be refused.

2.   An agent or customer requests that a payment due him be sent to him or a bank in a country other than the one where he earned the payment or in the principal country where he normally conducts business.   The request should be refused.

3.   An agent or customer requests that a payment due him be paid to a third party.   The request should be refused.

4.   An agent or customer requests that a payment due him be held indefinitely.   The request should be refused.   However, payment may be delayed and either (a) credited against an outstanding receivable of the payee or (b) held as a credit balance for the account of a payee of doubtful credit standing, in either case with full and proper accounting.

Business Conduct Guidelines, Guidelines F-1, Textron, November 1, 1978.

---

in the firm's internal policy manuals. To the extent that corporations make this link between policy positions and operational guidelines, it is important that such policies, or at least a summary statement of them, also be made available to outside observers of corporate practices as part of the firm's code of conduct.

This step can help convey the MNC's recognition of and respect for its international obligations, particularly in instances where corporations would not be violating U.S. law by an improper practice that may fall outside of the foreign country's effective legal jurisdiction as well. Corporate standards do exist above the minimum when they prohibit not only illegal acts, but also practices that aid others to act illegally.

An interesting if somewhat unusual variation on this same theme is presented in Monsanto's *Guidelines for Employee Conduct*. This booklet contains a section on "Policy on Inside Information and Trading in Securities," an issue addressed in many code documents to protect against violations of U.S. securities laws. This firm's policy statement goes further, however, to address the trading of securities in foreign countries, arguing for a basic business ethics standard even where local legal restrictions may not exist. After detailing U.S. legal requirements, the Monsanto document states:

Employees located outside the United States who trade securities in foreign countries should become familiar with, and observe, any laws applicable to their ex-U.S. transactions. As a matter of sound business ethics, such employees should also observe principles similar to those described above, even if not required by the laws of the country involved.[32]

Thus corporations can demonstrate responsiveness to many international issues by discussing specific topics in a code document that links general policy statements to operational business decisions and procedures. Another international concern exists that should also be addressed in an effective corporate identity code. This concern relates to issues involving an MNC's response to competing or potentially conflicting national government objectives and to questions relating to the nature of an MNC's ownership and control over its international affiliates.

Conflicting National Objectives

The easy and typical corporate position on the issue of conflicting national objectives is to state that the firm will abide by all laws in all countries where it does business. Such a standard is certainly a minimum requirement for MNCs, but unfortunately it does not constitute a good guideline for corporate conduct in many circumstances of overlapping governmental jurisdiction. Recognizing the sensitivity of national jurisdiction issues, it is perhaps surprising that a number of corporate documents actually do go beyond the minimum statement of obeying all laws in all countries by discussing corporate policies in ways that offer a range of national identity characterizations.

One approach that seems to emphasize a U.S. identity is represented by an excerpt from Motorola's summary of its code of conduct, which states: "Motorola will respect the laws, customs and traditions in each country in which it operates but, in so doing, will not engage in any act or course of conduct which may violate U.S. laws or its business ethics."[33] This type of statement suggests an operational standard that reflects the extraterritorial reach of U.S. laws in such areas as export controls, foreign boycotts, and the FCPA. A similar home country premise is contained in Digital Corporation's policy memorandum "Digital Business Ethics," which reads in part:

Since Digital, an American-based company, conducts business in many countries, we will conduct all worldwide activities well within the standards of U.S. business ethics. We will, of course, comply fully with local laws in all countries.[34]

An orientation that is more overtly responsive to the host country viewpoint is reflected in the "Legal Relationships" section of Armco Steel Corporation's *International Code of Conduct* (Exhibit 11). Further variations on how to handle conflict of law situations or differences over the application of local law are

Exhibit 11
Legal Relationships

It is our intent to be a good corporate citizen and to
obey all laws. Where there is conflict among the laws
of a host country in which Armco operates and the laws
of other nations, we intend to bring the conflict to
the attention of all proper authorities and abide by
the host country's disposition of the conflict. We
intend to abide by all regulations and procedures,
working with host country authorities to ensure that
Armco's dealings and reputation are as well regarded
around the world as they are within the United States.

International Code of Conduct, Armco Steel
Corporation, May, 1977.

represented by other codes of conduct. Ashland Oil's statement on business ethics directs that where laws are unclear or conflicting, corporate actions must be such that full disclosure will reflect well on the firm's integrity.[35] PepsiCo[36] and Union Carbide[37] advocate the use of international law and arbitration to help resolve legal differences. Caterpillar Tractor Co. establishes its intention to obey the law, but recognizing the diversity and possible conflicts between laws worldwide, the company, assuming a more activist posture, pledges "to offer, where appropriate, constructive ideas for change in the law."[38]

These corporate positions represent differences in orientation and approach rather than radical departures to either side of a minimum norm based on observance of all laws. Such differences do help establish a corporate identity, however. It is even possible to pursue these points further into more specific corporate statements on sensitive policy issues dealing with an MNC's role in relationships between home and host countries.

One of the problems that has plagued MNCs throughout the world is the suspicion that the firm will be most responsive to the needs of its home country. This feeling, which is often nearly as evident in other developed countries as in the developing world, goes far beyond the realm of economic cost-benefit calculations and into the world of international political intrigue. The MNCs generally like to portray themselves as purely economic entities, seeking to be in conformity with and supportive of each nation's developmental objectives. Nevertheless, it is growing ever more difficult to divorce the economic from the political in world diplomacy and MNCs find it hard to remain detached from the machinations of international politics.

To the extent that corporate codes address this issue, they tend to make positive statements of an intention to be responsive within each nation's framework of objectives, a position that essentially parallels the basic policy of obeying each country's laws. A few corporate codes go further to state a negative policy standard as well, usually framed in terms that would deny charges that MNCs act as tools of governments' foreign policies, particularly that of the home nation. The Dow Chemical Company offers an example of a positive/negative policy standard in its international business principles in two sentences excerpted from a section on its "Relationship with Host Governments":

We comply with the laws and regulations of those countries in which we operate, and we seek to conform to the policies and objectives of host nations. . . . We do not believe in and will resist becoming an instrument of the foreign policy of any government.[39]

Booz Allen takes this thought a bit further into a specific area that is seldom spoken about directly, much less placed in a written code. Under the heading "Corporate Citizenship," the company's *Statement of Professional Policies and Practices* reads in part:

In all countries in which we operate, the Firm and its employees will respect the spirit and requirements of all applicable laws and regulations. In addition . . . the Firm will not permit any of its business operations or employees to be used covertly by any government organization.[40]

Ownership and Control

The second element in addressing this aspect of broader international corporate identity is a firm's position on ownership, control, and influence relationships with affiliated entities in host nations. Ownership questions are perhaps the most traditional and easiest to address of these concepts. Many corporations explicitly state their preferences, ranging from 100 percent ownership of foreign subsidiaries to varying degrees of joint venture and local participation. The clear trend is away from full ownership as host countries increase their pressure for more substantive local involvement. An example of a concise corporate position statement on this issue is presented in Exhibit 12, drawn from Union Carbide's international code booklet.

As full or majority ownership standards decline, the issue shades into questions of control and eventually to the use of influence. Control issues are usually raised in relation to specific operational topics, many of which have already been discussed, such as exchange controls and accounting standards, procurement and marketing practices, and responsiveness in cases of conflicts over national objectives. Corporate codes must attempt to fashion process-related standards that address these control issues in a fashion that links general policy statements to operational business guidelines.

For example, in Exhibit 13, Johnson Wax commits itself to procedures that will provide local input to operating units so as to better adjust to local needs

Exhibit 12

Union Carbide prefers to have majority ownership of an
affiliate's equity. Experience has shown that this
policy minimizes managerial and operational problems
that arise, especially in the early stages of an
operation when start-up difficulties may mean a lack
of profits.

This policy, however, is not inflexible. Union
Carbide is sensitive to the responsibility to adjust
policies to respond to changing economic, social, and
political conditions within host countries.

We have accepted minority ownerships in ventures and
we will continue to consider joining with local
investors in arrangements where long-term results are
potentially beneficial and profitable to all parties
concerned.

The International Responsibilities of a Multinational
Corporation, Union Carbide Corporation, February,
1976, p.10.

---

and conditions. This pledge covers not just securing the assistance of legal, financial, and advertising consultants, but actually a commitment to elect outside national directors to each company's board. Despite the likely presumption of skeptics that only trustworthy local "yes-men" will be selected, this type of pledge cannot be dismissed so lightly. Boards of directors are at the heart of corporate management authority and a commitment to outside directors, much less to nationals in each country, addresses a substantive MNC control procedure. In fact, this corporate standard moves in the direction that some national government policies are evolving, but in advance of any such legal requirements in many nations.

Influence questions generally arise in negative terms, where critics seek to constrain excessive MNC economic power or to restrict MNC influence in what are thought to be inappropriate political or social areas. In a different sense, influence can relate more simply to the lower end of an ownership and control continuum, where an MNC's power over affiliated enterprises is the least. This type of issue is probably the most relevant to MNC relationships as applied to dealers, distributors, and agents. Most of these arrangements involve foreign entities or individuals that are independent of the MNC, yet are an important and often critical part of the MNC's identity. For the corporation, such low-power influence relationships can present some of the greatest challenges to defining a corporate identity and devising an operationally effective code of conduct.

Exhibit 13

We believe in contributing to the well-being of
the countries and communities where we conduct
business, and we commit ourselves to:

Seek actively the counsel and independent judgement
of citizens of each country to provide guidance
to local and corporate management, by:

-- Electing outside national directors to the
   board of each company.

-- Retaining distinguished associates and
   consultants in law, advertising, audit and
   banking to assist us in conducting our business
   according to the highest professional standards.

This We Believe, Johnson Wax, September, 1976, p. 6.

Caterpillar Tractor Co., for example, defines product support as an integral component of its quality standards. Many aspects of product support, however, are based upon the performance of the firm's worldwide network of independent dealers. While the dealers' relationship with Caterpillar is established under specific written agreements, there are naturally many important aspects of international business dealings that are not susceptible to precise legal formulations. Even more potentially difficult is the issue of the firm's identification with and influence upon dealers or others when much of the independent entities' business dealings do not directly involve the Caterpillar relationship, but can still indirectly impact upon Caterpillar's reputation and standards of proper business conduct.

The company seems to be cognizant of such difficulties in its code of conduct provisions governing "Relationships With Public Officials." This section commits the firm to both negative and positive standards. Caterpillar employees are prohibited from "payments of bribes, kickbacks, or other questionable inducements." They are also prohibited from assisting dealers or others in any questionable payment activities, while the firm additionally pledges that "we will discourage dealers from engaging in such practices."[41]

The Dow Corning Corporation's code of conduct is even more explicit in its commitment to use its influence with related but not controlled business entities to promote proper business conduct:

Dow Corning expects and encourages its agents, representatives and distributors to conduct business in a legal and ethical manner. The purchase of supplies, materials and services will be based on quality, price, service, ability to supply and the vendor's adherence to legal and ethical business practice.[42]

A further example of corporate action on this lower end of the ownership and control spectrum is Allied Corporation's pledge in its policy position on "Proper Business Practices." In the section on policy implementation, the firm states that its own employees associated with other enterprises will still be guided by Allied's policy standards and should attempt to influence corporate conduct to conform with such policy, reporting to appropriate officers any action believed to fall outside those standards.

The Corporation's employees associated with enterprises not controlled by the Corporation shall be guided in their conduct by the provisions of the Policy. They shall attempt to influence those enterprises to conduct their activities in conformity with all applicable laws and the Policy and shall report violations in accordance with the Policy.[43]

A corporate identity code must thus address issues involving both ownership and overlapping national jurisdictions in an internationally relevant fashion if the code is to respond in a meaningful way to global concerns about MNC activities. This challenge is usually dealt with, if at all, through minimal company standards that pledge the enterprise to little more than meeting its legal requirements. A more positive code approach, chosen by some international companies, is to define corporate positions in a more activist posture, setting forth the firm's intention to utilize its role and resources to aid problem resolution in these areas. By addressing such issues more directly and in greater detail the company is providing both a better self-identity code for outside observers and a more effective guidance tool for internal employee direction.

CODE IMPLEMENTATION

Purpose, form, operational content, and international application are all integral aspects of an individual corporate code of conduct, but actual code effectiveness also depends on building an implementation process to put into practice the business guidance mechanisms adopted in code policies. Implementation on the individual corporate level is just as critical to code success as is the development of implementation procedures on the international level that are giving increasing operational effect to voluntary intergovernmental codes. For companies, a code implementation process consists of several related steps, generally encompassing activities such as code distribution, interpretation, review, revision, training, and other forms of integration into internal corporate processes.

The principal objectives of a corporate code usually determine the document's initial pattern of distribution once final drafting has been completed. Most codes are aimed at corporate managers, so salaried employees are a central target audience. Some firms distribute their code to every employee, regardless of position. Documents that are more oriented to public relations purposes than to internal operational needs are channeled primarily to external groups and the media. Once distributed, codes must also provide for explanation or interpretation of the written policies, review and updating procedures to ensure the document's continuing effectiveness, and other implementation steps to link code objectives to operational business practices. A brief review of the case history of internal code development in a couple companies can help illustrate this process.

Examples of Code Development and Implementation

Caterpillar Tractor Co. was one of the first firms to develop an individual code of conduct that aimed at addressing specifically international business issues.[44] In fact, the initial Caterpillar *A Code of Worldwide Business Conduct* was subsequently used quite widely by other corporations as a reference guide in drafting their own documents in the late 1970s. The Caterpillar effort began in January 1974 when management commissioned the drafting of a company code to elaborate the basis for corporate policies and operations. This action was taken largely in response to increased public scrutiny of MNCs, particularly regarding political and ethical concerns about the societal role and operational methods employed by large, multinational business enterprises.

The Caterpillar Code was designed to address four specific objectives:

1. To cause reflective thought on what worldwide policies the company should follow. The code exercise allowed the time and structure for a directed self-assessment of the corporation's definition and purpose in relation to society. For example, conscious corporate policy was set or sharpened on a worldwide basis regarding equipment safety and pollution standards, political contributions, and support of free trade principles. These decisions helped establish clear corporate policy in areas of recognized concern in advance of specific governmental or other public pressures that might dictate less appropriate regulated actions.

2. To assure proper communication of corporate policies regarding business responsibilities and ethical practices to at least all management level employees. Any large organization, particularly one operating in different national settings with many thousands of employees, can experience communication gaps or breakdowns. A worldwide code provides a common core of policy based on corporate experience that is applicable throughout the entire organization.

3. To set high standards as a corporate challenge. Rather than simply cataloging present operating procedures, Caterpillar decided also to use the code to set forth its objectives for improvement, thereby providing a more complete self-definition. This approach means that the corporation is prepared to measure broadly its progress toward these higher goals, as well as its degree of adherence to normal operating standards.

4. To set forth Caterpillar's views regarding the responsibilities of governments in countries where the company is located. Operating on the premise that mutual confidence requires mutual commitment, this objective seeks to establish the basis for an open dialogue with public officials regarding the company's role in the society. Having stated the corporation's objectives and operational policies, the code seeks to register

related, reciprocal expectations the company has toward its treatment by government authorities.

These four objectives were the primary guides to the code drafting process. The exercise was undertaken with an essentially internal focus, to make the code meaningful in terms of corporate operations. Within a broader framework, however, the code can also be seen as advancing a self-regulatory approach with the purpose of avoiding the imposition of more inappropriate government regulation. Caterpillar viewed its code as an internal document. It did not actively promulgate its code as an example for other businesses to follow, but it has related its experience to others on request and generally supported public efforts to encourage voluntary corporate adherence to ethical business conduct standards.

The actual code drafting process was begun with a letter from Caterpillar's president to about eighteen senior managers requesting their input on the types of topics to be covered. This approach sought to gain a broad, worldwide perspective on corporate operations while also assuring top management involvement in the project. A first draft was then put together by the company's public affairs manager for review by Caterpillar's four operating directors. The revised draft was next reviewed by all corporate officers plus senior functional managers (general counsel, controller, tax manager, etc.). By the time an amended third draft was finally approved by Caterpillar's chairman, over two dozen people had been directly involved in the code's formulation.

While the ICC Guidelines and certain short business creeds were helpful referents in addressing certain code items, no general template was available at the time to provide a pattern for the code. Nearly one-third of the final product, published on October 1, 1974, represented new corporate thinking and positions. The other two-thirds of the content was drawn from various previous company statements.

Distribution of the Caterpillar Code reflected its primary internal focus. First copies were sent to the company's management group (approximately 14,000), with immediate follow-up sessions at most locations where plant managers led a discussion and answered questions on the code. Subsequently, the code has been published in French, Portuguese, Dutch, and Japanese to provide better local access to the document in several foreign plant locations.

Caterpillar officers also determined that the code must receive continual reinforcement through various mechanisms to demonstrate top management's commitment to it and to retain the attention and interest of general operating executives. Therefore sessions on the code were also introduced into the orientation of new personnel as well as the company's management training program; corporate publications, including the annual report, *Caterpillar World* magazine and *Caterpillar Folks* newspaper, all carried articles, interviews, or other information on the code. Strong endorsement of the code is given regularly by top officers in speeches both inside and outside the corporation.

A further step in assuring that the code was a meaningful, practical document was the company's willingness to engage in a follow-up review and revision exercise. On September 1, 1977 a second edition of the code was published to up-date earlier positions and address new issues arising in the company's constantly changing political and socio-economic environment. This revised document was about one-third longer than the original, with most new items added at the recommendation of senior executives. Among the new areas covered were information disclosure, integrity of financial information, illegal payments, and technology transfer. A section was also added to establish a reporting system for code compliance. Each officer, subsidiary head, plant or parts department manager and department head must now annually affirm knowledge and understanding of the code, and report any questionable events or activities to the company's general counsel.

Continuing the revision process, the company issued a third edition of the code in May 1982. The document again grew in length, from ten to fourteen pages. Several sections were retitled, generally improving the accuracy of their description, while several internal changes were made in code content. In addition, sections were added on Business Purpose, International Information Flow, Relationships with Suppliers, Human Resources, Inside Information, Privacy of Information About Employees, and Disposal of Wastes. One final adjustment was made that changed the document's title from *A Code of Worldwide Business Conduct* to *A Code of Worldwide Business Conduct and Operating Principles*. This change better reflects the company's approach to the code exercise and, at the same time, unintentionally symbolizes the linkage between policy positions and operational guidance that lies at the heart of a credible corporate identity code.

When it began its code effort, Caterpillar undertook a three-session business conduct seminar at both domestic and overseas locations to: (1) reinforce the code's importance, (2) provide information and answer questions, (3) probe general understanding of the code and its application to operational situations, and (4) provide another feedback channel for code clarifications or further revision. This seminar proved to be useful as both an educational and an evaluation device.

A limited, selective external distribution of the initial code was made by Caterpillar to certain legislators, association leaders, and company dealers and suppliers. No press release was made nor were general community mailing lists used. This decision stemmed from the primarily internal orientation of the code's objectives and from the view that broad public exposure could bring into question the document's credibility as a practical guide to business operations. Nevertheless, several press accounts, seminar presentations, and other events generated widespread interest in the code. Responding to numerous requests, over 25,000 copies of the code were sent to interested parties during the first five years after its initial publication.

The Norton Policy on Business Ethics dates from 1961, when the Norton

Company adopted a brief, rather general code during a period when U.S. public criticism of business was being fanned by instances of corporate misconduct involving price-fixing, conflicts of interest, and other illegal or improper practices.[45] The Norton Code was amended in 1967 to include a statement on non-discrimination in employment, reflecting contemporary civil rights concerns. Then, in the early 1970s, the overseas bribery scandals and ITT/Chile incident helped stimulate the firm to broaden its code to include issues relevant to its overseas operations.

In September 1973 Norton undertook a code revision process to consider questions concerning its international nature. Initial drafting by the firm's general counsel in consultation with other top executives was soon broadened to draw in advice from managers of overseas affiliates. The process was finally concluded in 1976 at a world conference attended by 200 top Norton managers. Some 20,000 copies of the final product were printed in eight languages and distributed to every U.S. employee and foreign affiliate, as well as to some suppliers, customers, shareholders, and other constituent groups and individuals. In foreign locations, the local managing director often signs the introductory letter to the code, making clear that local management is fully involved with and supportive of the company's statement of worldwide policy.

To ensure implementation of its newly revised international code, Norton also moved in 1976 to establish a Corporate Ethics Committee. This group was comprised of senior management including the chief executive officer and general counsel. All but one committee member were also on the board of directors, but two members were "outside" (non-corporate management) directors. The Committee's high-level composition thus assured that it could fulfill one of its functions, which was to emphasize the importance of the code within the company, while the presence of non-management individuals helped broaden the group's perspective and prevented its becoming more of a closed "insiders" activity.

The committee's other two objectives are also well served by the nature of its implementation activity. One committee function is to interpret gray areas of code application to practical work situations. For example, the Committee discussed the issue of accommodation payments and decided on company guidelines that would not permit third-country payments where they could aid others to violate the law. The interpretation process also helps fulfill the third objective, which is to assure that the code is retained as a meaningful document over time rather than as a one-shot effort. Thus the committee helps revise the document when needed, sometimes issuing bulletins on its interpretation decisions to include with the basic code document. Formal recommendations for changes in policy can be made to the board of directors whenever necessary, and a report on the company's compliance with the code is made to the board at least annually.

Managers must also review the Norton code annually with their supervisory personnel to assure an understanding of the document. Each executive down to a corporate department head must additionally sign a letter each year to be sent to the Corporate Ethics Committee affirming that a review of the code with subordinates was conducted, any suspicious conduct was investigated, and significant code violations were reported to the committee. Both internal and external auditors are also directed to report immediately to the committee any suspected code violations.

Weyerhaeuser is another firm that uses a Business Conduct Committee, established in 1977, to assist its code implementation. This committee is designed to provide in-house interpretation and advice regarding application of the policy standards outlined in the firm's code booklet. While the committee can recommend new or changed policies, its primary function is to provide a rapid response mechanism for employee inquiries. Committee composition is therefore kept deliberately diversified in terms of job functions, experience, age, sex, race, and other factors, drawing members from many different parts of the company's organization. While use of normal management channels is encouraged, employees have direct access to the committee, a process that has been facilitated by the publication of a supplement to the corporate code booklet that contains the committee members' names, telephone numbers, and a short background profile on each individual.[46]

A somewhat similar procedure was established by the Boeing Company. The firm has an Ethics Committee, appointed by the Board of Directors, but this group also has established a subordinate Business Ethics Review Board to provide guidance and clarification to company employees on matters relating to the application of Boeing's *Business Conduct Guidelines*. Employees unable or reluctant to pursue business conduct questions through normal management channels can contact the committee directly. The company's code booklet contains the telephone number of the Review Board's chairman to facilitate this process.[47]

Business conduct standards adopted by Cummins Engine Company are circulated to all exempt employees each year in the *Cummins Practice* manual. Group, division, and department heads are responsible for ensuring that new employees fully understand and comply with the standards. Each year these heads also review the policy guidelines with their staff and recommend any additions or changes that may be appropriate. International and regional managers also are instructed to review the business conduct guidelines with the firm's distributor principals in their territories at contract review time. Corporate auditing is responsible for auditing compliance with the standards. The director of corporate responsibility, a position discussed earlier, helps coordinate and support these activities.[48]

Other types of activities can also aid in the task of achieving effective code implementation. Textron's *Business Conduct Guidelines* relies heavily on individual employee actions, but it assists and reinforces this responsibility by providing a discussion section and several situation examples to help explain the application of most policy statements, as illustrated earlier in Exhibit 10. Some companies like Caterpillar, Chase, and Dow Corning arrange special seminars or dialogue sessions during which employees can discuss the application of code principles in everyday decision-making. A few firms such as IBM, Allied, and General Electric have even introduced specific modules on ethical issues into their management development programs.[49]

A final corporate example that serves to illustrate possible code implementation approaches is the follow-up procedure developed by Dow Corning.[50] This firm drafted its first code in 1976, using a Corporate Business Conduct Committee. When published and distributed the following year, the code was intended to provide guidelines for business conduct, but it was recognized that effective implementation was likely to involve case application questions, possible document revision, and a mechanism to evaluate corporate adherence to the adopted standards. Therefore a degree of latitude was provided for local application of the basic corporate guidelines within various world regions. A major role of the Business Conduct Committee was to conduct yearly audits in each major geographic area to monitor and assess code implementation. The Committee itself, appointed by the chief executive officer, is organized so that members represent a variety of backgrounds and experiences.

During the first two years, audits were conducted principally at area headquarters. Since then these audits have been expanded to include other regions and reach company personnel several levels below area management. This expansion is particularly significant since the process involves an increasing number of managers who are foreign nationals. During a typical day-long audit, Committee members will meet with from seven to fifteen people, covering a list of ten to fifteen questions that have been submitted by the Committee well in advance.

When a problem area is identified, discussion continues until there is agreement on the magnitude of the issue, after which area personnel are asked to suggest possible solutions that will allow them to operate within the code's guidelines. The Committee prepares written reports identifying major problem areas and recommending solutions. At the completion of an audit cycle, generally in May, the results are summarized and comprise the major part of a report to the corporation's Audit and Social Responsibility Committee, a subcommittee of the Board of Directors. At their request, this report has also been made available to the firm's outside auditors.

In 1980, the Business Conduct Committee decided that a revision of the corporate code was needed. About one-half dozen significant situations had been identified that the code either failed to address or where its provisions were outdated, while other emerging issues would also soon need attention. Early code practice had also developed a pattern whereby there were essentially several area codes that were being applied in different world regions. The code revision reconciled and consolidated these versions into a single global corporate code. The process included thorough discussions of the new draft during some nineteen audits over the year, giving literally hundreds of people input to the revision process. The resulting worldwide code was then published in 1981 and distributed in at least seven languages to corporate facilities throughout the world.

New or changed code sections included provisions dealing with privacy of employee records, proprietary information, conflicts of interest, distributor and agent relationships, purchase of supplies and services, recycling and waste disposal, intercompany pricing, and international business guidelines that deal with the relationship between corporate policies and law or conflicts of laws. The follow-up auditing process continues, now using the consolidated global code as a unified statement of corporate identity. The Business Conduct Committee also decided that the code should be reviewed every two years in light of rapidly changing legal and customary practices in the world. As a result of this commitment some further modifications were made in the code in 1983 and published in a revised edition the following year.

Beyond code drafting, distribution, revision, interpretation, training, and auditing functions lies a wide but still largely unexplored field of possible implementation activities that could integrate code guidelines more fully into operational corporate functions. Some approaches to this further integration have been suggested earlier. For example, Cummins Engine attempts to identify possible problem areas and build positive incentives for proper conduct into business decision-making situations where normal corporate incentives might tempt an employee to take questionable actions. The TRW plan for the 1980s, discussed earlier, links broad corporate identity goals to strategic planning, thereby integrating the objectives into operational and management processes. A slightly different approach to a similar objective is the evolution of issues assessment and strategic planning functions in a number of corporations.

In an essay on "The Mainstream of Business Responsibility," former General Electric Chairman Reginald Jones drew a connection between corporate codes and implementation activities as reflected in the comments reprinted in Exhibit 14. Having noted that GE had a code of conduct in the form of written policies since the early 1950s, Jones points out that a positive operational thrust must also be added to the typical constraints on actions that tend to dominate most written codes. General Electric began to develop such a strategic planning system in the early 1970s, forcing itself to assess external public policy issues and prepare for a measurement of corporate performance that would be conducted in both economic and non-economic areas.

Monsanto also is developing a strategic planning process that incorporates issues management, public responsibility concerns, and a growing international awareness and sensitivity. The firm's issues management function evolved in 1978 out of its social responsibility program that had been concentrated upon responding to issues such as affirmative action and environmental protection. From this basis the program quickly broadened into an assessment of economic and international issues as the corporation recognized its truly multinational character. This function then was merged into the corporate planning department so that, as described by Margaret A. Stroup, the firm's director of strategic issues analysis: "Now a formal vehicle for the identification of *all* issues

Exhibit 14

It is essential, but it is not enough to have a system of teaching and enforcing codes of conduct. These are aimed at assuring a minimum standard of good behavior--a safety net, as it were, to keep the Company and its people out of trouble. But these are essentially "thou shalt nots," and a preoccupation with constraints tends to interfere with the process of positive motivation of managers.

The overarching need is for a system of day-in, day-out decision-making and communications based on the active encouragement of our managers to move toward what we want this Company to be. We need continuous and positive interaction with the changing environment, so that we can respond creatively to emerging opportunities and constraints. We have been developing such a system for the better part of a decade.

Reginald H. Jones, "The Mainstream of Business Responsibility," in Business and Society: Strategies for the 1980's, Report of the Task Force on Corporate Social Performance, U.S. Department of Commerce, December 1980, p. 70.

---

impacting our business around the world not only existed but also was integrated into the regular management, planning, and decision systems of the corporation."[51]

These last two examples suggest one possible way in which code implementation can become integrated into operational decision-making. Issues management is itself a relatively new activity in terms of an organized corporate function. Obvious links exist between an issues assessment responsibility and code development or revision. When corporate codes are effectively implemented and serve as actual guidance mechanisms, they can bridge into corporate planning and operational control activities, as suggested in the Monsanto example. Thus, while actual corporate code activities may be directed and housed in a variety of locations, from board of directors' committees to law departments to public affairs offices, the need for implementational effectiveness suggests that further experience may forge ever stronger links between code activities and corporate planning or other operational and decision-making units of an enterprise.

INDIVIDUALIZING A CORPORATE CODE

The development of an individual corporate code of conduct depends upon matching a firm's particular circumstances and character with its external environment and societal concerns. For an MNC, this self-identification and matching process becomes more complicated due to overlapping political juris- dictions and cross-cutting socio-economic demands. Individualizing an MNC code therefore requires a careful examination of each firm's particular charac- teristics in relation to global product, operations, and marketing. Equally im- portant is the effective integration of code implementation procedures into the individual corporation's management style.

Previous examples in this chapter suggested some ways that companies have dealt with their product and operational characteristics in structuring an inter- national code of conduct. Obviously these examples are illustrative only and each firm must undertake its own self-identification exercise in order to for- mulate an effective individual code. Nevertheless, a few discernable conditions seem to exist that frame some initial parameters within which an MNC would begin its self-examination.

One important consideration is the relationship a firm's product has to gov- ernment activity. If the company's product is one that is heavily regulated or involves large government procurement markets, then special concerns must be addressed about an MNC's dealings with public officials and its responsiveness to national policy goals. On the other hand, products designed for mass con- sumer markets will call for codes that emphasize different constituency rela- tionships, as would products that meet intermediate, client-specified require- ments, such as in the machine-tool industry.

The levels of competitiveness, both within an industry and with regard to a particular product's standing, also constitute special circumstances that affect code development. In the past, firms under the least competitive pressures gen- erally emerged as the corporations with the most publicly responsible codes. A strong product leader apparently can afford to be a good corporate citizen as well, while firms struggling in a highly competitive environment seem less likely to adopt unilaterally a set of policies that go beyond minimum legal require- ments that all their competitors must meet. This apparent disparity in perform- ance might be overcome if an approach to code drafting stresses practical pre- positioning benefits that allow a firm to meet changing societal demands effectively in order to avoid incurring penalties and to exploit new opportunities.

For MNCs a pre-positioning strategy will require greater sensitivity to issues that may be of more concern abroad than at home. Too often American MNCs draft policies that respond only to prevailing U.S. concerns, thereby failing to recognize and respond to many issues that are important items on public agen- das overseas. On some issues, U.S. debate and action may have already created solutions that do not yet exist in other nations. For instance, public safety or consumer education levels abroad might require different corporate policy or implementation responsibilities than are necessary in the United States. In other cases, public concerns overseas can precede general U.S. interest, as was true until very recently of foreign concern over plant closure and job security issues. Some important topics may remain of interest only to foreign constituency groups.

The relevant point is that a global corporation must develop a truly global outlook. An MNC code of conduct should not be dominated by the decidedly parochial viewpoint that is reflected in most current MNC codes.

Code implementation is also an area where a corporation must individualize its approach. Management styles differ dramatically from company to company and an effective code of conduct must be attuned to the circumstances that govern the firm's own situation. In virtually any corporation the role of top management, particularly the chief executive officer, will be crucial to a code's success or failure. High-level support and involvement are required to allocate needed resources, demonstrate the importance of corporate principles, and actually integrate the code exercise into operational management decisions.

While top management style is fundamentally important to setting the tone of corporate operations, other objective circumstances will also affect the nature of individual code implementation. For example, a firm's past history will usually influence the approach taken toward code enforcement. Corporations with a substantial record of abuses or misconduct often place additional emphasis on establishing elaborate reporting and certification functions, as well as specific negative sanctions for code violations. Enterprises that have a relatively good record of conduct often rely on positive reinforcement and interpretation aids rather than emphasizing penalties for violators. While one may prefer to emphasize positive rather than negative enforcement, the actual circumstances surrounding an individual firm's situation should and do affect its approach to code implementation.

Overall, this attempt to take a closer look at individual corporate codes points up what an early stage the business community is at in developing truly international business codes. A number of corporations have taken steps in the right direction as they seek to link policy principles to functional operations in ways that are relevant to their own individual circumstances. This task is an evolutionary process that will take time, effort, and experimentation. The essential requirement now is to establish a broader, renewed business community commitment to developing international identity codes of conduct. While much of the original pressure for such action has slackened, at least temporarily, there are strong self-interest and public interest reasons to develop proactive code mechanisms that favor guidance over regulation in international business dealings.

NOTES

1. *CPC International Inc. Policy Manual*, CPC International Inc., December 1979, Introduction, p. 1.
2. *Business Conduct Guidelines*, International Business Machines, 1983.
3. *General Foods Basic Policies*, General Foods Corporation, no date.
4. *Code of Corporate Conduct*, ITT Corporation, no date.

5. For example, see *Statement of Corporate Objectives*, Hewlett-Packard, November 1980; and *Corporate Objectives*, PPG Industries, 1981.

6. *The International Responsibilities of a Multinational Corporation*, Union Carbide Corporation, February 1976, p. 1.

7. Ibid., p. 3.

8. See Irving Kristol, "The Complex Question of Business Ethics," *Singer Magazine*, The Singer Company, Winter 1979, pp. 12–14; and Peter F. Drucker, "What is 'business ethics'?" *Public Interest*, no. 63, Spring 1981, pp. 18–36.

9. Fletcher L. Byrom, Chairman of the Board, letter to management associates, Koppers Company, March 23, 1976, p. 2.

10. "Code of Conduct," *Clow Policy and Procedures*, No. AD-005, Clow Corporation, revised February 15, 1979, p. 1.

11. Peter A. French, "The Corporation as a Moral Person," *American Philosophical Quarterly*, vol. 16, No. 3, July 1979, pp. 207–215. For a reprint of this article and other views on this issue, see Thomas Donaldson and Patricia H. Werhane, eds., *Ethical Issues in Business*, 2nd ed. (Englewood Cliffs, N.J.: Prentice-Hall, 1983), pp. 105–145 and W. Michael Hoffman and Jennifer Mills Moore, *Business Ethics* (New York: McGraw-Hill, 1984), pp. 150–179.

12. "Ethical Standards," *Cummins Practice*, No. 1000–100, Cummins Engine Company, October 1, 1980, p. 3.

13. *Multinational Public Affairs Briefing Seminar*, Selected Proceedings (Washington, D.C.: Public Affairs Council, February 25, 1976), pp. 56–57.

14. Byrom, p. 1.

15. *Corporate Policies: A Summary for Employees*, Ashland Oil, Inc., March 1977.

16. *A Code of Worldwide Business Conduct and Operating Principles*, Caterpillar Tractor Co., revised May 1, 1982, p. 4.

17. *Statement of Professional Policies and Practices*, Booz, Allen & Hamilton, Inc., 1977.

18. *AMF Principles of Conduct*, AMF Inc., no date.

19. *This We Believe*, Johnson Wax, 1976, p. 4.

20. *Corporate Public Policy*, Foremost McKesson, Inc., no date.

21. "Warner-Lambert Policy Statements," *Public Affairs Report No. 71–1*, Warner Lambert, 1977.

22. *Code of Conduct*, PepsiCo Inc., 1976. Reprinted with permission of PepsiCo Inc.

23. *This We Believe*, p. 6.

24. *A Code of Worldwide Business Conduct and Operating Principles*, p. 10.

25. *This We Believe*, p. 7.

26. *Code of Worldwide Business Ethics*, Levi Strauss & Co., August 1, 1977.

27. *Corporate Mission and Philosophy of Management*, Dynalectron Corporation, May 1978.

28. "Questionable Payments," *Cummins Practice*, No. 1005–200, Cummins Engine Company, October 1, 1980, pp. 1–7.

29. *Business Conduct Guidelines*, Guidelines F–2, Textron, November 1, 1978.

30. "Proper Business Practices," *Policy*, Policy No. 102, Allied Corporation, June 29, 1984.

31. "International Distributor Accounts," *Cummins Practice*, No. 1010-075, Cummins Engine Company, October 1, 1980.

32. *Guidelines for Employee Conduct: Summary and Text*, Monsanto, July 1980, p. 32.

33. *The Highest Standards: A Summary of Motorola's Code of Conduct*, Motorola, Inc., no date.

34. "Digital Business Ethics," *Corporate Policy Memorandum*, No. 78–1, revision 2, Digital Corporation, October 1980, p. 1.

35. See *Corporate Policies: A Summary for Employees*; and *Code of Business Conduct*, Ashland Oil, Inc., no date, p. 5.

36. *Code of Conduct.*

37. *The International Responsibilities of a Multinational Corporation.*

38. *A Code of Worldwide Business Conduct and Operating Principles*, p. 12.

39. *International Business Principles*, The Dow Chemical Company, no date.

40. *Statement of Professional Policies and Practices*, p. 12.

41. *A Code of Worldwide Business Conduct and Operating Principles*, p. 12.

42. *A Code of Business Conduct*, Dow Corning Corporation, 1984.

43. *Policy*, p. 2.

44. Information for this description comes from interviews with Caterpillar executives and various company documents.

45. Description based on Theodore V. Purcell, S. J. and James Weber, S. J., *Institutionalizing Corporate Ethics: A Case History*, Special Study No. 71 (New York: The Presidents Association, 1979).

46. See *Weyerhaeuser's Reputation: A Shared Responsibility*, 2nd ed., Weyerhaeuser, March 1979; and *Weyerhaeuser Business Conduct Committee Guidelines*, Weyerhaeuser, no date.

47. *Business Conduct Guidelines*, The Boeing Company, January 1981.

48. "Ethical Standards," *Cummins Practice*, p. 3.

49. Purcell and Weber, p. 9.

50. John Swanson, Manager, Business Communication, Dow Corning, speech to a Business Ethics Class, Albion College, June 4, 1981, and presentation on "Developing a Working Corporate Ethic," given at the Fifth National Conference on Business Ethics, Bentley College, October 13–14, 1983.

51. Margaret A. Stroup, Director Strategic Issues Analysis, Monsanto, speech to the International Public Affairs Seminar, Public Affairs Council, Washington, D.C., September 8, 1983, p. 10.

8

Guiding International Business Conduct

Multinational corporations have expanded into a global marketplace that is still divided into self-governing nation-states. Some general international rules help regulate economic relations between these national units on trade and monetary issues, but no comparable framework exists on international investment matters. Foreign direct investment by MNCs cuts deeply into a nation's economy, creating social and political in addition to economic concerns. While MNC problems can lead to friction between countries, growing interdependence increases the need to find a harmonious resolution to these matters. Voluntary codes of conduct, directed primarily at MNCs, have emerged as a way to facilitate intergovernmental cooperation without compromising national sovereignty.

The business community views this new development with a mixture of curiosity and alarm. Preoccupied with a legal outlook on international business regulation, most companies are slow to perceive the voluntary codes' public affairs requirements and opportunites. A few international business standards have been promoted as self-regulation devices, but the key to guiding business conduct lies at the individual company level where standards are applied and performance is measured. Most individual MNC codes that now exist cannot meet this challenge because they are too limited in scope and lack a truly international orientation. By forging an international corporate identity code, MNCs can better define corporate goals and operations in a way that responds to societal concerns about international business dealings.

THE OUTLOOK FOR INTERNATIONAL CODES

Voluntary intergovernmental codes are not transitory phenomena that suddenly sprang into existence and will pass away just as quickly. These diplomatic instruments trace their roots to the international community's failure to achieve more binding agreements on foreign investment matters where issues involving MNCs reach too deeply into domestic life. As governments in both the industrialized and developing countries expand national controls over MNCs, the multijurisdictional nature of these firms' operations creates problems of counterpart effects occurring in several nations. In a world of nation-states pursuing diverse economic, political, and social goals, these overlaps can lead to confrontations over competing and sometimes conflicting national policies. Not only are diplomatic problems created, but MNCs can find themselves sandwiched uncomfortably between national sovereigns in a no-win situation.

Voluntary intergovernmental codes offer a possible way out of these multiplying conflict scenarios. The codes' non-binding nature permits governments to agree on general principles in areas where real policy harmonization is not yet possible. The accords identify issues of international concern about MNC operations while still maintaining sovereign independence of action case-by-case. General guidance is provided to the business community on issues of potential controversy while permitting companies to apply the principles flexibly to fit particular operating conditions. The discovery of these voluntary codes can thereby ameliorate political discord over MNCs, but it shifts an additional burden onto corporations for making the voluntary standards work.

These international codes are likely to proliferate since they meet governmental needs and are rapidly developing vested institutional interests in their survival and expansion. Already codes have been adopted that range from general principles (OECD Guidelines) to functional operations (UNCTAD RBP Code and OECD Privacy Guidelines) to specific industry practices (WHO Infant Formula Marketing Code).

Future code activity will vary as different interests are addressed in the ebb and flow of world events. The North-South debate will continue to stimulate code discussions, but the focus may become increasingly issue-specific. Developments in the industrialized nations will also generate code activity, as occurred on transborder data flows. Even the EEC's company law initiatives could turn to more code-like efforts: for example, if the Vredeling proposal or other draft Directives are blocked politically, and compromise, non-binding EEC Recommendations are adopted instead.

The international business community has made various attempts to structure its own standards that address international investment issues. Originally aimed at advising governments on the framework necessary to attract more investment, these efforts have broadened to include voluntary standards for business. The International Chamber of Commerce remains the central body for this attempt at self-regulation, but some industry-based activity is also underway. Such business efforts intersect with intergovernmental code developments in a reinforcing and interactive manner, as is occurring in the pharmaceutical field. Both movements will continue to influence each other in the coming years.

The outlook for international codes, whether intergovernmental or business, is therefore a continuation or even expansion of current efforts in an attempt to reduce friction over troublesome MNC issues. The success of these voluntary codes is dependent on one essential factor—endorsement and application at the company level. Individual firms can use these international codes as guidance, employing the inherent flexibility of situational adaptation to meet public concerns more successfully and creatively than is possible through externally imposed government regulation. Corporate codes of conduct play a vital role in this task as both a guidance mechanism and a communication device with interested constituencies.

A ROLE FOR INDIVIDUAL MNC CODES

The vast majority of individual company codes were created by U.S. enterprises during the foreign bribery scandals. The resulting documents are often poorly constructed in intent and operation, combining a few detailed directives on payments and conflict of interest with broad principles of a free enterprise ethic. International issues seldom receive substantive attention outside of antibribery procedures. Thus, with some notable exceptions, these codes do not address important international concerns about MNC operations nor reflect the firms' real international commitment.

Many business executives resist shouldering the extra burden of formal code standards, presenting numerous arguments that question their value and emphasize their difficulties. Certainly codes set high standards that critics can claim are not met by corporate performance, but the experience of firms with progressive codes suggests that the benefits more than outweigh this potential risk. While some immediate pressures on MNCs have decreased, emerging challenges make it imperative that corporations use this current opportunity to forge individual codes and implementation procedures that better reflect and communicate the firm's role in global society. To miss this opportunity now will simply condemn corporations to reacting again from a defensive posture when unresolved problems build to another crisis point in a few more years.

Business resistance to corporate codes is discussed by Jack Behrman in his book *Discourses on Ethics and Business*.[1] The two most common objections are based on a fear of the code's use against the company. First, a code could bring closer scrutiny by governments, critic groups, and the media. Having published a set of standards, corporate actions would then be measured against them, generating more inquiries or challenges to the firm's activities. This view sees these distractions as better avoided by a low-profile position. A related second concern is that corporate compliance with code standards can be misjudged or misrepresented, subjecting the firm to unfair criticism.

These objections are certainly understandable and examples of both will undoubtedly occur. Increased scrutiny of business appears inevitable, however, given the governmental concerns and nongovernmental activism that is driving the international code movement. Perhaps an individual enterprise might escape these general pressures for a while by remaining quietly on the sidelines, but such a strategy raises two problems. First, if too many corporations avoid public positions, the voluntary standards will fail, making binding but less appropriate regulations more likely for all. Second, whenever a reticent enterprise is pulled into the public arena, the job of explaining or defending its operations will become more difficult without a prior record of credible voluntary standards.

Explaining corporate policy and operations may be difficult and frustrating, particularly when critics challenge corporate interpretations and audiences lack technical sophistication regarding business requirements. This task's difficulty, however, does not make it any less necessary. Corporate operations must be made both understandable and acceptable to public constituencies. Many enterprises complain that they have not had a chance to explain themselves. A corporate code of conduct offers a good opportunity for such an explanation, ideally in advance of the time that specific criticisms are received.

Another objection to business codes is that they are perceived as public relations devices whose high principles and glowing self-portrait simply create further skepticism about corporations. This charge may be an accurate critique of some prior corporate efforts, but it is not a problem inherent in MNC codes. Standards that are clearly linked to operational conduct and backed by implementation procedures will gain credibility both inside and outside of the corporation. This book's description of a corporate identity code is designed to offer an approach to code development that can combine guidance and communication needs in a credible fashion.

A fourth business objection to codes identified by Behrman is the fear that corporate codes are a confirmation of misconduct. If companies were not doing anything wrong, there would be no reason to issue such standards. This reasoning is only partially correct in that there has been corporate misconduct. To some degree business codes are tied to this fact by the stimulus that code-drafting received from the overseas bribery scandals. In a broader context, however, the codes called for in this book are responses to expressions of public concern over MNC operations rather than corrective actions to specific abuses. By better communication of corporate policies and procedures, firms are answering public inquiries, not admitting wrong-doing. In fact, firms that have some of the best records also issue many of the best corporate codes that now exist.

Finally, codes could cause disturbances within a corporation, upsetting normal communication and chain-of-command channels by creating unusual monitoring and enforcement devices. This concern can be largely resolved through selecting those procedures, from a wide range of possible implementation mechanisms, that best fit an individual company's organization and management style. In practice, some firms have found that codes have very positive effects on internal communication, even relieving some of the pressure for "whistle-blowing" activities.

If these objections can be overcome, are there any counterpart benefits to justify the time and expense that code development will require? Reports from four companies on their own code efforts suggests at least seven areas where benefits can accrue. According to comments by executives from Dow Corning, Caterpillar Tractor, Norton, and Union Carbide,[2] their corporate codes help to:

- crystalize and update internal policy. Old, unchallenged procedures may be inappropriate under changed circumstances or may suffer from uneven administration; new or emerging issues may require early corporate action.
- provide a good management tool to aid internal communication, particularly in serving as a consistent policy guideline in cases of employee turnover.
- discover and stop situations that could develop into serious problems.
- improve employee morale and performance by showing the company cares about how it acts. Codes can also help employees resist possible pressures for inappropriate action.
- explain corporate policies and procedures in host countries. Codes offer a good introduction to a new area and set the stage for a discussion of counterpart government responsibilities.
- provide a basis for external communication with public constituencies that may have general inquiries or specific concerns about the company.
- evaluate and improve input to intergovernmental code of conduct exercises.

Continuing intergovernmental code discussions will force new corporate attention to individual MNC codes. These negotiations are not the most important reason to formulate a company code, but in responding to this activity firms may develop better international corporate standards and methods of general communication.

GLOBAL NEED AND CORPORATE EFFORT

Most of this book has been dominated by a discussion of political and business pragmatism. Governments settle upon voluntary intergovernmental codes to bridge differences without sacrificing national sovereignty. Corporations should respond to code pressures because the alternative is greater regulation or increased conflict. This concentration on such practical matters, however, undervalues a vital component of the picture that rests on subjective interpretations of an MNC's global responsibilities. The driving force behind calls for greater MNC responsiveness and international accountability really rests on an understanding of the dramatic and compelling needs in diverse parts of the modern world.

Not so long ago a debate raged in the United States over corporate social responsibility—not over its specific application as today, but as to the very notion about whether corporations have a social responsibility. For the most part this basic question has been resolved in favor of an expanded social contract for business. Corporations are involved in society far beyond the concept of "the business of business is business."

Today a similar issue is posed for MNCs in the face of disproportionately greater need on the global scale. The same initial objections are heard that MNCs are neither responsible nor capable of solving fundamental human problems in all countries around the world. This response is the right answer to the wrong question. It is neither the right nor the responsibility of MNCs to determine the fundamental standards that govern a society. It *is* a company's obligation, however, to communicate its own standards and procedures so that a society is able to judge accurately the appropriateness and role of that enterprise in meeting the society's needs.

Corporations do not have an independent right of existence in the sense that is embodied in a notion of human rights. To be granted a right to exist within a society, and to maintain that right over time, corporations must at a minimum do two things. First, they must produce economic goods for that society, since this objective is the fundamental reason for the enterprise's existence. Second, they must not do harm in the process, violating the society's norms and non-economic values. To the extent that harm is incurred as a trade-off for economic benefits, the firm's existence becomes proportionately more problematic.

In the face of world need, however, MNCs should also accept a social responsibility "to reach beyond the minimal." The question is not "can you solve all the problems?" but rather "can you do better?" This question is too often considered only in the sense of extracurricular philanthropic activity, leading to legitimate protests that there are limits to corporate largess that have to do both with a proper societal role and fiduciary obligations to shareholders. While philanthropic involvement is desirable and should be encouraged and recognized for its contribution, this activity too often distracts attention from the central questions of business performance. Doing "good deeds" will not save a corporation whose basic operational standards fall below societal demands, nor will the absence of corporate giving lead to unnecessary business regulation. In short, the primary evaluation of good corporate citizenship rests not on its good deeds, but on corporate decision-making about the nature of the firm's basic products and operations in relation to societal needs.

A corporate identity code provides a self-adapted statement of voluntary standards that a firm can accept "beyond the minimal." Such a code will not satisfy all critics, nor does it guarantee that the stated standards will never be overstepped. What a corporate code does offer is a challenge and an opportunity to do better than what is simply required of a corporation by law. Particularly for an MNC that operates in so many needy areas of the world, this opportunity should not be missed.

INTERNATIONAL CODES FOR MULTINATIONAL BUSINESS

Much of the fire seems to have gone out of MNC issues lately. Hard economic times and a relative shortage of capital make foreign investors welcome in most overseas capitals. Several developing countries have even joined the ranks of home countries, sending their own MNCs abroad in search of greater returns on investment and, in turn, becoming less committed themselves to proposed restrictions on MNCs. The rhetoric in international organizations often does not square with practical business dealings taking place on the national level.

This respite is likely to be quite brief. Many traditional MNC issues will surface again because basic jurisdiction problems and pressing global needs remain unresolved. Perhaps equally significant are a set of emerging issues that may make businesspeople wish for the simple anti-MNC polemics of the past.

For example, the increased use of nationalistic trade performance requirements places greater pressure on MNCs in ways that directly affect global decision-making and leave the firm exposed to competing demands in home and host countries. In industries such as transportation and electronics there is also a trend toward inter-MNC integration where tie-in arrangements are being expanded through such devices as equity purchase, joint research and development, coproduction, component supply, and marketing and distribution agreements. These changes will cause increased government concern over corporate national identities and will require a clear explanation of their significance for national policy objectives such as greater local employment and technological innovation.

Events in the 1970s forced MNCs onto the defensive. An opportunity now exists to change this posture into a positive forward outlook and plan of action. One step in this direction is to build a public affairs program that uses the intergovernmental code movement as public guidance rather than just defending against it as possible law. Individual MNC codes can play a vital role in this effort, counterbalancing the use of intergovernmental codes as political levers while also creating a better understanding of corporate operations that could preclude more restrictive actions in the future.

National sovereignty is not at bay in today's world of MNCs, but interdependence between countries has created a greater need for a harmonious reconciliation of the pressures created by multijurisdictional business dealings. Intergovernmental codes can help relieve these pressures and, through their expressions of concern, guide corporate self-regulation. The hard task now falls on MNCs to use the flexibility of individual application to formulate corporate codes that can direct and communicate the basis for company operations. A corporate code is not an answer to all of an MNC's problems, but it is a good public affairs mechanism that can and should be used to better effect.

This book has not been written by an avowed MNC critic, but by one who believes in the general good conduct of most companies, and in their potential to do still better. Sometimes it is easier to gain attention by castigating business performance and threatening dire consequences if things do not change. The approach here has been to encourage action by arguing somewhat more dispassionately that it is in business' self-interest to develop meaningful codes of conduct. The point that should not be missed, however, is that such a self-interested business action is also very much in the public interest wherever MNCs operate. Businesspeople, and particularly business leaders, should respond to this notion as well.

NOTES

1. Jack N. Behrman, *Discourses on Ethics and Business* (Cambridge, Mass.: Oelgeschlager, Gunn & Hain, 1981), pp. 136–138.

2. See *Codes of Conduct*, proceedings from the Public Affairs Council Workshop on Corporate Codes of International Business Conduct (Washington, D.C.: Public Affairs Council, September 16, 1975), pp. 57–63, 87–103; Theodore V. Purcell, S. J., and James Weber, S. J., *Institutionalizing Corporate Ethics: A Case History*, Special Study No. 71 (New York: The Presidents Association, 1979); and John Swanson, Manager, Business Communications, Dow Corning, speech to a Business Ethics Class, Albion College, June 4, 1981.

Appendix: OECD Declaration*

THE GOVERNMENTS OF OECD
MEMBER COUNTRIES

CONSIDERING

-- That international investment has assumed increased importance in the world economy and has considerably contributed to the development of their countries;

-- That multinational enterprises play an important role in this investment process;

-- That co-operation by Member countries can improve the foreign investment climate, encourage the positive contribution which multinational enterprises can make to economic and social progress, an minimise and resolve difficulties which may arise from their various operations;

-- That, while continuing endeavours within the OECD may lead to further international arrangements and agreements in this field, it seems appropriate at this stage to intensify their co-operation and consultation on issues relating to international investment and multinational enterprises through inter-related instruments each of which deals with a different aspect of the matter and together constitute a framework within which the OECD will consider these issues:

Reprinted by permission from *International Investment and Multinational Enterprises: Revised Edition 1984* (Paris: Organization for Economic Cooperation and Development, 1984), pp. 11–22.

DECLARE:

Guidelines for Multinational Enterprises	I.	That they jointly recommend to multinational enterprises operating in their territories the observance of the Guidelines as set forth in the Annex hereto having regard to the considerations and understandings which introduce the Guidelines and are an integral part of them;

National
Treatment

II. 1. That Member countries should, consistent with their needs to maintain public order, to protect their essential security interests and to fulfil commitments relating to international peace and security, accord to enterprises operating in their territories and owned or controlled directly or indirectly by nationals of another Member country (hereinafter referred to as "Foreign-Controlled Enterprises") treatment under their laws, regulations and administrative practices, consistent with international law and no less favourable than that accorded in like situations to domestic enterprises (hereinafter referred to as "National Treatment");

2. That Member countries will consider applying "National Treatment" in respect of countries other than Member countries;

3. That Member countries will endeavour to ensure that their territorial subdivisions apply "National Treatment";

4. That this Declaration does not deal with the right of Member countries to regulate the entry of foreign investment or the conditions of establishment of foreign enterprises;

International
Investment
Incentives and
Disincentives

III. 1. That they recognise the need to strengthen their co-operation in the field of international direct investment;

2. That they thus recognise the need to give due weight to the interests of Member countries affected by specific laws, regulations and administrative practices in this field (hereinafter called "measures") providing official incentives and disincentives to international direct investment;

3. That Member countries will endeavour to make such measures as transparent as possible, so that their importance and purpose can be ascertained and that information on them can be readily available;

Consultation
Procedures

IV. That they are prepared to consult one another on the above matters in conformity with the Decisions of the Council on the Guidelines for Multinational Enterprises, on National Treatment and on International Investment Incentives and Disincentives;

Review   V. That they will review the above matters within three
                                 years (1) with a view to improving the effectiveness
                                 of international economic co-operation among Member
                                 countries on issues relating to international
                                 investment and multinational enterprises.

NOTES AND REFERENCES

1.   A first review was undertaken in 1979. The present review took place
         in the OECD Council meeting at Ministerial level on 17th and
         18th May 1984. It was decided to review the Declaration again at the
         latest in six years.

ANNEX TO THE DECLARATION OF 21st JUNE 1976 BY GOVERNMENTS
OF OECD MEMBER COUNTRIES ON INTERNATIONAL INVESTMENT AND
MULTINATIONAL ENTERPRISES, AS AMENDED IN 1979 AND 1984

GUIDELINES FOR MULTINATIONAL ENTERPRISES

1.   Multinational enterprises now play an important part in the economies
of Member countries and in international economic relations, which is of
increasing interest to governments. Through international direct investment,
such enterprises can bring substantial benefits to home and host countries by
contributing to the efficient utilisation of capital, technology and human
resources between countries and can thus fulfil an important role in the
promotion of economic and social welfare. But the advances made by
multinational enterprises in organising their operations beyond the national
framework may lead to abuse of concentrations of economic power and to
conflicts with national policy objectives. In addition, the complexity of
these multinational enterprises and the difficulty of clearly perceiving their
diverse structures, operations and policies sometimes give rise to concern.

2.   The common aim of the Member countries is to encourage the positive
contributions which multinational enterprises can make to economic and social
progress and to minimise and resolve the difficulties to which their various
operations may give rise. In view of the transnational structure of such
enterprises, this aim will be furthered by co-operation among the OECD
countries where the headquarters of most of the multinational enterprises are
established and which are the location of a substantial part of their
operations. The Guidelines set out hereafter are designed to assist in the
achievement of this common aim and to contribute to improving the foreign
investment climate.

3.   Since the operations of multinational enterprises extend throughout the
world, including countries that are not Members of the Organisation,
international co-operation in this field should extend to all States. Member
countries will give their full support to efforts undertaken in co-operation
with non-member countries, and in particular with developing countries, with a
view to improving the welfare and living standards of all people both by
encouraging the positive contributions which multinational enterprises can
make and by minimising and resolving the problems which may arise in
connection with their activities.

4.   Within the Organisation, the programme of co-operation to attain these ends will be a continuing, pragmatic and balanced one. It comes within the general aims of the Convention on the Organisation for Economic Co-operation and Development (OECD) and makes full use of the various specialised bodies of the Organisation, whose terms of reference already cover many aspects of the role of multinational enterprises, notably in matters of international trade and payments, competition, taxation, manpower, industrial development, science and technology. In these bodies, work is being carried out on the identification of issues, the improvement of relevant qualitative and statistical information and the elaboration of proposals for action designed to strengthen inter-governmental co-operation. In some of these areas procedures already exist through which issues related to the operations of multinational enterprises can be taken up. This work could result in the conclusion of further and complementary agreements and arrangements between governments.

5.   The initial phase of the co-operation programme is composed of a Declaration and three Decisions promulgated simultaneously as they are complementary and inter-connected, in respect of Guidelines for multinational enterprises, National Treatment for foreign-controlled enterprises and international investment incentives and disincentives.

6.   The Guidelines set out below are recommendations jointly addressed by Member countries to multinational enterprises operating in their territories. These Guidelines, which take into account the problems which can arise because of the international structure of these enterprises, lay down standards for the activities of these enterprises in the different Member countries. Observance of the Guidelines is voluntary and not legally enforceable. However, they should help to ensure that the operations of these enterprises are in harmony with national policies of the countries where they operate and to strengthen the basis of mutual confidence between enterprises and States.

7.   Every State has the right to prescribe the conditions under which multinational enterprises operate within its national jurisdiction, subject to international law and to the international agreements to which it has subscribed. The entities of a multinational enterprise located in various countries are subject to the laws of these countries.

8.   A precise legal definition of multinational enterprises is not required for the purposes of the Guidelines. These usually comprise companies or other entities whose ownership is private, state or mixed, established in different countries and so linked that one or more of them may be able to exercise a significant influence over the activities of others and, in particular, to share knowledge and resources with the others. The degree of autonomy of each entity in relation to the others varies widely from one multinational enterprise to another, depending on the nature of the links between such entities and the fields of activity concerned. For these reasons, the Guidelines are addressed to the various entities within the multinational enterprise (parent companies and/or local entities) according to the actual distribution of responsibilities among them on the understanding that they will co-operate and provide assistance to one another as necessary to facilitate observance of the Guidelines. The word "enterprise" as used in these Guidelines refers to these various entities in accordance with their responsibilities.

9.   The Guidelines are not aimed at introducing differences of treatment
between multinational and domestic enterprises; wherever relevant they
reflect good practice for all. Accordingly, multinational and domestic
enterprises are subject to the same expectations in respect of their conduct
wherever the Guidelines are relevant to both.

10.   The use of appropriate international dispute settlement mechanisms,
including arbitration, should be encouraged as a means of facilitating the
resolution of problems arising between enterprises and Member countries.

11.   Member countries have agreed to establish appropriate review and
consultation procedures concerning issues arising in respect of the
Guidelines. When multinational enterprises are made subject to conflicting
requirements by Member countries, the governments concerned will co-operate in
good faith with a view to resolving such problems either within the Committee
on International Investment and Multinational Enterprises established by the
OECD Council on 21st January 1975 or through other mutually acceptable
arrangements.

        Having regard to the foregoing considerations, the Member countries set
forth the following Guidelines for multinational enterprises with the
understanding that Member countries will fulfil their responsibilities to
treat enterprises equitably and in accordance with international law and
international agreements, as well as contractual obligations to which they
have subscribed.

GENERAL POLICIES

Enterprises should:

1. Take fully into account established general policy objectives of the
   Member countries in which they operate;

2. In particular, give due consideration to those countries' aims and
   priorities with regard to economic and social progress, including
   industrial and regional development, the protection of the
   environment and consumer interests, the creation of employment
   opportunities, the promotion of innovation and the transfer of
   technology (1);

3. While observing their legal obligations concerning information,
   supply their entities with supplementary information the latter may
   need in order to meet requests by the authorities of the countries
   in which those entities are located for information relevant to the
   activities of those entities, taking into account legitimate
   requirements of business confidentiality;

4. Favour close co-operation with the local community and business
   interests;

5. Allow their component entities freedom to develop their activities and to exploit their competitive advantage in domestic and foreign markets, consistent with the need for specialisation and sound commercial practice;

6. When filling responsible posts in each country of operation, take due account of individual qualifications without discrimination as to nationality, subject to particular national requirements in this respect;

7. Not render -- and they should not be solicited or expected to render -- any bribe or other improper benefit, direct or indirect, to any public servant or holder of public office;

8. Unless legally permissible, not make contributions to candidates for public office or to political parties or other political organisations;

9. Abstain from any improper involvement in local political activities.

DISCLOSURE OF INFORMATION

Enterprises should, having due regard to their nature and relative size in the economic context of their operations and to requirements of business confidentiality and to cost, publish in a form suited to improve public understanding a sufficient body of factual information on the structure, activities and policies of the enterprise as a whole, as a supplement, in so far as necessary for this purpose, to information to be disclosed under the national law of the individual countries in which they operate. To this end, they should publish within reasonable time limits, on a regular basis, but at least annually, financial statements and other pertinent information relating to the enterprise as a whole, comprising in particular:

   i) The structure of the enterprise, showing the name and location of the parent company, its main affiliates, its percentage ownership, direct and indirect, in these affiliates, including shareholdings between them;

  ii) The geographical areas (2) where operations are carried out and the principal activities carried on therein by the parent company and the main affiliates;

 iii) The operating results and sales by geographical area and the sales in the major lines of business for the enterprise as a whole;

  iv) Significant new capital investment by geographical area and, as far as practicable, by major lines of business for the enterprise as a whole;

   v) A statement of the sources and uses of funds by the enterprise as a whole;

vi) The average number of employees in each geographical area;

vii) Research and development expenditure for the enterprise as a whole;

viii) The policies followed in respect of intra-group pricing;

ix) The accounting policies, including those on consolidation, observed in compiling the published information.

COMPETITION

Enterprises should, while conforming to official competition rules and established policies of the countries in which they operate:

1. Refrain from actions which would adversely affect competition in the relevant market by abusing a dominant position of market power, by means of, for example:

   a) Anti-competitive acquisitions;

   b) Predatory behaviour toward competitors;

   c) Unreasonable refusal to deal;

   d) Anti-competitive abuse of industrial property rights;

   e) Discriminatory (i.e. unreasonably differentiated) pricing and using such pricing transactions between affiliated enterprises as a means of affecting adversely competition outside these enterprises;

2. Allow purchasers, distributors and licensees freedom to resell, export, purchase and develop their operations consistent with law, trade conditions, the need for specialisation and sound commercial practice;

3. Refrain from participating in or otherwise purposely strengthening the restrictive effects of international or domestic cartels or restrictive agreements which adversely affect or eliminate competition and which are not generally or specifically accepted under applicable national or international legislation;

4. Be ready to consult and co-operate, including the provision of information, with competent authorities of countries whose interests are directly affected in regard to competition issues or investigations. Provision of information should be in accordance with safeguards normally applicable in this field.

FINANCING

Enterprises should, in managing the financial and commercial operations of their activities, and especially their liquid foreign assets and liabilities, take into consideration the established objectives of the countries in which they operate regarding balance of payments and credit policies.

TAXATION

Enterprises should:

1. Upon request of the taxation authorities of the countries in which they operate, provide, in accordance with the safeguards and relevant procedures of the national laws of these countries, the information necessary to determine correctly the taxes to be assessed in connection with their operations, including relevant information concerning their operations in other countries;

2. Refrain from making use of the particular facilities available to them, such as transfer pricing which does not conform to an arm's length standard, for modifying in ways contrary to national laws the tax base on which members of the group are assessed.

EMPLOYMENT AND INDUSTRIAL RELATIONS

Enterprises should, within the framework of law, regulations and prevailing labour relations and employment practices, in each of the countries in which they operate:

1. Respect the right of their employees to be represented by trade unions and other bona fide organisations of employees, and engage in constructive negotiations, either individually or through employers' associations, with such employee organisations with a view to reaching agreements on employment conditions, which should include provisions for dealing with disputes arising over the interpretation of such agreements, and for ensuring mutually respected rights and responsibilities;

2. a) Provide such facilities to representatives of the employees as may be necessary to assist in the development of effective collective agreements;

   b) Provide to representatives of employees information which is needed for meaningful negotiations on conditions of employment;

3. Provide to representatives of employees where this accords with local law and practice, information which enables them to obtain a true and fair view of the performance of the entity or, where appropriate, the enterprise as a whole;

4. Observe standards of employment and industrial relations not less favourable than those observed by comparable employers in the host country;

5. In their operations, to the greatest extent practicable, utilise, train and prepare for upgrading members of the local labour force in co-operation with representatives of their employees and, where appropriate, the relevant governmental authorities;

6. In considering changes in their operations which would have major effects upon the livelihood of their employees, in particular in the case of the closure of an entity involving collective lay-offs or dismissals, provide reasonable notice of such changes to representatives of their employees, and where appropriate to the relevant governmental authorities, and co-operate with the employee representatives and appropriate governmental authorities so as to mitigate to the maximum extent practicable adverse effects;

7. Implement their employment policies including hiring, discharge, pay, promotion and training without discrimination unless selectivity in respect of employee characteristics is in furtherance of established governmental policies which specifically promote greater equality of employment opportunity;

8. In the context of bona fide negotiations (3) with representatives of employees on conditions of employment, or while employees are exercising a right to organise, not threaten to utilise a capacity to transfer the whole or part of an operating unit from the country concerned nor transfer employees from the enterprises' component entities in other countries in order to influence unfairly those negotiations or to hinder the exercise of a right to organise (4);

9. Enable authorised representatives of their employees to conduct negotiations on collective bargaining or labour management relations issues with representatives of management who are authorised to take decisions on the matters under negotiation.

SCIENCE AND TECHNOLOGY

Enterprises should:

1. Endeavour to ensure that their activities fit satisfactorily into the scientific and technological policies and plans of the countries in which they operate, and contribute to the development of national scientific and technological capacities, including as far as appropriate the establishment and improvement in host countries of their capacity to innovate;

2. To the fullest extent practicable, adopt in the course of their business activities practices which permit the rapid diffusion of technologies with due regard to the protection of industrial and intellectual property rights;

3. When granting licences for the use of industrial property rights or when otherwise transferring technology, do so on reasonable terms and conditions.

NOTES AND REFERENCES

1. This paragraph includes the additional provision adopted by the OECD Governments at the meeting of the OECD Council at Ministerial level on 17th and 18th May 1984.

2. For the purposes of the guideline on disclosure of information the term "geographical area" means groups of countries or individual countries as each enterprise determines is appropriate in its particular circumstances. While no single method of grouping is appropriate for all enterprises or for all purposes, the factors to be considered by an enterprise would include the significance of operations carried out in individual countries or areas as well as the effects on its competitiveness, geographic proximity, economic affinity, similarities in business environments and the nature, scale and degree of interrelationship of the enterprises' operations in the various countries.

3. Bona fide negotiations may include labour disputes as part of the process of negotiation. Whether or not labour disputes are so included will be determined by the law and prevailing employment practices of particular countries.

4. This paragraph includes the additional provision adopted by OECD Governments at the meeting of the OECD Council at Ministerial level on 13th and 14th June 1979.

Selected Bibliography

Baldridge, Malcolm. Secretary of Commerce. Letter to American business leaders concerning the OECD Privacy Guidelines. July 20, 1981.

Barnet, Richard J., and Muller, Ronald E. *Global Reach*. New York: Simon and Schuster, 1974.

Black, Robert; Blank, Stephen; and Hanson, Elizabeth C. *Multinationals in Contention*. New York: The Conference Board, 1978.

Behrman, Jack N. *Discourses on Ethics and Business*. Cambridge, Mass.: Oelgeschlager, Gunn & Hain, 1981.

————. *National Interests and the Multinational Enterprise*. Englewood Cliffs, N.J.: Prentice-Hall, 1970.

Bergsten, C. Fred; Horst, Thomas; and Moran, Theodore H. *American Multinationals and American Interests*. Washington, D.C.: The Brookings Institution, 1978.

Blanpain, Roger. *The OECD Guidelines for Multinational Enterprises and Labor Relations 1976–1979*. Hingham, Mass.: Klower Law and Taxation Publishers, 1979.

Business and Industry Advisory Committee to the OECD. *A Report for Business on the OECD Guidelines for Multinational Enterprises*. Paris, 1980.

Campbell, Duncan C., and Rowan, Richard L. *Multinational Enterprises and the OECD Industrial Relations Guidelines*. Multinational Industrial Relations Series No. 11. Philadelphia: University of Pennsylvania, 1983.

Centre on Transnational Corporations. Report of the Secretariat. *Transnational Corporations: Issues Involved in the Formulation of a Code of Conduct*. New York: United Nations, 1976.

————. *The CTC Reporter*. United Nations Centre on Transnational Corporations. New York: United Nations. Various issues.

Chamber of Commerce of the United States. Specialized Task Force of the National Chamber's Multinational Corporations Panel. "Elements of Global Business Conduct for Possible Inclusion in Individual Company Statements." Washington, D.C.: January 1975.

"Chasing the Multinationals: The OECD guidelines for multinationals are, after all, being given some real effect." *The Economist*. June 4, 1977, pp. 93–94.

Chatov, Robert, *An Analysis of Corporate Statements on Ethics and Behavior*. Prepared for the Standards of Performance Task Force, California Roundtable. June 1978.

――――. "What Corporate Ethics Statements Say." *California Management Review*. Vol. 22, No. 4, Summer 1980, pp. 20–29.

"Code of Behavior for Japanese Investors Overseas: JFTC." *The Journal of the ACCJ*. August 5, 1973.

Code of Conduct Adopted for EC Companies in South Africa. Background Note No. 24. Washington, D.C.: European Community Information Service, September 23, 1977.

Codes of Conduct. Proceedings from the Public Affairs Council Workshop on Corporate Codes of International Business Conduct. Washington, D.C.: Public Affairs Council, September 16, 1975.

Code of Conduct for Companies with Interests in South Africa. Government Guidance to British Companies on the Code of Conduct Adopted by the Governments of the Nine Member States of the European Community. London: Her Majesty's Stationary Office, 1978.

"Codes of Conduct: Worry over restraints on multinationals." *Chemicalweek*. July 15, 1981, pp. 48–52.

Coolidge, Phillip; Spina, George C; and Wallace, Don, Jr., eds. *OECD Guidelines for Multinational Enterprises: A Business Appraisal*. Washington, D.C.: Institute for International and Foreign Trade Law, Georgetown University, 1977.

Coombe, George W., Jr., and Kirk, Susan L. "Privacy, Data Protection, and Transborder Data Flow: A Corporate Response to International Expectations." *The Business Lawyer*, Vol. 39, No. 1, November 1983, pp. 33–66.

The Corporate Examiner. Vol. 10, No. 8–9. New York: Interfaith Center on Corporate Responsibility, September 1981.

Davidow, Joel. "Multinationals, Host Governments and Regulation of Restrictive Business Practices." *The Columbia Journal of World Business*. Summer 1980, pp. 14–19.

DeGeorge, Richard T. *Business Ethics*. New York: Macmillan Publishing Co., 1982.

Donaldson, Thomas, and Werhane, Patricia H. *Ethical Issues in Business: A Philosophical Approach*. 2nd ed. Englewood Cliffs, N.J.: Prentice-Hall, 1983.

Drucker, Peter F. "What is 'Business Ethics'?" *Public Interest*. No. 63, Spring 1981, pp. 18–36.

"EEC and South Africa: Will the Code Stick?" *The Economist*. September 24, 1977, p. 96.

The Ethics of Corporate Conduct. The American Assembly, Columbia University. Englewood Cliffs, N.J.: Prentice-Hall, 1977.

Fejfar, Mary A. *Regulation of Business by International Agencies*. St. Louis: Center for the Study of American Business, Washington University, 1983.

Feld, Werner J. *Multinational Corporations and United Nations Politics: The Quest for Codes of Conduct*. New York: Pergamon Press, 1980.

Franko, Lawrence G. *The European Multinationals*. Stamford, Conn.: Greylock Publishers, 1976.

French, Peter A. "The Corporation as a Moral Person," *American Philosophical Quarterly*. Vol. 16, No. 3, July 1979, pp. 207–215.

Gerlach, Luther. "Milk, Movements and Multinationals: Complex Interactions and Social Responsibilities." *Responsibilities of Multinational Corporations to Society*.

Vol. III. Proceedings from a conference. Washington, D.C.: Council of Better Business Bureaus, June 1–2, 1978.

Glynn, Leonard. *Multinationals in the World of Nations*. New York: U.S. Council for International Business, 1983.

Goldberg, Paul M., and Kindleberger, Charles P. "Toward a GATT for Investment." *Law and Policy in International Business*. Vol. 2, No. 2, Summer 1970, pp. 295–325.

Hellman, Rainer. *Transnational Control of Multinational Corporations*. Translated by Marianne Grund Freidberg. New York: Praeger, 1977.

Hewson, Barbara C. "Influencing Multinational Corporations: The Infant Formula Marketing Controversy." *International Law and Politics*. Vol. 10, No. 125, 1977, pp. 125–170.

Hoffman, W. Michael and Moore, Jennifer Mills. *Business Ethics*. New York: McGraw-Hill, 1984.

"How Organized Labor Uses OECD Voluntary Code to Harass International Firms." *Business International*. April 15, 1977.

Hughes, Kent H. *Trade, Taxes, and Transnationals*. New York: Praeger, 1979.

IFPMA Code of Pharmaceutical Marketing Practices. Zurich: International Federation of Pharmaceutical Manufacturers Associations, 1981.

The Impact of Multinational Corporations on Development and on International Relations. Department of Economic and Social Affairs. New York: United Nations, 1974.

Implementation and Enforcement of Codes of Ethics in Corporations and Associations. A report prepared for Ethics Resource Center. ORC Study #65334. Princeton, N.J.: Opinion Research Corporation, August 1980.

International Business Principles: Codes. Stanford Research Institute International. No. 24. Menlo Park, Calif., 1975.

International Chamber of Commerce. *Extortion and Bribery in Business Transactions*. Paris: International Chamber of Commerce, 1977.

———. *Guidelines for International Investment*. Paris: International Chamber of Commerce, 1972.

———. *International Code of Sales Promotion Practice*. Paris: International Chamber of Commerce, 1973.

International Confederation of Free Trade Unions. *Trade Unions and the Transnationals, A Handbook for Negotiators*. Madrid, November 1979.

"International Investment and Multinational Enterprises—OECD Ministerial Review." Press Release No. 181. Paris: OECD Information Service, June 14, 1979.

International Labour Office. *Multinational Enterprises and Social Policy*. Geneva, 1973.

———. *International Principles and Guidelines on Social Policy for Multinational Enterprises: Their Usefulness and Feasibility*. Geneva, 1976.

———. *Tripartite Declaration of Principles Concerning Multinational Enterprises and Social Policy*. Geneva, 1977.

The International Organizations Regulatory Guidebook. International Business-Government Counsellors, Inc. Washington, D.C.: International Organizations Monitoring Service, 1982, 1983, 1984.

Jacoby, Neil H.; Nehemkis, Peter; and Eells, Richard. *Bribery and Extortion in World Business*. New York: Macmillan Publishing Co., 1977.

Kindleberger, Charles P. *A GATT For Foreign Investment: Further Reflections*. New York: The Carnegie Center for Transnational Studies, 1980.

Kline, John M. "Entrapment or Opportunity: Structuring a Corporate Response to International Codes of Conduct." *The Columbia Journal of World Business*. Summer 1980, pp. 6–13.

———. *State Government Influence in U.S. International Economic Policy*. Lexington, Mass.: Lexington Books, D.C. Heath, 1983.

Kristol, Irving. "The Complex Question of Business Ethics." *Singer Magazine*. The Singer Company. Winter 1979, pp. 12–14.

Kugel, Yerachmiel, and Gruenberg, Gladys W. *International Payoffs*. Lexington, Mass.: Lexington Books, D.C. Heath, 1977.

Landsorganisationen I Danmark. Letter to TUAC. Report on the conflict between the HK and the Hertz Rent-a-Car in Denmark. January 26, 1977.

Michaud, Lucien, ed. *Multinational Corporations and Regional Development: Conflicts and Convergences*. International Federation of Catholic Universities. Center for Coordination of Research. Rome: Herder, 1983.

Multinational Corporations in World Development. Department of Economic and Social Affairs. New York: United Nations, 1973.

Multinational Public Affairs Briefings Seminar. Selected Proceedings. Washington, D.C.: Public Affairs Council, February 25, 1976.

"OECD vs. Badger-Belgium Settled 'Out of Court'; Unions Claim Victory." *Business International*. July 15, 1977.

Organization for Economic Cooperation and Development. Communication by the Belgian Delegation to the Committee on International Investment and Multinational Enterprises. Paris, March 23, 1977.

———. *International Investment and Multinational Enterprises*. Paris, 1976.

———. Note from the General Secretary of the TUAC to the Chairman and Members of the Committee on International Investment and Multinational Enterprises. Paris, March 25, 1977.

———. Review of the 1976 Declaration on International Investment and Multinational Enterprises. Documentation for meeting of Council at Ministerial Level. Paris, June 13–14, 1979.

———. *Report on the 1984 Review of the 1976 OECD Declaration and Decisions on International Investment and Multinational Enterprises*. Report by the Committee on International Investment and Multinational Enterprises. Paris, 1984.

The Pacific Basin Charter on International Investments: A Declaration of Basic Principles. Adopted at PBEC Fifth General Meeting in Wellington, New Zealand, May 19, 1972. Menlo Park, Calif.: PBEC, 1972.

Purcell, Theodore V., S. J. "The Ethics of Corporate Governance." *Review of Social Economy*. Vol. XL, No. 3. December 1982.

Purcell, Theodore V., S. J., and Weber, James, S. J. *Institutionalizing Corporate Ethics: A Case History*. Special Study No. 71. New York: The Presidents Association, 1979.

Recent Developments Related to Transnational Corporations and International Economic Relations. Economic and Social Council. Commission on Transnational Corporations. New York: United Nations. E/C.10/1982/2, July 16, 1982.

Robinson, John. *Multinationals and Political Control*. New York: St. Martin's Press, 1983.

Rolfe, Sidney. *The International Corporation*. Paris: International Chamber of Commerce, 1969.

Rubin, Seymour J. and Hufbauer, Gary Clyde, eds. *Emerging Standards of International Trade and Investment*. Published under the Auspices of The American Society of International Law. Totowa, N.J.: Rowman & Allanheld, 1984.

The Search for Common Ground: A Survey of Efforts to Develop Codes of Behavior in International Investment. A Special Report to the United States Committee, Pacific Basin Council. New York: The Conference Board, 1971.

Servan-Schreiber, Jean-Jacques. *The American Challenge*. New York: Atheneum, 1968.

Standards of Conduct in Business. The Colgate Darden Graduate School of Business Administration. University of Virginia. Charlottesville, Va: Center for the Study of Applied Ethics, 1977.

A Study of Corporate Ethical Policy Statements. The Foundation of the Southwestern Graduate School of Banking. Dallas, Tex.: Southern Methodist University, 1980.

Summary of the Hearings before the Group of Eminent Persons to Study the Impact of Multinational Corporations on Development and International Relations. Department of Economic and Social Affairs. New York: United Nations, 1974.

A Survey of Business Roundtable Members on Business Conduct Guidelines. The Business Roundtable, December 1975.

Trade Union Advisory Committee to the OECD. Speech by TUAC President at the Occasion of the Consultation with the CIME Committee on April 11, 1978.

Transnational Corporations in World Development: A Re-Examination. Economic and Social Council. Commission on Transnational Corporations. New York: United Nations, 1978.

Transnational Corporations in World Development: Third Survey. United Nations Centre on Transnational Corporations. New York: United Nations, 1983.

U.S. Commerce Department. *The Multinational Corporation: Studies on U.S. Foreign Investment*. Vol. 1. Washington, D.C.: U.S. Government Printing Office, 1972.

United States Council of the International Chamber of Commerce. *Guiding Principles for Codes of Conduct: The Business Viewpoint*. New York, 1980.

United States Council for International Business. *Corporate Handbook to the OECD and Its Business and Industry Committee*. New York, 1982.

———. *EC Update*. Newsletter. Various issues.

———. *International Information Flows*. Newsletter. Various issues.

———. *OECD Update*. Newsletter. Various issues.

———. *UN Report*. Newsletter. Various issues.

———. *U.S. Employers and the International Labor Organization*. Proceedings of a seminar. New York, 1982.

U.S. State Department. Advisory Committee on International Investment, Technology and Development. Minutes from a meeting held in Washington, D.C., November 13, 1980.

———. *Current Status Report: Selected International Organization Activities Relating to Transnational Enterprises*. Washington, D.C.: Office of Investment Affairs, July 1982, August 1983 and August 1984.

USA-BIAC Committee on International Investment and Multinational Enterprises. *A Review of the OECD Guidelines for Multinational Enterprises: Employment and Industrial Relations*. Prepared by Vernon O'Rourke. New York, May 1978.

———. *A Review of the Declaration on International Investment and Multinational Enterprises*. New York, November 1976.

————. *A Review of the OECD Guidelines for Multinational Enterprises: Competition.* Prepared by Barry E. Hawk. New York, 1977.

————. *A Review of Standards and Guidelines for International Business Conduct.* New York, September 1975.

————. *U.S. Corporate Response to OECD Guidelines: Examples of Voluntary Cooperation.* New York, April 1978.

Vernon, Raymond, ed. *Big Business and the State.* Cambridge, Mass.: Harvard University Press, 1974.

————. *Sovereignty at Bay: The Multinational Spread of U.S. Enterprises.* New York: Basic Books, 1971.

Verhaegan, Thierry. *International Codes of Conduct for Business: Some Legal Implications.* New York: United States Council of the International Chamber of Commerce, January 1981.

Waldmann, Raymond J. *Regulating International Business Through Codes of Conduct.* Washington, D.C.: American Enterprise Institute, 1980.

Wallace, Cynthia Day. *Legal Control of the Multinational Enterprise.* The Hague: Martinus Nijhoff Publishers, 1983.

Wallace, Don, Jr., ed. *International Control of Investment: The Dusseldorf Conference on Multinational Corporations.* Institute for International and Foreign Trade Law, Georgetown University. New York: Praeger, 1974.

————. *International Regulation of Multinational Corporations.* New York: Praeger, 1976.

Walton, Clarence C., ed. *The Ethics of Corporate Conduct.* The American Assembly. Columbia University. Englewood Cliffs, N.J.: Prentice-Hall, 1977.

World Health Organization. *International Code of Marketing of Breast-milk Substitutes.* Geneva: WHO, 1981.

Index

About the Author

JOHN M. KLINE is Deputy Director of the Karl F. Landegger Program in International Business Diplomacy at the Georgetown University School of Foreign Service in Washington, D.C. Dr. Kline teaches courses in international business ethics and business-government relations. From 1973 to 1979, as Director of International Economic Policy at the National Association of Manufacturers, he worked on many international code developments. He is the author of *State Government Influence on U.S. International Economic Policy* and numerous articles on international economics and multinational corporations.